LIFELINES

LIFELINES

FOR AFRICA STILL IN PERIL AND DISTRESS

COLIN FRASER

Hutchinson
London   Sydney   Auckland   Johannesburg

Plate 1   Chad – mother and child, drought victims, at a relief camp in Ati.   (UN Photo)

Hutchinson Education

An imprint of Century Hutchinson Ltd

62–65 Chandos Place, London WC2N 4NW

Century Hutchinson Australia Pty Ltd
P O Box 496, 16–22 Church Street, Hawthorn,
Victoria 3122, Australia

Century Hutchinson New Zealand Limited
P O Box 40 –086, Glenfield, Auckland 10,
New Zealand

Century Hutchinson South Africa (Pty) Ltd
P O Box 337, Bergvlei, 2012 South Africa

First published 1988

Set in Linotron 10/12 Baskerville
by Saxon Printing Ltd., Derby

Printed and bound in Great Britain by
Anchor Brendon Ltd, Tiptree, Essex

British Library Cataloguing in Publication Data
Fraser, Colin
   Lifelines: for Africa still in Peril and distress
   1. Africa. Famines
   I. Title
   363.8

ISBN 0 09 173232 8

CONTENTS

GLOSSARY

AMC	Agricultural Marketing Corporation (Ethiopia)
CFA	Committee on Food Aid Policies and Programmes
CSO	Central Office of Statistics (Ethiopia)
EEC	European Economic Community
EWS	Early Warning System
FANA	Food and Nutrition Administration
FAO	United Nations Food and Agricultural Organisation
IEFR	International Emergency Food Reserve
ILO	International Labour Organisation
ITHS	International Transport and Handling Subsidy
ITN TV	Independent Television Network (UK)
MALT	Management and Logistic Team
MSF	Medecins sans Frontièrs
MT	Metric Tons (*All references to tonnage are in metric tons*)
ODA	Disaster Unit of UK Overseas Development Administration
OEOA	United Nations Office for Emergency Operations in Africa
OEOE	United Nations Office for Emergency Operations in Ethiopia
OPAM	Office des Produits Alimentaires du Mali
OPEC	Oil Producing Export Countries
RAF	Royal Air Force
RRC	Relief and Rehabilitation Commission

SPLA	Sudan Peoples' Liberation Army
UN	United Nations
UNDP	United Nations Development Programme
UNDRO	United Nations Disaster Relief Co-ordinator
UNHCR	United Nations High Commission for Refugees
UNSO	United Nations Sudano-Sahelian Organization
USAID	United States Agency for International Development
WFP	World Food Programme
WTOE	World Food Programme Transport Operation in Ethiopia
WTOS	World Food Programme Road Transport Operation Sudan
US$	All monetary amounts are given in US dollars

ACKNOWLEDGEMENTS

I have incurred numerous debts of gratitude in researching and writing this book. In fact, without the support of the many people who helped, it could not have been written. Everywhere I travelled in Africa, and during the research and writing in Rome, people unstintingly gave of their time to provide me with information, ideas, and comments. Many of them are identified and quoted in the text, but many who also helped are not. I regret this, but in the interests of readability and the structure of the book, it has not been possible to quote everyone who provided information. I hope that those left out will accept my apologies, and at the same time, my assurance that their help was invaluable and much appreciated.

The World Food Programme provided support without which the undertaking, and the travel in Africa to gather first-hand information, would not have been possible. The staff of the WFP offices in Chad, Niger, Mali, the Sudan, and Ethiopia all went out of their way to facilitate the work, providing transport, setting up contacts with government officials on my behalf, travelling into remote areas with me, patiently answering my questions, and providing invaluable insights. WFP is far from being the only source of food aid for relief and development in Africa – though it is the only multilateral one – and if WFP and its staff are mentioned so often, it is because of the support and help they provided.

The staff of WFP in the Rome headquarters were equally helpful, providing me with vast amounts of information and documentation. Personnel of UN bodies are not always forthcoming when faced with a journalist or author, but wherever I went in WFP , people were frank and open in describing successes and failures, strengths and weaknesses. This, and the moral support I received, were as important as the material and logistical backing. I wish to express my thanks to all the WFP staff who helped, but in particular I wish to mention Paul Mitchell, Neil Gallagher, and Diana Dixon of the Public Affairs and Information Branch; they were the focal point in making all the necessary arrangements and contacts for me, and for providing information and encouragement. I also wish to make clear that WFP did not try to influence the book beyond checking the text for factual accuracy concerning their operations.

My thanks go to Fiona Morrison who went through a stack of documents almost a metre high and created an index system for the information they contained. Her efficient research and cataloguing saved many days of precious time. Her comments on the draft of the book were also invaluable. Tom Morrison applied his knowledge and experience of African agriculture to checking the draft for technical accuracy in this area.

Every writer needs a good editor. I was fortunate to have Bonita Brindley take on the task as a labour of love. She went through the first draft with meticulous care and made numerous and creative editorial suggestions for improvements.

My colleagues and partners in Agrisystems provided support and encouragement for this book project from the start, but their most important contribution was that they ensured that I was left in peace to get on with the writing.

My wife Gerdy patiently put up with my long absences, my mainly incommunicado status for weeks on end while I wrote, and the general trauma the project brought to our domestic life. She was also a sounding board for ideas and did much of the initial proof reading.

To all these people, and to those many who are not named, goes my heartfelt gratitude.

★　　　★　　　★

Acknowledgements are also necessary in respect of source material. I have deliberately not burdened the text with footnotes, bearing in mind the saying, attributed to Winston Churchill, that, "Reading footnotes is like having to go downstairs to answer the doorbell when you are in the middle of making love!"

Much of the material on the situation in Africa is drawn from such outstanding works as *Africa in Crisis* by Lloyd Timberlake (Earthscan/IIED 1985), and *The Greening of Africa* by Paul Harrison (Earthscan/IIED – Paladin 1987). These books are essential reading for anyone requiring more detailed information on the malaise that afflicts Africa and of some of the initiatives in course to rectify it. *African agriculture: the next 25 years*, published by FAO in 1986, is an authoritative study of the African situation and of the future prospects for the continent. It contains a wealth of information. On desertification and other environmental matters in the Sudan, key information and statistics were found in the series of papers published recently by the Institute of Environmental Studies of the University of Khartoum with support from USAID.

For background information concerning the famine of 1984-85, and in addition to official reports and contacts, I drew heavily on three works: *A Year in the Death of Africa* by Peter Gill (Paladin 1986); *The Ethiopian Famine* by Kurt Jansson, Michael Harris and Angela Penrose (Zed Books 1987); and a typescript, as yet unpublished, entitled *Cleft Stick – Dilemmas in the Development of a Disaster – Ethiopia 1974-84* by Tom Franklin.

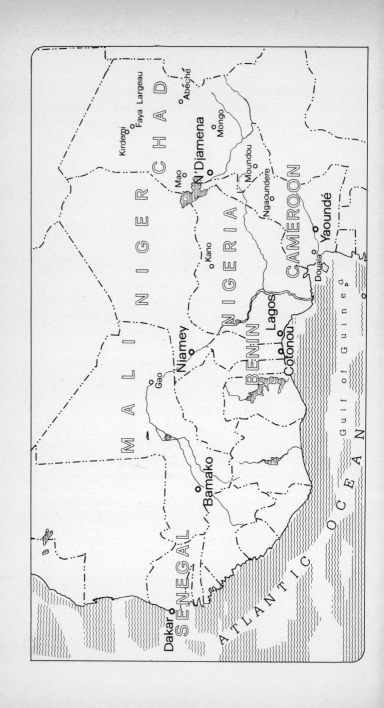

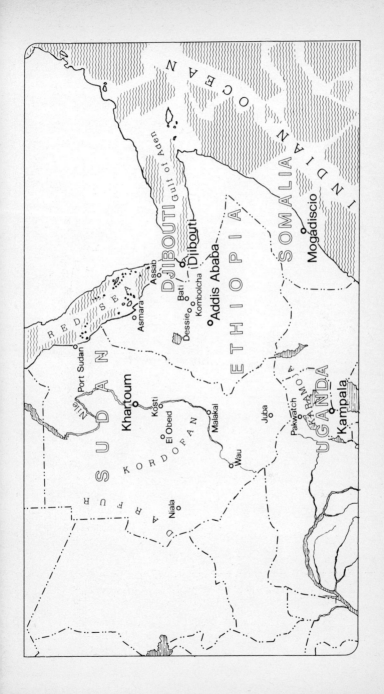

1

IN PERIL AND DISTRESS

The last weeks of the dry season are the time of sandstorms in the desert and semi-arid areas of Africa. This particular June morning dawns clear and very hot in Khartoum, but throughout the morning a dusty haze builds up. It seems harmless enough, but in fact it is a prelude to an apocalyptic *haboub*, the short-lived but violent sandstorms of the Sudan.

A creeping – and very creepy – gloom settles over the city during the late morning. There is an oppressiveness in the still air. Then, a fitful and hot breeze sighs through the trees along the Nile, stirring their leaves. They seem to be fidgeting in expectation.

The gloom becomes deeper and deeper until a veritable "darkness at noon" has descended. Any vehicles still trying to circulate have their head-lights on full beam as they creep along, but most cars have stopped. Suddenly, in the deep twilight, the wind springs up. The trees sway furiously in the sand-laden blast for about ten minutes, and then the wind subsides again, as rapidly as it came.

A distant and continuous rumbling sets in. Is it wind or thunder? It could be either or both, for in a few moments the rain is lashing down through the murk, and the wind has returned with a vengeance. It rains mud.

The next day, we go to El Moelle, a vast squatter area in the outskirts of Khartoum. Here, the destitute live in

Plate 2   Upper Volta – refugees from Mali wait for food rations to be distributed.   (FAO/Florita Botts)

improvised dwellings. Some have managed to build cube-like hovels out of mud bricks, but the majority live in shelters made of straw, matting, and any other materials they can lay their hands on. Strips of tin with circular holes cut in them feature prominently as building material; they are remnants from a canning factory after the disks for lids have been punched out. Nothing goes to waste when there is such poverty.

A squatter area like this is bad enough in warm, dry weather. After rain, it is horrendous. There are large areas of water through which people must wade, often up to their knees. The shelters are sodden and there cannot be a dry item of bedding anywhere. Children paddle through the deep puddles, and since there are no drains, and no sanitation, it takes little imagination to realize the gravity of the health risk. It is life in a septic tank.

The tens of thousands of people living in El Moelle are refugees from drought. Most came from Darfur and Kordofan Provinces in 1984 and 1985. They were driven eastwards towards the Nile in a desperate search for food and work after their crops failed and their livestock died, in effect unravelling the whole fabric of their existence.

Saleh Mohamed El Nour, 40-years-old, tells the story of what happened in his village, El Halba in Kordofan.

There were seven years of poor rains before 1984. In the last three of those years, you could say that it hardly rained at all. Our village had been prosperous once. We grew good crops of dura, sesame and groundnuts, and we had plenty of livestock too. But all this changed over those years. The crops became less and less, and the livestock began to die because there was no grazing for them.

In 1984, it did not rain at all. We had no crops and most of our animals had died. We had to leave. El Halba was a big village, with many people, and we all had to leave. It was the same in many villages. We came towards the Nile hoping to find land that we could cultivate or work so that we could buy food. We walked for 5 days.

People went to many different provinces. I do not think the people of El Halba will ever be together again. I would go back there but I have nothing. We have no seeds, no tools, and no food to eat while we wait for a crop. It is difficult getting enough food here for my eight children. For some months after we arrived we were given food, but not now. I sell charcoal... [He trails off, shrugging hopelessly.] I wonder what happened to El Halba, whether anyone has gone home.

★   ★   ★

It is late afternoon near Mao, in western Chad. We labour over the dunes, groping our way though a sandstorm until, finally, we arrive on a barren hilltop of such bleakness that it shrinks the heart. There, in that wilderness, barely visible through the wind-driven dust, are scattered the makeshift tents of refugees. They have fled from the Libyan forces occupying the northern part of Chad.

A small group of men sit in front of one tent, seemingly oblivious to the sandstorm that blasts around them. Their possessions consist of a few woven mats, some cooking pots, and a battered oil barrel for water.

Ogou Wollimi, a man in his fifties, is the leader of this small group. He wears a *galibia* that was once white, but it has taken on the hue of the desert dust. He is a calm man, fully sure of himself. His features remain at peace, his voice unemotional as he tells their story.

We are farmers from a village called Kirdemi, near Faya, in the northern part of the country. The Libyans occupied our area about 3 years ago. When they came, they told us that they were going to help us and make life better for us. But about one year ago, they began to take our sheep and our goats. They would just come and take them, and they never paid. We asked Goukouni Oueddei [1] to help us but he could not. He was without power with the Libyans. It got worse. They began to take our camels too.

So we protested more. They became angry, and after that they began to kill people. They would arrive, just like you have now, but they would say nothing. They would descend from their vehicle in front of a house and spray our people with machine-guns. A few months ago they were killing as many as ten people a day. A relative of mine was killed by them.

3

It was too dangerous to stay in our villages. But we knew we could not leave together in a big group because we would have been hunted in the desert. So we made plans to leave in small groups, at night, hoping they would not notice we had gone.

I brought 23 people here. We had just enough camels to carry food and water and to allow the smaller children to ride when they became tired. We set out at night, and we travelled by night too. We were frightened of being seen from helicopters. We did not know where to go, but we had to leave the area to be safe.

It was very hard, especially for the small children. Our journey took more than 40 days and nights. We did not have enough food and water, but people helped us when we found their villages or camps. And they told us that we should try to come to Mao because we would find help and food here.

We had no money because the Libyans only allowed their own money to be used in the areas they occupied. For one period of five days we had no food at all.

We were very tired and weak when we arrived here. We needed food urgently. Monsieur Etienne here [he indicated the young Chadian World Food Programme Officer based in Mao who was sitting among us] he gave us rations from his store. He has been giving us rations every month for the three months we have been here.

Thanks to Allah, we have been saved. And now that the Libyans have been forced to leave our area, we shall return. I hope the authorities will help us to find transport. I do not think we could walk those 800 kilometres again.

While we are taking our leave, a refugee approaches to say that another group has just arrived from the north. Etienne takes note of the numbers, promises to check and to make food available next morning.

The new group will join the 500 people already there, to wait stoically on this desolate hilltop, flayed by sandstorms. They are the innocent victims of strife and turmoil. But they are alive; food is assured, and they can realistically hope to return to their villages soon. Such a hope would be unrealistic for many of the more than 5 million people who are now refugees from strife and drought in Africa.

★   ★   ★

Mao is almost 4OO kilometres north of N'Djamena, the capital of Chad. It perches on high ground, a sparse collection of stone buildings with flat roofs that rise into pointed protuberances at the corners and midway along the sidewalls. As in other architectural styles in this part of the world, these protuberances provide anchorage for the roof timbers set beneath them.

The town has the austere beauty of unadorned simplicity, a reflection of the harsh austerity of the desert that surrounds it. But Mao also gives the impression of a town under siege, for it is embattled by the desert, under siege by sand. Its open areas, and its "streets" are filled with sand, and where a wall is open to the prevailing wind, waves of it are building high against the stonework. Local people remember wistfully the years of prosperity before the drought began in the early 197Os, to let up only slightly in the following years, and return with cataclysmic vengeance in 1984–85.

A young man, Musa Batran, from a once well to-do family in Mao recalls that his family had 1,5OO camels in the 196Os. During the drought beginning in 1972, they took their livestock to Niger, but the animals did not adapt well to the grazing there and many died. The family was never able to rebuild its herd properly. Then the drought of 1984-85 took a mighty toll, and today they have only 1OO camels.

Livestock has always been the basis for any prosperity in the area. Its loss in these recent cycles of drought has brought havoc to the local economy, and to the minds of some people. There is a man in Mao who literally went crazy when his last animals died in 1984. He has never recovered his sanity; he wanders about, pitiably importuning people to listen while he extolls the virtues of his magnificent animals, and with wild and tear-filled eyes, affirms that they are about to return to him in all their glory.

★   ★   ★

The market of Mao is an open area of sand with ramshackle

stalls covered by straw roofs supported by gnarled branches garnered from the desert. These roofs normally ward off the ferocious sun, but they provide no shelter from the sandstorm that has been blasting Mao for 11 days. Most of the stalls are deserted, for even the locals, resilient survivors that they are in this harsh environment, tend to stay at home to avoid the whirling, penetrating grit outside. But in one stall, behind a sewing machine that would be a collector's item in an industrialized country, sits a man who is working despite the sandstorm. He is Mohamet Mahmud Khalil, 41-years-old, the father of four children, a nomad until 1984.

He is slim and has restless eyes in the dark face beneath the red and white *kufia* on his head. He recalls the life of the desert with nostalgia.

If I had some livestock, I would not spend another day here in Mao. But there is no hope. That life is finished. Things were never the same after the drought of 1972. We lost most of our animals in that first drought. We did manage to build up our herd again afterwards. There were three quite good years before things began to get worse again.

The grazing has been getting less and less. There are more sandstorms too. Before the great drought of 1972, we did not need to go far to find grazing. After that, it became more and more difficult.

I had 27 camels and 30 sheep when the last great drought came. We went further and further looking for grazing that someone else had not found. It was no good. My animals began to die in March 1984. Their heads seemed to swell and they lost their hair. They fell to the ground one after the other and could not get up again.

My last camel died in June 1984. I remember it well. We were about 30 kilometres from Mao. My sons were aged 12 and 10 and my daughters 8 and 6. We walked here. We had heard that food was being given out. We were given help until I had learnt tailoring and could keep my family.

If the government would help us now to buy livestock, perhaps we could go back. But livestock are expensive, especially camels, and it is no use being a nomad with only sheep and goats. Nomadism is finished for us.

He stops, hawks, and spits into the dust – eloquent punctuation for his views on the non-future of nomadism.

★　　　★　　　★

The crews of Trans-Saharan Rally cars that blast down the sand track which leads into eastern Mali from Algeria would certainly not notice the village called Kalinsar that lies off to their right, about 5 kilometres out of Gao.

But the village of Kalinsar may be of historic significance; for it is being built by Tuaregs, people who for centuries despised any life not lived in tents. The almost mythical "blue men of the desert", who roamed the vast expanses of the Sahara, made rich by the milk, meat, and wool of their livestock, have been brought down by years of drought and hardship. The traditional way of life of these bellicose, proud and independent people has been shattered. They are building houses in Kalinsar, and they are growing crops nearby. These light-skinned Caucasians, who abhorred manual work as being beneath their dignity and kept black slaves to do their menial chores, are coming to terms with a new reality.

The baked-mud walls of Kalinsar are a russet brown that merges into the surrounding desert. From outside the village, there is not a single leaf of green to be seen. However, the village will one day be canopied by foliage, for as you enter it, you are faced by scores of small, round towers about a metre high and made out of a latticework of mud bricks. They are set in neat straight lines in all the spaces between the houses. Each of these little towers is built around a sapling and is protecting it from the searing winds.

We go through a door set in a perimeter wall and inside there is an open yard surrounding a large adobe house. More trees are growing in this yard, and we are proudly shown a new type of clay stove, designed to burn wood more efficiently, that has been built in one corner.

An open-sided tent is pitched in the opposite corner of the yard, and a group of men are seated beneath it and in front of it. It is early evening during Ramadan, and these are the tribe's religious scholars and ascetics, the marabouts.

7

The elderly chief is elegant in white robes. His face, like that of everyone in the group, is covered by a *tagilmust*, the traditional blue, olive-green, black or white litham that is carefully wound around the head and face to conceal all but the eyes. (It is considered offensive for a Tuareg to show his mouth.)

The chief, who looks frail and whose eyes are watery behind his ultramodern gold-rimmed, tinted glasses, greets us gravely and then returns to his seated position on the mat and to the study of his enormous Koran. It has large handwritten calligraphy and is bound in red leather. He has asked a younger brother to speak on his behalf.

This younger brother is in his forties. Unusually, his *tagilmust* is loosened from his face so that his mouth is visible. Perhaps the 44°C shade temperature is as trying for him as it is for me. He is olive-skinned and the features of his clean-shaven face are strong and regular. He looks me directly in the eyes for what seems an eternity, assessing me with the cold stare of a bird of prey. The sheer presence of the man is daunting, and I have to steel myself to hold that stare. Finally, in abrupt and emphatic-sounding Tamashek, their Berber language, he begins to respond to my question. His voice is deep and modulated.

We have always lived thanks to our livestock. Our camels, cows, sheep, goats, and donkeys provided wealth for us. But now our livestock are gone, and we are here. It is not possible to live from animals anymore.

We were rich. We had more than 2OO camels, 1,OOO cows, 3,OOO sheep, 3,5OO goats, and many donkeys. There were 1,6OO people in our group. The drought that began in 1972 was bad enough. We had to go far in those years to find grazing. Many of our people went into Niger and Burkina Faso. Our group went to Niger. Many animals died – about half of them did – in about nine months. But then conditions got better again and we rebuilt our herds. We thought that the drought of the '7Os would be like the one of 1913, which our people still talk about. It was terrible but many years of good rainfall came after it had passed.

So we did not expect what happened in 1984. We were camped about a hundred kilometres from here. The grazing from 1983 was finished and we knew that conditions were very bad everywhere. We needed the mango rains, [2] but they never came. There was nowhere for us to go. Our animals died in about five weeks in May and June.

[I was incredulous, and I interrupted: "You mean they *all* died in five weeks, all 9,OOO of them, or however many you had?"]

Yes, it was as I say. They all died in a few weeks. Death has no preference, but it was the cows that began to die first, then the sheep, goats, and the camels last. The land was littered with carcasses. There was no more hope for us.

Our group split up. Some went to other countries. We have not seen them since 1984. We had a truck and we came here to Gao. There were many thousands like us coming to Gao for food and help. Later, when we had decided to build this village and grow crops, World Food Programme gave us rations until our first harvests. We got help from UNICEF which drilled three boreholes for us. We built an irrigation canal, we have planted hundreds of trees, and we are growing crops of vegetables and grain.

Our ancestors and parents have never done such work. You must see what we are doing. Why can we not have food-for-work for the building we are doing? Yesterday we sent a truck to Mopti to buy food for the community. It is going to cost us 5OO,OOO CFA. [3] We could have spent that money on building materials, or on improvements to our cropland.

We are working to build this village, and each Friday in our mosque, we pray to Allah to help us, because the life in the desert is finished.

[He pauses, raises his arms aloft, and looking up at them, goes on] A man's strength is in his arms. If he dies because he does not use them, he is at fault.

[He fixes me again with those lambent, disturbing eyes, but now there is humour in them, and a sardonic smile twitches at the corner of his mouth.]

Well, I have helped you by telling you what you wanted to know, and now you must help us. We do not want you to leave the village

9

until you have seen what we are doing. You must walk around and see it all. And you must tell people that we need help.

We set off on the tour that had been requested, and we find that what has been achieved in so short a time is indeed impressive. The group of marabouts has stayed in the tent and delegated some young men to show us around, which they do with evident pride. The houses are well-built and laid-out according to a plan provided by the government. There are two mosques. The first is an adobe structure of arched vaults. It is large, about 50 metres square. The second, almost as large, is just behind the first and is still under construction. It is more elaborate and has roof timbers cut from doum palms, a highly-prized wood for construction in the Sahel. They have spent the equivalent of US$2,000 on these timbers which were brought a considerable distance.

We are shown into more courtyards of houses, each with recently-planted trees. We stop by the village pump where women and children are furiously spinning the hand-wheel while others cluster around with a variety of containers to catch the precious water as it spills from the spout.

We return to the tent where the marabouts are gathered and I am vigorously cross-examined about my impressions. They must be pleased with my reaction, for the chief's brother reaches behind him and brings forward a small cushion. Its cover is hand-woven and brightly-coloured, a minor masterpiece. "This is the work our women do," he says. "It is for you."

I express my appreciation, and also my regret that I have nothing to offer in return. "Ah, but you have," one of the assembled company says. "That ball-point you have been writing with!"

It had never occurred to me that ball-point pens could be so prized in this society. As we take our leave, followed by the repeated reminder that I must tell the outside world what they are doing, children clamour around asking for pens. Luckily I have several more in various pockets and in my camera case, but it is quite a struggle to keep just one for my own use until such time as I can buy another.

On the way out of the village, there is a final sight they want us to see. A traditional Tuareg tent is pitched in an open area. It is made of hide carefully stretched low between poles driven into the ground. Neatly arranged under its fawn canopy are some coloured carpets and cushions. Clearly, this is a nostalgic display of their past traditions. It begs the question of whether these people and others like them will really stay in villages; or will the lure of the desert prove too strong if, and when, favourable conditions return?

It seems that they probably will stay, for they have invested much effort in creating such villages. At least, the villages will become a permanent part of the nomadic groups' lives with part of the family staying in them to practise sedentary farming, while others graze livestock, perhaps of better quality, and roam less far than in the past.

In some Tuareg settlements started since the last drought, the women have begun to work in the fields, though this is not yet the case in Kalinsar. If this practice becomes generalized, one could expect to see the women working the land while the men graze their livestock within a few kilometres' radius.

★   ★   ★

It had rained more than usual during May 1987 in the highlands of Ethiopia. They were an emerald paradise at the time. It was difficult to imagine this verdant land had been parched, barren, and the scene of so much distress and death in recent years, particularly in 1984 and 1985. Nor was it easy to imagine that only a few months later, drought and despair would again stalk these hills.

The road from Kombolcha to Bati, in the region of Wollo, twists through the hills, following a river that rushes and tumbles in May 1987, but which drought has often reduced to a lifeless litter of dry boulders in recent years.

Bati is a small town lying on a slope in the rolling countryside. It is a place few people had heard of until late

1984. Then, an area just outside the town became one of the many camps for refugees from starvation. During the subsequent months, journalists and aid-workers descended on it in droves.

We turn off the main road. At the corner is the local mill where people come to have their grain ground. A roar of machinery emanates from the interior, while outside donkeys and camels await their owners. The donkeys are impassive and seem half asleep in the strong sun of that high altitude, but the camels are wide awake, sneering and disdainful as always.

We enter a dirt track that twists down into a ford through a stream. We climb away from the ford and continue up the dirt track until, suddenly, we are overlooking the Bati camp site. Now, it consists only of six long corrugated-iron buildings with open space around them. At the height of the crisis in 1985, there were almost 30,000 people in this camp, and a further 8–10,000 were squatting outside in the hope of receiving help.

During the worst time, as many as 130 people a day were dying in Bati. At better times, 40–50 people died each day. Trucks carried the bodies to the far side of the scrub-covered hills east of the camp where funeral parties buried them in unmarked graves.

There is still a roughly-painted sign over a door into one of the corrugated iron sheds that says, "Save the Children Fund Office, Bati". A less imposing office would be hard to imagine; it is a striking reminder of the harsh and primitive conditions in which relief agencies so often work. By the end of 1985, most of the adults had left the camp, although a few were unable to do so until the harvest of 1986, and Bati became a shelter for orphans. It has looked after 1,450 children from a wide area, and helped re-settle them or re-unify them with members of their family.

When we visit Bati in 1987, the camp is still looking after 261 children orphaned by the drought or separated from their parents. They are being cared for and given education. The life of the camp, the summoning for food or lessons, is regulated by a large and unusual bell hanging from a wooden frame in an open area between the sheds. It is an enormous brass casing from an artillery shell which emits a loud clang when struck with a stick.

We sit on the steps outside an information and briefing tent on a hillock overlooking the camp. During the crisis, journalists and visitors were taken to this same vantage point for a bird's eye view of the misery below. They could also read off the figures of daily deaths, new arrivals, children in supplementary feeding, and malnutrition rates displayed on boards in the tent.

Now, we talk to Zerebe Yimer. He is 10 years old, lively and optimistic despite his harrowing past. He proudly writes his name for me in Latin script.

I come from the village of Tchake, in the Dessie Zuria area, far from here [he tells us]. My mother died when I was very small and I don't remember her. I lived with my father and a brother who was bigger than me. My brother went away to the army.

We had a cow and a heifer calf. My father often talked about the hard years we were having. We never seemed to have enough to eat. Then the drought came and there was no grass for the cow. She got very thin and she died, and then the heifer died too. It rained a little and my father and I sowed some seeds, but the drought came back and the plants died.

My father began to sell firewood to make some money to buy food, but he was very tired. He became ill with malaria and had a big fever for many days. Then he died too. We had no food left and the president of our Peasant Association took me to his home. He did not have much food either and he asked Concern [4] whether they would take me to their camp. They said that I could go next day. I slept outside and was very hungry until they came for me. I came to Bati later.

Zerebe Yimer and his 260 companions in Bati represent a sort of hardcore for whom the camp management is facing difficulties finding a home, or relatives with whom to re-unite them. Meanwhile, the resilience of children comes to their rescue. "What would you like to do in life?" I ask Zerebe. "I want to be a doctor", he replies.

★   ★   ★

We negotiate a track in the hinterland beyond Bati. The Land Cruiser is in its lowest gear, heaving and rolling so that we have to hang on grimly. The track, normally used only by animals and people on foot meanders through scrub, up and down rocky ledges and through tight hairpins. The wheels scrabble for purchase; the engine labours. Finally, we come around a last shoulder in these majestic, rolling highlands and we are met by a scene of idyllic beauty. There is a group of *tukols* – traditional round thatched Ethiopian houses – on a hill-top, surrounded by eucalyptus. Cattle are grazing in a lush landscape below, and just before us a farmer is ploughing a small field with a pair of oxen.

We gather in the shade of a magnificent spreading tree, and the ploughman, Said Ahamet, joins us. He is of medium height, very thin and with the fine features of so many Ethiopians. He tells a story that seems hardly credible in 1987 as we look on this scene of apparent pastoral fertility. But the Wollo region was desperately hit by the last drought, and also by many earlier ones.

I was born here in Kame and I have lived here all my life. I think I am about 35-years-old, but I do not know exactly.

In May 1984 we planted our sorghum as usual. There had been some rain and the crop began to grow. But there was no more rain and it withered. We would have planted again if there had been any rain, but there was none, not a drop. The animals ate the dried-up crop.

I can remember many difficult years here, but never one with no crop at all like 1984. I had a wife and two children to feed. We had some stocks of food from the 1983 harvest, enough for us until the next harvest, if there had been one.

We were very careful with our food, but by September it was running out. I had eight cows and I began to sell them to be able to buy food in Bati. The prices were very low, only about a quarter of their proper price. But we were luckier than some other people here. They tried to keep their cattle, and prices went even lower. So they still refused to sell, and then most of their cattle died.

We also had 26 goats. We tried to eat goat meat, but we could not eat it alone, without cereals. We also sold a necklace belonging to my wife. We had paid 4O Birr [5] for it and they gave us 1 Birr for it. When we had nothing left, we began to sell the goats...

[He pauses, looking pained.]

No, 'sell' is not the right word [he goes on]. I do not like talking of these matters. Selling is when you have something that someone else wants and you negotiate a price. Nobody wanted what we had. We had to take whatever they would give us. That is not selling.

The normal price of a goat would be about 3O Birr, but everyone was trying to sell their animals and I could only get 5 Birr for mine, or sometimes even less. With that I was able to buy about one kilo of food, enough for two days for my family if we were very careful. By October we had 18 goats left.

The enormity of his situation suddenly hits me. "You were able to buy food for 36 days," I said. "But you couldn't expect any crop, even if it did rain on schedule, until the Belg [6] crop in June of the next year. What were you going to do?"

"We expected to die," Ahamet replies, simply and without emotion. "But we were lucky," he goes on. "One day, some people taking firewood to Bati came back and told us that tents were being put up on a flat area outside the town. A few days later, we heard that some food was being given out. When we had finished all our food, we walked to the camp at Bati. Everyone from Kame went there when they had finished their food, about 3O families in all. Only two old couples didn't go. They were very weak and they preferred to stay here and die in their homes."

Notes

1 Goukouni Oueddei: the leader of a faction fighting the government of Hissan Habre and who had, at the time, formed an alliance with Libya.

2 Mango rains are the short rains that normally arrive in these areas of the Sahel in March-April and create enough growth of pasture to carry the livestock over until the main rains begin in June.

3 CFA 5OO,OOO was equivalent to about US$1,65O in that period.
4 Concern: An Irish voluntary agency that does relief and development work in the field.
5 There are about 2 Birr to the US Dollar.
6 With the exception of Tigray and Eritrea in the northern part of the country, Ethiopia generally has two rainy seasons, the Belg and the Meher. The short, Belg rains should peak in March–April to provide a crop around June. The Meher, the long rains, should peak in July–August to produce the main crop in November. In a normal year, the Belg crop, though not as important as the Meher crop, provides significant quantities of food grains, especially in the southern and eastern Highlands, including the region of Wollo. More details will be found on rainfall patterns in Chapter 4.

2

"A BIBLICAL FAMINE" AND ITS MAKING

The people described and cited in the preceding chapter were tiny fragments in a vast mosaic of human suffering that covered, and still cover, many parts of Africa. Let us turn now to the broader picture of that suffering, and to some of the underlying factors that helped to bring it about.

The situation in Ethiopia was the first to be drawn to world-wide attention, arousing enormous public concern for what was going on both there and in other countries of Africa. The words that follow were delivered by Michael Buerk of the BBC as commentary to two TV reportages which he made in Makelle and Korem feeding camps in northern Ethiopia in October 1984.

Dawn, and as the sun breaks through the piercing chill of night on the plain outside Korem, it lights up a biblical famine, now, in the twentieth century. This place, say workers here, is the closest thing to hell on earth.

The situation in Ethiopia has gone well beyond the stage at which words like tragedy and disaster have any meaning. It's a situation that is out of the control of the government here, or of the international voluntary agencies. It will be nearly a year before Ethiopians can expect proper rains again. By that time, thousands of people, perhaps even millions of people, may have died.

Plate 3   Senegal – a child stands beside the remains of cattle destroyed by drought near the village of Rose Bethio in the north.   (FAO/Yannick Muller)

The cameraman working with Buerk was Mohamed Amin, a highly talented film and video man who works with Visnews out of Nairobi. He recorded and edited his images so skilfully that when they were broadcast in prime time in Britain on 23 and 24 October, and when they were subsequently shown on 425 of the world's TV networks, they shocked hundreds of millions of people to the very core.

Some two-and-a-half years later, Buerk was asked during a radio interview how he had felt when putting together those reportages from Makelle and Korem. He replied to the effect that the sight of such suffering, and on such a scale, affected him deeply. He was seeing, hearing and smelling the scene, and his worry was whether he would be able to convey that misery and distress to people sitting in their armchairs in front of their TVs, and seeing it only in two dimensions.

It is a matter of history that he succeeded brilliantly. His spare commentary made no attempt to go into the complexities of the causes of famine. He allowed the horrifying pictures to speak for themselves, minute after minute of scenes and sounds of holocaust; there were few, but well-chosen, words by Buerk in commentary. The coverage unleashed a wave of sympathy the world over. Most people dug deeply into their pockets and contributed to relief work on an unprecedented scale. At the same time, the growing weight of public opinion forced many donor governments to take urgent action.

The Buerk/Amin coverage was complemented by widely broadcast radio reports from Mike Wooldridge, the BBC's East Africa correspondent. These BBC reports in October 1984 were certainly not the first information about the Ethiopian famine to reach audiences in the industrialized countries. In July 1984, Irish TV had shown a film called *When the Crying Stops*. British ITN news and TV channels in twelve other countries had picked up the story. There was also Charles Stewart's 60-minute documentary *Seeds of Despair* shown on British screens, also in July 1984, but it was not taken up by the US networks, perhaps because the presidential election campaign was in full swing and the Los Angeles Olympic Games were due to start shortly.

However, long before the major items of TV and radio coverage just mentioned, the news media had been reporting on famine conditions in parts of Ethiopia. As early as April 1980, the international media had given coverage to an appeal for help launched by the Ethiopian government. In the same year, there were appeals broadcast by voluntary agencies. At one time or another in the four years that followed, most of the news media in the industrialized countries carried items about the worsening situation in Ethiopia and in some other African countries. These reports did trigger responses in some quarters, but the scale of the aid provided was too small to avert the disaster.

The scenes of starving Ethiopians on TV that were broadcast long before those shot by Amin, even though equally harrowing, did not have the impact of the Buerk/ Amin reportage in mobilizing public opinion. The sheer power of the reporting, as already described, was certainly instrumental in creating this effect, but there were probably many other elements that also played a part. For example, the Buerk/Amin coverage went on the air at prime time on two successive evenings, when there was little other world news of importance. Furthermore, in autumn and winter, more people watch TV than they do in summer.

Whatever the precise reasons for the impact of the Buerk/ Amin reports, compared to earlier ones, it was their footage that finally made an information breakthrough. At last the world at large became concerned and mobilized; and it also began questioning why earlier action had not been taken to prevent the misery and death they were seeing on their TV screens.

Ethiopia got most of the media coverage in the west. As journalists gave the situation increasing attention, some of the coverage became negative and critical about the Ethiopian authorities. Some of that criticism was less than fair, as we shall see later.

★ ★ ★

Even if Ethiopia was the centre of attention for much of the time, in fact much of the African continent was in desperate straits. There had been the catastrophic drought of the early 1970s that had hit the Sahelian countries and Ethiopia in particular. It is never announced afterwards, and probably no one even knows, how many people have died during a famine. It is a statistic that no one wants to publicize, for it has negative reflections on governments and on aid agencies alike. However, it has been estimated that about 100,000 people died in the Sahelian countries, and about 200,000 in Ethiopia during the drought of 1973–74.

But as we have learnt from the testimony of the people heard in the first chapter, the drought of the early 1970s heralded a period of over 17 years in which conditions have continued to be adverse in Africa. Little news about these adversities ever made headlines until they developed into another, and even bigger, catastrophe in 1984–85. Tom Franklin, an American who worked for the UN in Ethiopia during the last crisis has put together a history (so far unpublished) which he calls *Cleft Stick – Dilemmas in the Development of a Disaster – Ethiopia 1974–1984*. He makes the point that Ethiopia has been on the brink of the precipice for a very long time. During the 20-year period between 1958 and 1977, about 20% of the country was under famine conditions *each year*, he states. Only one of those famines ever became known through media coverage – that of 1973–74 – but Franklin states that there were "silent emergencies", as he terms them, in most years.

Franklin believes that between 2 and 5 million people starved to death in those "silent emergencies", but he does not document these figures. In fact, the inaccessible vastness of the Ethiopian Highlands, in which people are scattered in dwellings on remote hilltops, coupled with the guerrilla activities in some parts of the country, make it difficult to obtain reliable and detailed information. There is little reason to doubt Franklin's point about the "silent emergencies", but how many people may have died in them remains speculative.

Ethiopia had been a net exporter of cereals in the years after World War II, but from 1976 onwards, it became clear that the need for relief food aid each year had become endemic. There were droughts or excess rainfall at the wrong time; there were attacks by crop diseases or pests; the limited land resources were degrading at an accelerating pace as a result of the excessive human and livestock pressure on them and of their improper use; and political strife compounded all these problems. Hundreds of thousands of people, and more often millions, were condemned to suffer food shortages each year. And slow take-off from the ports and lack of transport were making it impossible to prevent people from starving even when imported or donated food was available.

People uninitiated in relief and development work often think of famine as a disaster *event*, something that happens merely because it does not rain or because some other act of God intervenes. However, famines occur for a series of complex and underlying reasons related to such issues as poverty and environmental degradation, and of course to a general state of agricultural underdevelopment. Many countries or regions in Africa are now afflicted by all the basic and underlying conditions that can easily produce a famine with only a relatively small triggering cause. Therefore, the problems in Africa should not be considered in the context of one-off famines for which food is rushed to the scene. Rather, they should be looked at in a broader context of prevention, which implies sustained, long-term development action if the underlying problems are to be resolved.

For the rural poor, there is a slippery slope with, at the top, the assured basic needs of food, clothing, and shelter, while at the bottom, lie destitution and starvation. When people are hanging on near the bottom of that slippery slope, as millions in Africa are, and something happens to tumble them to the bottom, there is a humanitarian and moral obligation to rush in with relief aid. That relief aid may save many and lift them back on to the slope again. But they will still be in that precarious position near the bottom, ready to be knocked off again by some quite small triggering factor. The only way to break the cycle is to help people to reach the top of the slope. There, they will have the resources and capacity to withstand all but the most major of factors that could tumble them back to the bottom. In other words, long-term assistance to the poor to help them create sustainable assets is the only way to break the vicious circle of poverty that makes them so vulnerable to disaster.

Famines triggered by drought or by events such as locust plagues are nothing new in Africa. In the past, most of them went unnoticed. People withered on the vine, and there was no mass media to report that withering. Nor were there the international and private development and relief organizations to call on. However, it is a fact that the recent 17-year-period of drought and famines is the longest on record.

The alarm bell for the 1984–85 crisis that was maturing in much of Africa was rung in early 1983. The Food and Agriculture Organization of the UN (FAO) has a Global Information and Early Warning System that it had set up in 1975 in the aftermath of the famine of 1972–73. It uses satellite imagery to provide information about cloud cover and vegetation, which, of course, are guides to rainfall and drought. Linking this information to other data, the System aims at providing a timely alert to an impending crisis.

In May 1983, FAO telexed donors identifying 22 "needy" countries in Africa and asking for increased assistance to those countries. The number of countries in Africa that FAO identified as being "calamity affected" later rose to 24, and at one stage to 27, before dropping back to 21 in 1985.

In the event, and as the months passed, there were nine countries that really had disastrous situations on their hands. They were: Ethiopia, the Sudan, Chad, Niger, Mali, Burkina Faso, Mauritania, Mozambique and Angola. FAO has been criticized for raising an alarm for so many countries, thereby diminishing its credibility and distracting attention from countries that really had millions of people facing doom. But it is easy to criticize with perfect hindsight, and we shall look into early warning systems later in this book.

The response of the international donor community to the African crisis was late almost everywhere. Pride, politics and so-called diplomacy were often the principle causes of delay. In the Sudan, President Gaafar Nimeiry did not want to admit to what was happening in his country. Not so many years earlier, he had been declaring that his country could become the bread-basket for the Middle East, for it had vast unused tracts of land and the abundant waters of the Blue and White Niles. On this premise, he had courted oil-rich countries of the Middle East to invest in Sudanese agriculture.

Now, however, his country was in economic shambles, and in these already difficult circumstances, it was hit by the worst drought in memory. In many regions, rainfall in the years 1982–84 inclusive ranged from 10–50% of the previous 30-year average, and it was unevenly spread.

As early as March 1983, and in the face of government resistance, UNICEF sponsored a baseline study of nutritional levels among children in the Red Sea Hills. The Department of Community Medicine of Khartoum's Medical School carried out the survey among almost 3,500 children under the age of five in 73 different locations. They found that a third of the children were undernourished, and they clearly stated in their report that there was "evidence of a crisis situation". UNICEF took this information to the Minister of Health in October 1983. There was no reaction, no request for assistance.

The Red Sea Hills are essentially a nomadic area in which few food crops are grown. Thus, the suffering of the people revealed by the nutritional survey was not necessarily an indication of what was going on in the more agricultural areas of the Sudan. However, in the cropping areas, too, the

23

drought was having disastrous consequences. It was devasting the Sudan's vital sector of rainfed agriculture which normally produced almost all the sorghum and millet consumed by the population as its staple diet. After a bumper harvest of almost 4 million tons of cereals in 1981–82, the annual harvest dropped to less than 1.5 million tons in 1984. There was a shortfall of 1.4 million tons to meet the nation's needs. Two-thirds of the livestock died. Grain prices were soaring and were to increase by 400% during 1985. Farmers and pastoralists were flocking towards richer areas and towns. A mission on a fact-finding visit in January 1984 drove 50 kilometres out of El Fasher in Darfur; they passed 14 deserted villages in which they found that all the sorghum planted had either not germinated or had withered in the seedling stage.

An economic and human catastrophe was at hand, yet Nimeiry went on trying to conceal it. He did not ask for international help on an appropriate scale until November 1984. Before that request for help, the United Nations agencies could take no action, for they can step in only when officially asked to do so by the government concerned.

However, the United States was not held to such conditions. The US had an important aid presence in the Sudan, since it is the largest recipient of US aid in Africa south of the Sahara. American officials in Khartoum identified the crisis on the horizon in March 1984; by July 1984, they were advising Washington that the harvest would probably be only 50% of normal; and by September, a request for 82,000 tons of grain had been processed. The first of the shipments reached Port Sudan in November, before the Nimeiry government had officially acknowledged the crisis. Perhaps the Americans were out to show the world that their allies were well looked after, in contrast to the allies of the Soviet Union in the neighbouring country who had been getting plenty of military help, but nothing to alleviate the suffering caused by famine.

★   ★   ★

In Ethiopia, too, politics got in the way of an early

24

international response. The widespread dislike for, and distrust of, Mengistu's Marxist regime was to play an important role in the development of the crisis. A look at the build up to the famine there is instructive, and at the same time shocking when one realizes how human lives were sacrificed to politics, pride, and to some unfair media coverage at certain critical moments.

Ethiopia has a Relief and Rehabilitation Commission (RRC) that was set up in 1974 to deal with the emergency of the time. It started with a staff of six. It now has a staff af about 6,OOO, and during the crisis of 1984 and 1985, it employed over 12,OOO people. The RRC has an Early Warning System that has also been functional for several years; in fact it was the first to be set up in Africa. It attempts to identify impending crises and estimate how much relief food will be required.

From 1976 onwards, in each and every year, the RRC produced reports in which they called for food aid. They identified areas likely to be affected by drought or other problems, and estimated the number of people who would be in need of help. But international agencies usually considered that these figures were inflated, and that calls for help were based on insufficient hard data. They found the RRC reports useful in so far as identifying parts of Ethiopia that were at risk, but they tended to dismiss the figures for numbers of people likely to suffer.

A WFP evaluation report on the response to the 1984–85 famine in Ethiopia states that RRC's credibility had been eroded because in every year since 1976 the RRC "reported drought and millions in need of assistance without any major famine developing until 1984". In fact, the relief aid donated to Ethiopia in the years 198O–83 averaged only 2O% of the amounts requested by RRC. However, even if no "major famine" developed in those years, we should perhaps ponder for a moment whether Franklin's "silent emergencies" might not have been causing persistent suffering that went largely unnoticed in remote parts of the country.

Whenever a country has a looming or actual food deficit that requires external relief aid, there are discussions between the government and potential donors to determine the deficit as exactly as possible, the numbers of people at risk, in what areas, and so on. Some governments are more open than others in discussing these matters and in trying to come up with reasoned figures for agreeing supplies of emergency food aid. In Ethiopia, there were often polemics after the RRC produced estimates of its food aid requirements. The RRC would stand by its figures, while the donors would push for more information and generally query the data and methodology behind the figures.

In sum, there was mistrust between donors and the RRC, and food aid was not being supplied on the scale required. People were already suffering greatly by 1982, for the effects of drought were widespread. In December 1982, the Save the Children Fund (UK) opened a selective feeding programme at Korem and immediately admitted about 400 severely malnourished children. The Catholic Relief Services (US) asked for 838 tons of food from the American government for Makelle. WFP provided a first consignment of 12,000 tons of food for the Ethiopian Food Security Reserve. Meanwhile, drought victims from northwest Wollo had begun to trek towards Gonder in search of food.

In early 1983, the first FAO early warning report for the year confirmed the RRC's forecast of very grave food shortages. There were people in distress migrating all over the northern part of the country. About 15,000 farmers and their families had left their land to come to the town of Makelle, and the RRC had registered 14,000 people in the Korem camp. The situation continued to worsen. Various TV networks in industrialized countries gave coverage to the Ethiopian famine in the first quarter of 1983. In March of that year, the RRC estimated that more than 5.25 million people would be in need of assistance in the coming nine months.

Ethiopia now began to receive increased attention. The UN and numerous voluntary agencies were on the alert, the media had given coverage to the situation, and appeals had been launched. But then, on March 27, an article in the *Sunday Times* of London did severe damage to the Ethiopian cause. Under the headline, "Starving Babies' Food Sold for Soviet Arms", the journalist Simon Winchester wrote that "there was mounting evidence" to the effect that food aid to Ethiopia was being diverted to the army and that increasing amounts of it were also being sent to the Soviet Union as payment for arms.

Voluntary agencies in Ethiopia and the UN at once carried out an investigation. At the end of it, they pronounced that "there was no information to support allegations of misuse of relief food as cited in recent media reports". The EEC delegation in Ethiopia also carried out an investigation and wrote: "Allegations that food aid had been re-exported to third countries are unfounded." The report also said: "So far, no conclusive evidence has been produced to show that food aid has been systematically diverted to the armed forces."

Simon Winchester had not been to Ethiopia to research his piece. His sources were recent defectors from Ethiopia, spokesmen for guerrilla movements fighting the government, or for charities unhappy with the Mengistu regime.

The *Sunday Times* piece was grist for the mill of the many people in authority in western governments who were opposing food aid to Ethiopia. The story stuck as no favourable story ever sticks. When I was researching this book, countless people told me, with complete conviction, that Ethiopia was re-exporting food aid to the Soviet Union during the famine.

Quite apart from any enquiries carried out, it should be mentioned that Assab is a small port, and there were relief agency staff in that port day and night. There was no way that food cargoes could have been reloaded without it being widely noticed. Perhaps the story started from the fact that the Soviet Union had given 300 army trucks to Ethiopia, complete with army drivers, to move food within the country. People saw food being loaded on to these trucks and drew the wrong conclusion.

While on the subject of diversion of food, it does seem probable that some went to the armed forces. But it has also been pointed out that in the areas of the country with active guerrilla movements, local people often stored their food in the nearest army post, since it would be better defended there than anywhere else. Overall, and towards the end of the emergency, the major donors concluded that the total diversion of food aid had been less than 5%.

The overwhelming opinion of most people who have worked in Ethiopia and elsewhere in Africa is that the RRC is a far superior organization to similar ones in the continent, and that it does a very creditable job, given the enormous problems it faces. The head of the RRC in the most critical period was Major Dawit Wolde-Giorgis. Dawit had previously been the military governor of Eritrea. He was tough, and an excellent orator who also spoke perfect English. But he was often blunt to the point of arousing antagonisms. In particular, he seemed to raise the hackles of the Americans, not only because he was prone to hectoring donors, but also because he was prone to propounding the Marxist government's hardline policies. But an expatriate adviser to him during the critical early-1985 period described him as deeply concerned for the people of his country and one of the most impressive men he had ever worked with. In passing, it is paradoxical to note that Dawit later defected to America.

Quite apart from any irritation caused by Commissioner Dawit, the Mengistu regime is so unpopular in many western countries that no opportunity is lost to vilify it. There can be little doubt, in fact, that some people in positions of power in the west hoped that the Mengistu government would be brought down by the famine. Food is power, after all. Plenty of governments have been brought down in the wake of famines, including that of the Emperor Haile Selassie. Perhaps, therefore, some governments preferred to wait on the sidelines while Ethiopia collapsed under the stress of famine, thus hastening the demise of its detested Marxist regime.

However, it should also be said that the regime has often laid itself open to criticism. The Ethiopians sometimes seemed to go out of their way to be belligerent and difficult. Even after America was finally providing assistance on a massive scale, in fact paying for over a third of all the famine relief, the regime made difficulties about the number of USAID officials in Ethiopia helping to administer that aid. The regime restricted the number to five people. Furthermore, Mengistu attacked the West during a May Day parade and accused it of waging "psychological warfare" against his people. At the same time, aid from the West was flooding into Ethiopian ports.

Ethiopians are tough, proud people who do not mince words. Their uncompromising stance, and the fact that many in command give the impression that the sun rises and sets on the Soviet Union, alienates many potential friends in western countries.

The regime is dictatorial and harsh even with its own people on occasion, and this does not help it either. There was the infamous and widely publicized incident when a fanatical local party secretary had people forcibly evacuated from the feeding camp at Ibenat, in the Gonder region. By the time the UN and voluntary agencies had taken action and got the people back from the hills where they had taken refuge from the troops, many were suffering from exposure. The UN showed some teeth on that occasion, and Chairman Mengistu admitted to Kurt Jansson, the UN Assistant Secretary General for Emergency Operations in Ethiopia, that a mistake had been made. The party secretary was disciplined, but not before much damage had been done both to the people forced out of the camp, and to Ethiopia's reputation.

The Ibenat incident was first reported in the *Washington Post* and was then taken up world-wide by the media, creating an uproar of outraged criticism of the Ethiopian regime. In this case, there was good cause for such criticism, even if it was a maniacal local official who had acted on his own initiative. According to Jansson, however, the world press embellished the story of Ibenat by inflating the number of people who had been evicted from the camp and by saying that the camp itself had been burned. Jansson's monitoring staff had ascertained the number of people evicted as 36,000 – much lower than many figures cited by the press– and Jansson personally flew into Ibenat immediately after the incident and later stated that the camp itself had not been burned.

Embellishment, and inaccurate reporting, plagued much of the media coverage. Some of the western press remained hostile, quick to leap on rumours and to use them to denigrate the government. For example, the *Sunday Times* returned to the attack with another, but less prominent, article in December 1983 which reported on a cover-up carried out by RRC in respect of 15,000 tons of WFP food that had gone astray. There was proof of this cover-up in the form of a letter to RRC staff from its management telling them to do it and to destroy the evidence after the WFP auditor had finished his work.

However, the food was not missing at all: the intended beneficiaries had received about the same quantity of grain, but it had come from another donor. In effect, the RRC had carried out a swap, which under WFP regulations they were not allowed to do without prior consultation. What RRC was in fact covering up was that they had done the swap without permission, *not* that the food had been diverted.

The sad aspect of unfair reporting was that every time the government got a bad press, and unfounded stories of food diversion or of the government deliberately withholding aid in certain areas were concocted, they sabotaged the efforts to find the resources required to prevent millions from dying. So it was the stricken and long suffering people of Ethiopia who were being put even further at risk by inaccurate journalism. In sum, media coverage of the Ethiopian crisis was a mixed blessing: on the one hand, without coverage such as that of Buerk and Amin, the

general ignorance of the plight of millions, and the indif-
ference to it in many government circles, might have
continued; on the other some of the media coverage made it
harder to help the people in need.

The early months of 1984 were a crucial period in the build
up of the "biblical famine" in Ethiopia. Many people have
stressed that the first few months of that year were the latest
time in which the worst of the catastrophe could still have
been averted, if rapid international action had been taken.
The events in those fatal months leading up to October
1984, when the world was finally aroused to the tragedy, are
instructive and could be a useful lesson for the future. What
follows is an outline of those events. It has been pieced
together from various written and verbal sources. Some of
those sources contradict each other, or at best have a
different slant on the events according to their role in them,
or to their prejudices. Indeed, providing this outline is like
stepping into a minefield with big boots, but the issues are
too important not to make an *attempt* to provide an unbiased
view of what happened.

On 30 March, the RRC called a donors' meeting in Addis
Ababa. Commissioner Dawit spoke compellingly of the
disaster facing the country, and a video of the drought
conditions and of the people's suffering was shown. A
document produced by the RRC was then distributed. The
document pointed to problems of drought in many parts of
the country and came up with the staggering figure of 7.4
million people that would be in need of food aid that year.
Of these, about 2.2 million were people displaced by war,
but the remaining 5.2 were drought-affected. To feed the
latter, 912,OOO tons of food would be required that year.
To most of the donors, it seemed like yet another in the
series of exaggerated assessments made by the RRC for
earlier years.

According to Tom Franklin's detailed account, a fatal
tactical error was made by the RRC in its appeal of 3O

March 1984: the RRC admitted that with the existing state of the ports, and the limited transport and road system, it would be unlikely that it could distribute 912,OOO tons of food. The RRC therefore limited itself to reaching only half of those affected and wrote: "This brings the ... food aid requirements down to 45O,OOO tons." Taking into account the stocks of 6O,658 tons it had set aside for an emergency food reserve, the RRC had what it termed a "deficit" of 389,342 tons. The report went on to say that even this lower amount could only be properly administered if the donor community provided logistic help and ancillary supplies such as medicines, tents, water supplies, agricultural inputs, etc.

In other words, the RRC was basically saying that they *needed* 912,OOO tons of food to feed their people, but that they could not physically take delivery of such an amount and distribute it. They therefore requested less food, and they thereby introduced the notion that logistic capacity to deliver food should be the criterion by which to judge how much food aid the country should receive, implicitly accepting that many people would go short.

This notion was later perpetuated by a three-man FAO/WFP Food Supply Assessment Mission that visited Ethiopia in February–March 1984, the same period in which the RRC was preparing its appeal of 3O March. The Mission consisted of an agricultural economist, a logistics specialist (both of them consultants recruited by FAO), and a very junior officer from WFP. It terms of experience, it was not a strong mission, and it did not include a nutritionist. This proved a serious omission.

The Mission's report was not published until June 1984, even if its main findings were available to the Ethiopian government at the end of the Mission's month-long stay in the country. The conclusions of the report, or rather the way they were interpreted, provoked acrimony and scorn. For the impression left by the report was that the UN's official estimate of the quantity of food *required* in Ethiopia was only 125,OOO tons, against the 389,342 tons *requested* by RRC, which in turn was against their estimated real *requirement* of 912,000 tons (the amount that would be needed to feed everybody adequately, if it could have been unloaded from ships and distributed). The report of that Mission was almost certainly an important factor in delaying the mounting of an effective relief operation. In effect, it influenced attitudes among potential donors until the famous BBC TV coverage proved that things were at least as bad as the RRC had said they would be.

We have seen how a 912,000-ton requirement became a "deficit" of 389,342 tons according to the RRC, but how did the FAO/WFP Mission's report lead to the impression that only 125,000 tons were "required"? The opinion of some observers has been that the Mission was grossly incompetent, but this is too simplistic a view by far, even if it is true that the Mission's performance was below par in certain areas.

To set the scene, Tom Franklin makes an interesting observation regarding the context in which the Mission had to work. He states that the Mission was in a very difficult bind because, on the one hand, the "Ethiopian government wanted UN support for its position", while on the other, "most donors were reluctant to believe anything that looked as though it had been influenced by government figures".

In essence, Franklin argues that because of this situation, the Mission was reluctant to pronounce itself clearly in its report and avoided direct and open commitment. Firstly, in a muffled way, the Mission said that it agreed with the RRC's assessment of requirements and went on to say: "Thus the total requirement is estimated at approximately 684,000 tons."

This immediately looked like a massive reduction from the RRC figure of 912,000 tons. However, the Mission was referring to the *9-month* period to the year end, while the RRC was referring to the *12 months* beginning in April 1984. In both cases, the requirement was identical at 76,000 tons per month.

However, the report went on to say: "Considering the present and potential logistic capacity for the transport and distribution of relief goods (mainly food aid), as well as accessibility to the affected areas, the Mission concluded that 125,000 tons can be transported from the ports to the drought-affected areas and distributed internally between April and December 1984 to supply the drought-affected people in the northern regions."

In effect, this was a figure of about 14,000 tons per month. To donors inherently unwilling to give to a Marxist regime which they thought was diverting food to the military, and also deliberately trying to starve out its enemies, it was easier to conclude that the country only *required* 125,000 tons than to delve into what the Mission was really saying in its diplomatic circumlocutions – which was that the country could only *distribute* 14,000 tons a month but that it *required* 76,000 tons a month.

It will be seen that words such as "requirement" and "deficit" were incorrectly used by the RRC, and the Mission did not clarify these issues. Later, there was even more confusion when official UN documents referred to a "requirement" of 125,000 tons.

Quite apart from these issues of terminology, there were some even more important problems and confusing factors that embroiled the Mission. These problems were of such a fundamental nature that they are worth mentioning here, for they could raise their heads again, at any time and in any place, to plague a food supply assessment team.

Firstly, the Mission that worked in Ethiopia in early 1984 was there about three–four months after the 1983 harvest. They could not make their own independent assessment of the crop and had to base their analysis on figures provided by the Central Office of Statistics (CSO). These indicated a total production of cereals and pulses of 7.3 million tons, only 6% lower than the record crop of 1982. But after the Mission's visit, the CSO revised its production figures downwards to only 6.1 million tons. Thus, for its analysis, the Mission had used a total crop production figure that was 1.2 million tons more than the reality.

Furthermore, the official population figure for the country used by the Mission was 35 million people. In 1984, a population census was carried out, but the results were not available at the time of the Mission's visit. When they were published later, they revealed that the real population of the country was 42 million, so there was a discrepancy of 7 million extra people.

The Mission did not travel as extensively in the countryside as would have been desirable, partly because of difficulty over government permits. They did visit parts of Tigray, Eritrea, and Gonder, saw the drought conditions there, and also noted that people had begun to gather at food distribution centres. But the problem they observed was still relatively small. There were only about 3,000 people in the Ibenat centre, for example.

Another confusing factor in trying to assess the real situation was that the Agricultural Marketing Corporation (AMC) had been holding a carryover stock of 240,000 tons of cereals on 1 November 1983. This was the result of good harvests in some parts of the country in 1982 and 1983. At the time of the Mission's visit, AMC was trying desperately to get rid of its surplus stocks at below the already low official prices. (It had also promised the aforementioned 60,658 tons to an emergency food reserve.) It would seem therefore that even the AMC was not aware of the impending crisis, or they would not have been unloading their stocks as they were. The manager of the AMC was later removed from his post, perhaps because of his actions during this critical period. Certainly, there can have been little coordination between RRC and AMC if the former was shouting for food aid while the latter was selling off grain at rock bottom prices. Admittedly some of it was being sold to drought-affected people along the roads in Wollo, but there was no point in generally promoting extra purchases and consumption by lowering prices to all and sundry at such a critical time. With the market situation as easy as it was, the Mission was led into believing that there must also be good on-farm supplies of cereals.

The Mission's findings in respect of Ethiopia's *overall* cereal deficit, based on a daily need per person of 500 grams, was that 400,000 tons of food aid would be needed for the rest of the year. This figure was based on the assumption that surpluses in the central parts of the country would partly offset shortages in the drought-hit north. However, this would have implied, firstly, that people in the drought areas had the means to purchase the grain, and secondly, that it could be delivered to them, despite transport and security problems. Realizing that there would almost certainly be problems on both these counts, the Mission decided to accept the RRC's higher estimate of requirements, but expressed it as 684,000 tons for 9 months, rather than the RRC's 912,000 tons for 12 months.

The logistics aspects of the Ethiopian situation was also fraught with problems and contradictions. The RRC's record of food distribution was abysmal. For the year 1981–82, it had averaged only 3,500 tons per month, and for the year 1982–83, it had averaged only 6,350 tons per month. So bad was the situation that the Office of the UN Disaster Relief Coordinator (UNDRO) had raised money from the EEC in the last part of 1983 to help RRC resolve some of its transportation problems. When the FAO/WFP Mission was in the country, it found that the funds supplied through UNDRO had not even been spent in full. This helped influence the Mission towards the notion, already promoted by RRC, that the main criterion for establishing the quantity of food to be provided was the RRC's distribution capacity. Thus, they reached their figure of 125,000 tons. Even this quantity of food to be distributed over 9 months would be almost 14,000 tons a month, more than twice RRC's best delivery rate in previous years. And this would not take into account any stocks of food already in Ethiopia that would need to be distributed.

Having sketched out the complications and confusing issues faced by the Mission, we should also examine where they did, in fact, perform poorly. Firstly, the language used in the report and the way the findings were presented were so roundabout that it was too easy to miss the points being made. Secondly, although the Mission did recommend that US$12 million be provided to improve logistics, they should have hammered home the point that logistics were the key factor. They should have stated clearly, and without hedging, that the country *needed* 76,OOO tons of food a month, *and* an enormous injection of logistics help to get the food through the ports and delivered to those in need. When the relief operation was at its height, well over a year later, these were approximately the quantities of food that were passing through the ports and being delivered each month. It was, in fact, the first time in history that such an enormous increase in port throughput and overland delivery had been achieved. It is understandable, therefore, if the members of the Mission were unable to envisage such levels of improvement being possible, but they should, at least, have identified the need for them.

Another point that totally escaped the Mission was the cumulative effect of several years of drought and civil strife on the populations in the northern parts of the country. In fact, the shortage of emergency food supplies in previous years had critically narrowed the margin between bare survival and death from starvation. Evidence of this was available in the country, and a nutritionist in the team would certainly have identified it.

However, even the best assessment mission in the world could not have foreseen the total failure of the Belg (short) rains that normally provide some food crops around June in the central parts of Ethiopia. That these short rains would be followed by very poor Meher rains, which provide the main crop, was also beyond prediction. The Mission did mention that the Belg rains were late, but this is quite common in Ethiopia and it does not necessarily imply a failure of the Belg crop. A really experienced mission, which included a nutritionist and which gathered more information in the field, would probably have raised the warning that *if* the rains failed to arrive, or were poor, the situation could rapidly turn into a disaster. For this is exactly what happened, turning a chronic situation of many years standing – and one which had not drawn sufficient donor attention – into a major catastrophe.

There was a final element in the forging of the Ethiopian tragedy, and the government was entirely to blame for it. September 1984 marked the 10th anniversary of the coming to power of the Marxist regime. Big celebrations were to be held in the capital, and the North Koreans were called in to organize them. US officials have claimed that Ethiopia spent US$200 million on the celebrations, which is probably an exaggeration, but large sums certainly were spent that might instead have been used to purchase food. Even more serious, however, was that the Politbureau concentrated all its attentions on the anniversary festivities and paid little heed to the RRC and the worsening famine in the preceding months. In effect, the RRC was being spurned by donors and by its own authorities alike in a critical period for millions of Ethiopians. In addition, the Politbureau did not want their celebrations marred by drawing attention to the famine ravaging their people, so journalists were not allowed to go to see what was happening in the drought areas until after the September festivities.

However, whatever the Politbureau did or did not do, it is worth mentioning that the RRC's estimate of the food aid required, 912,000 tons, turned out to be almost exactly right.

It will be clear from the foregoing outline of events that the situation during the build up to the Ethiopian disaster was extremely complex. Many factors and people were to blame for what happened. Nothing can be done about factors such as rainfall, but it is to be hoped that the people have learned some lessons for the future.

Elsewhere in Africa, matters were less controversial and

political. But on the practical level of what was happening to the wretched and the destitute, things were much the same.

Chad is the most land-locked of countries, with only about a third of it – the part below the 16th parallel – humorously referred to as "useful Chad". And even that "useful" part contains much desert. A population estimated at about 4.5 million lives in this vast and mainly inhospitable tract buried in the middle of Africa. In addition to its natural problems, it had had a civil war going on for about twenty years. Drought had the country in a grip that slowly tightened from 1981–82 onwards. Two million of Chad's people were in its clutches. Some of the worst suffering was in the southern, agricultural parts of the country. Two years of crop failures caused by localized droughts produced acute famine conditions, and hundreds of people died.

In the early stages of the drought, these sedentary farmers were less well able to cope than the nomads and semi-nomads further north. The latter, hardened by conditions in the desert, seem to have developed ways of hanging on to life when drought hits. They eat fewer cereals than ordinary farmers at the best of times, and when their animals are producing less than normal, they eke out their existence with things such as dates from the wadis. But when the crunch really came and their livestock began to totter and fall all over the barren waste, they too were reduced to looking for help. There were about 70,000 people who had newly arrived in N'Djamena, the capital. It is estimated that 600,000 people moved into Western Sudan, 40,000 into the Central African Republic, and about 8,000 into Cameroon.

All over the Sahel too the drought was causing severe suffering. In Niger, the President was slow to ask for help and in the end was prompted to do so by representatives of foreign aid agencies. The government declared its emergency and asked for help on the last working day of 1984. Out of a total population of about 6 million, 2.5 million needed help. There were distress migrations of about 400,000 people. The government stopped these people from coming into towns and instead installed them in areas where dry season cultivation was possible. They were given food there rather than in camps.

In Mali, there were 200,000 people uprooted by the drought and about 1.5 million seriously affected by it. In neighbouring Mauritania, 800,000 people, or almost half the population, needed food aid, and there were 200,000 people displaced.

In Southern Africa, drought and strife joined forces to create catastrophe. In Angola, already in an economic and political crisis, cereal production was down 40% from its levels of 5 years earlier, and there were almost half a million people who had to leave their homes and land and look for food in camps. In Mozambique, 2.5 million people were in need of food aid in 1985.

The litany could go on but would add little to the picture of human suffering. Throughout Africa, 35 million people were affected by the drought, and 10 million people left their homes and land in search of food and water.

Many of these people ended up in camps, part of those apocalyptic scenes brought by TV to millions around the world. The prophecy made many years ago by the British author C. P. Snow was thus realized. He had predicted that the day would come when we would sit in the comfort of our homes and watch people starving to death on our television screens.

It took many months before some semblance of order was brought to those feeding camps, which in effect were initiated by spontaneous gatherings of people who had come towards towns in search of help. People often arrived in desperate straits. In Ethiopia, more than 60% of the people live more than a 2-day walk from the nearest road, and some had had to walk for many more days than that before arriving at a shelter. Many were being carried or helped by others who were still a little stronger. But none could have been very strong: the average weight of adults arriving at the Korem feeding camp was 33 kg (72.6

pounds), and the average newborn child weighed 2.5 kgs (5.8 pounds).

The camps needed wire and guards to allow entry only to those in the greatest of need. In the early months of the crisis, there was not enough food to go around, and so the aid workers were usually forced to apply triage, in other words, often deciding who was to die and who was to live by giving help only to those most in need and turning away those who seemed not to be in immediate danger. However, the aid workers knew full well that those children they turned away today would return in a week or so in desperate need and have to be admitted for help or die. They also knew that when they were ultimately admitted, they would be in such a state of distress that their chances of making a full recovery would be curtailed. A young volunteer nurse working in the hell-on-earth of an Ethiopian camp was asked by a television journalist what she felt about having to make such decisions. "It breaks my heart!" she said, with moving sincerity.

There, within those compounds, thousands upon thousands of people gathered, while thousands more waited outside hoping for food. There were seas of tents, improvised shelters, and in the early days before the relief operations got fully into gear, seas of people sitting in the open. They huddled in whatever shawls and ragged clothing they had managed to salvage. People whose bodies had been deformed by their suffering, grotesque stick figures with arms and legs that were nothing but bone, children with bellies and limbs bloated by kwashiorkor, or wasted by marasmus with their little behinds so emaciated that the skin had puckered into "tobacco pouches"; all lethargic with heads that appeared larger than normal because of the gauntness of the rest of their frames, with suffering and grief in their eyes, and with sores and ulcers on their skins.

The disease problems in such compounds were horrendous. People living in such close proximity, already debilitated by hunger, and with no sanitation, were prey to all manner of infectious illnesses. In many camps, measles killed thousands of children, as did respiratory infections. Apart from the whimpering and crying of those in distress and pain, coughing was the constant background sound.

Severe diarrhoea took the lives of thousands, especially children. Their intestines were so ravaged that sometimes, when defecating, they would excrete part of them before lapsing into death. There was cholera in many camps, although it was not always officially identified as such, perhaps to limit alarm and also to avoid possible travel and movement restrictions.

The relief staff working in these camps pushed themselves to the limits of their endurance. They were often sick themselves, and nearly always exhausted. At least initially, the less experienced volunteers were also overwhelmed by the scale of the human suffering and damage that confronted them. I once met a nurse in the Sudan who had spent over a year in relief camps. When we met, she had transferred to preventive health care. She said that she had reached the end of her tether in the camps. Emotionally and physically, she could take no more.

According to the UN, the total emergency needs in 1985 in response to the great African famine were estimated at $3.38,000 million worth of food, transportation, health services, water supply and sanitation, clothing, shelter, agricultural inputs, and so on. Of these needs, about 85% were met by the end of that year. The unmet needs, worth about $500 million and mainly in the non-food sector, were reassessed and where appropriate, brought forward into 1986.

About 6 million tons of emergency food were donated, transported and distributed in 1985, and more than 2 million tons followed in 1986. With what had gone before as the effect of the drought built up to its climax, a total of about 10 million tons of food was provided.

The largest donor was the US which shouldered the responsibility for almost half of all the emergency assistance. The EEC, World Food Programme, and Canada, were also major donors, but this, the largest relief operation in history, mobilized numerous donors world-wide. Private voluntary agencies of every conviction and creed – and some with no creed except human compassion – gave money, time, and services to those in need. Countries that not so long ago faced frequent famines themselves, such as India and China, gave large quantities of food.

From the organizational side, the African emergency was surrounded by some of the infighting which is unfortunately so common among the UN agencies. An outsider could be forgiven for expecting that the Office of the United Nations Disaster Relief Co-ordinator (UNDRO) would play a central role in planning and coordinating the relief work in Africa. For it was set up in 1971 with the responsibility of directing and coordinating the relief work of the UN system, and to coordinate that work with assistance coming from other inter-governmental and non-governmental organizations. However, although "coordination" and the need for it are constant themes in UN circles, none of the major agencies ever likes to be "coordinated" by someone else. UNDRO's rather vague mandate forces it to cross other people's path, which at once makes life difficult for it. Its problems in asserting its coordinatory role and authority were also compounded by some careless mistakes. For example, it once said that 5.2% of the population was at risk when it meant 5.2 million people, and it had to correct the mistake two weeks later with further telexes to donors.

The UN bodies that have direct mandates for disaster relief operations usually work rather well together. They are UNICEF, WFP, and the UN High Commission for Refugees (UNHCR). The quarrelling tends more to involve the bodies that are peripherally involved in disaster relief; its basis is the fighting for territory that generally goes on in bureaucracies.

In the UN, the difficulties of delineating responsibilities among exisitng bodies has led to the classic response of setting up a new organization or office to deal with a new problem. The African drought was no exception, but at least the United Nations Office for Emergency Operations in Africa (OEOA) was set up with a mandate limited to two years when it came into being at the end of 1984. It terminated its work as planned in October 1986 and was duly dissolved.

The New York-based OEOA had in fact been preceeded by an Office for Emergency Operations in Ethiopia. The chief instigators for setting up that Office in Addis Ababa were James Grant, the head of UNICEF, and James Ingram, the head of WFP. The former is an American, and the latter an Australian. Although they are quite different in their personal styles – Grant being more outgoing than Ingram – they have a similar sense of urgency and purpose; and they both pursue what they believe in with remarkable determination and energy. They met in New York and discussed the immediate need for the UN to assume its natural role as leader in the Ethiopian relief operations. They realized that highly-experienced senior people would be required to coordinate operations in a key country such as Ethiopia, and they agreed that Kurt Jansson would be the ideal man for the job there. Jansson, a Finn, had many years' experience of organizing relief work. In particular, he had been in charge of the UN relief operations in Kampuchea in the early 1980s.

Following the discussions between Grant and Ingram, the former conveyed their views and their urgent proposal to the Secretary General of the UN. As a result, the Office for Emergency operations in Ethiopia was set up, and Kurt Jansson was called out of retirement in the South of France to go to Addis Ababa. Later, and after the setting up of the OEOA in New York, Winston Prattley was assigned to organize and coordinate similar relief operations in the Sudan. Prattley, a New Zealander, had many years of development experience with the UN.

Some noses within the UN system were put out of joint by the creation of the OEOA, and by the organizational responsibilities assigned to it. However, during the crisis, the OEOA in New York, the Office for Emergency Operations in Ethiopia, and its counterpart in the Sudan, played an important role in negotiating with donors and with governments alike, and in coordinating the relief work.

It is certainly true that the relief operation started late in most countries, and the predictions were that millions would die. However, despite the bunglings, the politics, and the enormous problems, many fewer people than expected actually did die. Kurt Jansson has made an estimate of 500,000 famine deaths in Ethiopia, and certainly the death roll must have run into many hundreds of thousands throughout Africa. In fact, a figure of 2 million dead has been suggested. However, millions were also saved. More could have been had there been better information as the crisis developed, better planning, better logistics, and less pride and politics.

3
AFRICAN CRISES

There is a chronic, underlying crisis in most African countries upon which acute crises like those of 1984–85 easily superimpose themselves. Many adverse factors combine to create the chronic crisis, among them drought, population growth, insufficient food production, the cost of energy, international debt, and environmental degradation. Certainly, the drought was the triggering cause of the 1984–85 catastrophe, but it would not have caused the damage it did were so much of Africa not in a downward economic and environmental spiral.

Statistics need to be viewed with caution anywhere in the world. Particularly in Africa, however, many countries are enormous and have populations scattered over vast tracts of territory, sometimes totally inaccessible for several months each year. For this reason, the statistical data that is gathered there may be less than perfect. However, having entered that caveat, according to statistics issued by FAO, food production per head in Africa is now almost 20% less now than it was in 1960. This is because the population is growing faster than food production.

In fact, Africa's population is growing faster than any population has ever grown in any other part of the world. While the population of the rest of the world is doubling every 40 years, in Africa it is doubling every 24 years. As an

Plate 4   Mali – women have to walk miles to find firewood for cooking and heating.   (FAO/Franco Mattioli)

example, let us look at Kenya, one of the most prosperous and best managed of African countries. Today, Kenya's population is 2O million. Even if families limited the number of their children tomorrow to two per family, instead of the current average of eight, the population of the country would stabilize at 53 million because of the many young people now coming into the marriage-age bracket. As it is, projections are that Kenya will only stabilize its population when it has 121 million people, in the year 2O3O. Kenya has a limited amount of agricultural land; estimates are that, even it it were farmed with very high levels of technology of the sort used in, say, Holland today, the country could only feed 51 million.

Of course, many countries in Africa are far less densely populated than Kenya. Because of this, many African leaders in the past have resisted suggestions that they should limit their population growth, saying that they do not have an over-population problem compared to, say, Asia. Fundamentally, from the point of view of available space, they are right. But the problem is not one of space and available land; rather, it is a question of the economic stability and growth potential that a country has to support a burgeoning population. For with limited economic resources, how can a country develop food production, create jobs, and provide health and education services for a rapidly growing population, when it cannot even satisfy these requirements for its *existing* levels of population?

The last decades have seen Africa squeezed unmercifully by economic forces originating elsewhere in the world. The prices of Africa's exports of raw materials and agricultural commodities have fallen greatly. To quote some examples, cocoa prices fell by two-thirds in the five years leading up to 1983. The traditional export commodities such as coffee, groundnuts, cotton, sugar, tea, cocoa and palm oil fell by 27% between 198O and 1982. These dropping prices can be attributed to various factors that may work alone or in concert. Among the factors are: world over-supply, protectionism, changes in consumer demand, and the introduction of new technologies in industrialized countries. On the other hand, import prices, especially of petroleum, have risen enormously. In 1971, the beef from one Sahelian steer would buy one barrel of oil, whereas in 1981, nine steers were needed.

By 1984, only a few oil-exporting countries in Africa had positive trade balances. Most African countries borrowed heavily when their commodity prices were firm – especially in the early 1970s – and when they therefore had a good credit rating. Now Africa is saddled with enormous debts and debt-servicing costs.

At the human level, especially among rural people, incomes have been declining by about 2% per year. An International Labour Office survey established that between 1974 and 1982, the proportion of Africans who could not meet their basic needs of minimum diet, shelter, and clothing rose to 69% of the population (whereas in other regions of the world the proportion was dropping). In those eight years, the number of Africans who could not assure their basic needs rose from 205 millions to 258 millions.

Few would deny that the development policies of most African countries have been disastrous in the decades since independence. This perhaps has been the most important factor of all in determining the plight of so many countries today. Considering that in most of Africa, at least 70% of the people live in rural areas and depend on agriculture for their livelihood, the concentration on urban and industrial development in so many countries has been gravely misplaced. Africa is full of modern cities thronging with Mercedes and other prestige cars. But go a few kilometres beyond the city limits, and you find yourself in the Africa of old, the bush that has not changed in a hundred years – except that in many areas it is suffering environmental degradation – and where farmers' methods of cultivation have hardly changed either.

The concentration on the urban sector is understandable, for it is the urban people who provide political support, or who create difficulties, for rulers. Therefore, those in the towns must be looked after. They must have cheap food, even if the producers of that food, illiterate peasants stuck out in the boondocks, cannot make enough income from their labours to cover their basic needs. In such circumstances, we should not be surprised if peasants decide that it is not worth the time and sweat under the hot sun to produce for the market.

To overcome poverty and periodic famines, the rural and agricultural sector in Africa needs far more development attention than it has had in the past. Even with that attention, however, we must bear in mind that agriculture in tropical areas is not as easy as it is in temperate areas. Firstly, there are fewer hours of daily sunshine during the growing season in tropical areas. In Europe, during the main growth months of summer, there are about 14–15 hours of daylight, but in the tropics, day and night are roughly equal. Furthermore, in the tropics, the growing season is also the rainy season, so there is cloud cover during parts of many days, further reducing the hours of sunshine.

In addition to these problems affecting the tropics in general, much of Africa has a particularly harsh environment. It is geologically older than most temperate areas. Because of this, and often because of extremes of heat and rainfall too, its soils are more weathered. Consequently, many soils in Africa are coarser than most in the world. The heavy tropical rains easily leach out the soluble plant nutrients from such soils. Highly weathered tropical soils may also have high levels of aluminium oxide, which is basically toxic to plants, as well as large quantities of iron oxides which produce the reddish hues of so much of Africa. These iron oxides easily develop into hard layers, or pans, which plants cannot penetrate. Similarly, in many areas, silt and clay soils form surface crusts which hamper plant growth and inhibit the infiltration of rain water. Humous, that great mollifier of soils in temperate zones, quickly oxidizes in the higher temperatures of the tropics, and with less of it, crusting and soil compaction are common.

Erosion is a serious problem all over Africa. The intense rain storms and strong winds play havoc with any land unprotected by vegetation. And sand moved during sandstorms can bury germinating crops and ruin good farmland over time.

This tendency for rain to fall with tremendous intensity when it does come not only causes erosion but also results in more run-off and less infiltration and water storage in the soil. In addition, many parts of Africa have highly irregular rainfall, so crops may get away to a good start after planting, only to shrivel where they stand when a dry spell then sets in.

Even when climate, weather and soil conditions are good, some of the most fertile valleys have been rendered unusable because of adverse health conditions. The hideous affliction of River Blindness (onchocerciasis) has made whole areas of good valley bottoms uninhabitable in west and central Africa. The disease is spread by a black simulium fly that breeds in fast-flowing, aerated water. When it bites humans it transmits the disease, which first shows as small lumps under the skin. These lumps are formed by groups of tiny filaria worms. As long as they stay under the skin, they cause little harm, but in heavy infestations they usually get behind the eyes as well, thereby blinding the person. The disease tends to affect men more than women, and in some river valleys of Africa, as many as 70% of the men have been blinded. Fortunately, there is now an internationally-supported project trying to eradicate the disease, apparently with some success.

Much of Africa is infested by tsetse fly which spreads trypanosomiasis among cattle. This disease makes it practically impossible to carry out economic livestock activities, or even to use oxen for ploughing. Furthermore, trypanasomiasis, as sleeping sickness, is a serious disease in humans. Then there is bilharzia in most of the lakes and ponds, and once that parasite gets into people, it is debilitating and often fatal. Malaria is prevalent almost everywhere in the continent; it is responsible for many days of work lost per year, and for many other days of below-par performance. During an evaluation mission for a project in the Sudan in which I participated, we were told that on any given day during the rainy season, a third to a quarter of the project staff would be sick with malaria.

However, perhaps even more economically significant than these dramatic diseases are more insidious ailments such as chronic malnutrition and diarrhoea. These are the consequences of poverty and poor sanitation. In many countries of Africa, children suffer 4–5 severe bouts of diarrhoea a year, especially during the rainy season. It is a prime killer of infants under five years of age.

As for food and agriculture, national policies for health have been urban-biased. Governments have often invested heavily in high-technology medical services, such as modern hospitals with the latest equipment, but these only serve the more prosperous urban sectors. Many countries have expended 80% of their investment in health services to reach 20% of the population, virtually ignoring primary health care and preventive medicine among the rural people who make up the largest sector.

This urban bias in Africa has been a major negative factor from almost every aspect of national development. The contrast with countries like China is marked. There, every-thing has been done to improve the rural sector. After the founding of the People's Republic, there was an all-out drive for food production. This involved the development of production infrastructures, and so people were set to building small and large dams for water harvesting, digging irrigation canals, carrying out soil conservation work, reforestation, and so forth. Then, about ten years ago, when a flourishing agriculture was in a position to assure the country's basic food requirements, an emphasis on agri-cultural mechanization began freeing growing numbers of people from work on the land. This labour began to undertake a wide variety of small and medium manufacturing and servicing industries in the countryside. Today, the rural Chinese in many parts of the country are better off than the city-dwellers. Production incentives provide them with the possibility of earning a reasonable income; and services such as health and education in the rural areas generally match those in the cities.

Compared to China, most African countries face a number of quite different problems, including having fewer people spread thinly over the countryside. The Chinese example has been cited merely to bring into relief the question of national policies with respect to the rural sector. One outcome of policies in favour of the rural sector is that life in the countryside can be as rewarding and pleasant as life in the cities. And this means that there is little problem in finding well-qualified government staff ready to live and work there.

In Africa, however, to be sent to the countryside is often tantamount to a punishment. The living conditions may be primitive in the extreme, and in addition, the official or development worker may have to take a cut in salary because the living costs, at least theoretically, are lower in the rural areas. This is hardly a formula for attracting good staff and encouraging them to become front-line troops in the battle for rural development. Ministry offices are certainly important, but the victory over rural poverty is to be won in the field, not in those offices.

How many internationally-supported projects have failed because no good government staff could be attracted to work in them, and to stay in them? How much development money has been wasted though making do with lower-quality staff who do not have the capacity to make the project succeed? Such problems are legion, to the extent that some donors now pay salary supplements to national staff to attract them. This may be satisfactory as long as the donor is supporting the project. But in this scenario, whatever happened to the principle that a development project, even if it has external assistance to start it, is a *national* initiative which should be taken over by the government once it is up and running?

Certainly, governments are short of cash to pay their cadres, but why not look for other inducements to persuade the very best to work in the field, where they are needed? For example, would it be so difficult to arrange that people working in hardship posts earn extra seniority while they are there? Such seniority could take the form of faster promotions or more simply, each year in a rural area could count for, say, 15 or 18 months of service. If such inducements have seldom been made available hitherto, it is probably not because of inherent and insurmountable difficulties: a more likely cause is that the issue of having first-class staff in the countryside to help propel development has not been a major consideration. It will have to become one if African governments are now serious about their rural sectors.

The legacy of colonialism is another cause that is often cited for Africa's agricultural problems. During colonialism, the agricultural priority was certainly on cash crops, and it is said that this priority has been imprinted on Africa. There are elements of truth in this, but it is not the straightforward cause–effect relationship it might appear to be. If predominantly agricultural countries, like most in Africa, do not export agricultural commodities, how can they generate the foreign currency they require for their essential imports? For those not endowed with mineral wealth, there is no real alternative in their present state of development. Furthermore, many African governments have been very happy to promote cash crops as a source of foreign exchange, certainly, but also as a source of internal revenue. They often pay their producers prices far below world market prices and put the difference into the national exchequer. This is yet another blow at the rural economy. In many countries, such tactics are killing the goose that lays the golden egg.

An emphasis on cash crops often means that this sector receives favoured treatment in terms of such important inputs as credit, marketing, extension, and so forth, while the food crop sector receives little such support. This phenomenon is not confined to Africa: in the centre and south of Italy, for example, the only well-organized and effective applied research and extension activities are connected to tobacco!

Overall, it is true to say that pessimism about Africa's situation is based on its failure in agriculture. Fortunately, most African leaders today seem to have recognized the problem for what it is and have recently agreed to spend 20–25% of all future public investment in the agricultural sector, as opposed to the 6–10% they were investing before. It was high time that this change of heart took place. Previously, Africa was the only Continent in which investment in agriculture had been declining for several years. Perhaps the scene is now finally set for an agriculture-led recovery in Africa. Its farmers have proven themselves time and again to be competent and resourceful; all that is required is the right economic environment, inducements and technical support for them to produce far more than they produce at present. In effect, this means a reform of policy in respect of prices paid to farmers for their produce, an overhaul of the inefficient and costly parastatal marketing boards that exist in many countries, and properly organized services to farmers to provide credit and other imputs.

Many experts agree that Africa, despite its harsh environment, could very easily feed itself. And it is not only the fault of government policies if it does not do so today. For experts also agree that Africa has been ill-advised by development assistance teams. The World Bank's own evaluations have led to the conclusion that about a third of all its agricultural projects in West Africa, and about half of the same type of project in East Africa, have been failures. This compares with a failure rate of only one agricultural project in twenty in South Asia.

A consensus is emerging that too many projects have been planned without proper consultation with the intended beneficiaries. People in rural communities usually see their own problems in quite a different way than a superficial and external observer sees them. And unfortunately, too many projects are formulated on the basis of superficial and external observation of people's needs and capacities, and of their existing production methods and systems. It is hardly surprising, therefore, that so many projects have come up with proposed solutions that do not reflect local realities and the problems as the people perceive them.

For example, in Africa in recent decades, there has been much emphasis on irrigation in the semi-arid countries. Thus, capital and technology intensive projects have been developed. However, most of those irrigation schemes have turned into economic disasters. One cause of the problem has certainly been that large-scale irrigated agriculture is a totally new concept in many countries, and there have not been sufficient local people prepared to practise it effectively.

Irrigated agriculture is appealing to donors and recipients alike. Donors somtimes have a vested interest in selling equipment and construction services to establish irrigation schemes, not to mention that some donors tie their aid to equipment and supplies to be provided from their own industries. Recipients of aid often feel that irrigation and other relatively high-technology inputs are prestigious for their nation. Some of these problems can be illustrated by an experience I had some 15 years ago when I worked briefly on a project in the Jebel Marra area of Western Sudan. This mountainous area has a considerable agricultural potential, and the project was in effect a pre-investment study to determine the best crops to grow, systems of irrigation, and so on. The main snag with the Jebel Marra is that it is about a thousand kilometres in line of flight from Khartoum; and it is considerably further by the desert tracks that are impassable during the rainy season, and by the narrow-gauge railway to Nyala which is notorious for its precarious functional state.

There is good ground water in the Jebel Marra, often at quite shallow depths where it can be reached by hand-dug wide-mouthed wells. The first international project manager, who was Dutch, imported two windmills from Holland for water pumping. One was erected, but there was seldom enough wind to stir its blades; the other was still crated when I was there a year or more after its arrival.

The second project manager, who was in post at the time I was there, was a canny Swiss. He came up with the idea of bringing in two artisans from the Nile area to teach some local people how to make *saquias*, or Persian wheels, those water-lifting devices driven by a bullock harnessed to a shaft and plodding slowly in a circle around the well-head. The *saquia* and the *shadoof*, another simple water-lifting device, are the main stay of the irrigation in much of the Nile Valley, which holds some of the most intensive agriculture in the world.

However, when the canny Swiss mentioned his proposal to the local authorities in the project area, they turned it down flatly. They were scornful of such simple technology and wanted diesel pumps. The project manager argued that if a pump broke down, it would take weeks to get a part from Khartoum, even if the part were available in Khartoum. And if it were not, it would take months. And what about diesel fuel for pumps? The Sudanese were adamant, however, and virtually accused the Swiss of trying to keep them in a state of under-development by foisting primitive technology on to them.

There is little doubt that in areas of Africa like the Sahel, where each country has a relatively high rainfall area in the southern part, attention to improving traditional rainfed cereal crops such as sorghum and millet could have paid off with relatively little investment. In Mali, for example, millet yields average only about 700 kg per hectare. Starting from such a low base, it is often easy to bring about major yield increases. Merely using improved varieties and improved cultivation practices could almost certainly bring considerable gains.

All these considerations, and many others too, will need to exercise the minds of Africa's decision-makers if they are to pull their countries out of their crises. And if they do not, according to FAO estimates, Africa by the year 2010 will see its per capita food production decline by a further 30%; cereal self-sufficiency will drop from the present 85% to 56% in sub-Saharan Africa, which would mean a cereal deficit of 100 million tons a year, compared to little more than 20 million tons per year in 1979–81. The cost of importing so much food would be about $28,500 million, more than twice the projected value of agricultural export earnings.

No discussion on Africa's woes can ignore the chaos and misery caused by internal strife, as well as war between countries on occasion. It seems as though there has hardly been a moment in the last 25 years without there being at least one civil or international war in course in Africa. This state of constant turmoil usually has its origins in one or more of the following causes: the general absence of democracy in Africa; the lack of religious tolerance; rivalries between peoples, tribes and clans; and the instability of the new political regimes. Needless to say, the conflicts are more often than not fuelled by external interests.

These wars are an enormous drain on resources. For example, in recent years Chad has been spending 40% of its GNP on armaments. Firstly, it had a civil war, and then it took on the Libyans, who had occupied parts of the north, and successfully ousted them from most of it in early 1987. And Chad is perhaps the poorest country in Africa. We are forced to say "perhaps", for there is no knowing for certain whether its people are poorer than Ethiopians – who figure as the poorest in the World Bank's World Development Report for 1987 – because Chad is in such chaos that the World Bank can report few statistics for it.

At the time of writing, there seems a chance that peace may break out in Chad, after about 20 years of war.

However, the whole country seems geared to war and it will not be easy to adjust to peace. Weapons even seem to be part of the domestic scene. When I joined the *Prefet* of Mao in his home for a glass of beer, he said something in Arabic to a young man who was standing by. He went away and came back with the loaded magazine of a sub-machine gun from which he extracted two cartridges. He then used the magazine to lever the caps off the beer bottles!

Even if there is peace in Chad, the cost of repairing the damage wrought in all those years will be enormous. The capital, which the French used to call Fort Lamy, got its present name of N'Djamena after independence. The name is based on an Arabic term for "shady tree", and indeed the town has many acacias, lush-green or brilliant red flam-boyants, lining its dusty streets. However, any illusions of peace and rest for the soul that the words "shady tree" might conjure up have been shattered by events of recent years. At one point in 1980, eleven different factions were fighting in the town, and the place is still a wreck. It must have been rather elegant once. Apart from its trees and general air of spaciousness, the architectural style is Moorish and it has a natural grace. The low buildings, mainly of a warm, sandy colour and with many arcades, seem to fit the surroundings. The River Chari flows along one side of the town, set deep between sloping banks that are topped by trees.

However, there is hardly a wall to be seen anywhere in town that is not riddled with the pock marks made by bullets. At a guess, almost half of the buildings are without roofs, and many of them have livid scorch-marks on the walls above the window openings as evidence of a fire-devastated interior. Many of the roofless, windowless, and doorless houses have been taken over by pastoralists from the north who lost all their livestock in the 1984–85 drought. They have rigged mats and other materials to make improvised shelters within the four walls, and somehow they manage to stay alive. In the early morning, they brew a little tea on an open fire and sit in the dust in front of their impromptu home to drink it before going off to seek, by hook or by crook, something more sustaining for their emaciated bodies. Their poverty is absolute, but it seems that many are too proud to seek manual work.

At the time of my visit, a Japanese TV crew was in the country to record a distribution of rice donated by their country. As backgound footage, they were rushing around filming the damage in N'Djamena. A Chadian remarked to me: "I don't know what they are filming all that for. If they think the town is damaged now, they should have seen it four or five years ago. It really was bad then. A lot has been repaired since."

A lot may have been repaired, but there is still a lot to be done, and at what cost for a country so poor!

★　　　★　　　★

Strife brings terrible hardship to innocent bystanders. Mozambique is another country that has been at war for years, and as in so many countries, it seems to be a war that neither side can win. And so it drags on, disrupting production and making transport and communications difficult, if not impossible. It is estimated that about 5.5 million people, out of a total population of about 14 million, now depend on external food. Drought has compounded the hardship in recent years so that, by the early months of 1987, the alarm went out. People were dying of famine.

Peter Simkin of WFP was part of a mission sent to assess the situation. Simkin, who was trained in social anthropology and psychology, has long experience of working among the hungry and the poor in many countries of the world, including during the famine in Ethiopia in 1974. He is a man of compassion, and of mature and sober judgement. He describes a visit to the town of Inhaminga, in Sofala Province of Mozambique, during April 1987.

Inhaminga was an important town. It used to be the main railway workshop and shunting yard on the railway connecting Beira with Malawi and Tete. That railway line is now cut in several places. The bridge over the Zambesi has been damaged, and there are several trains that we could see from the air that appear to have been burned out or otherwise damaged. They're blocking the line.

Similarly, the road that runs alongside the railway line is impassable, and no vehicles, at least from the south, have been able to get through recently, as far as we know. So Inhaminga is cut off and has been for about three years. The only food that has arrived has been flown in. It used to have a population of about 40-50,000. We were told that it now has about 13,000 people.

From the air, there is no sign of any cultivation going on around the town. No sign of any movement of vehicles on the roads. There is an army garrison defending the town, which has been captured twice by the rebels and then recaptured by government troops. There has been a lot of intense fighting in that area, so virtually every building is damaged or burnt, and there are railway trucks in the sidings with rocket holes through them.

We were taken around the town by the military commander, and we went to see a number of families. They told us that many men had been taken away by the guerrillas. A few had escaped and come back, but certainly there were more women and children than men around.

Nearly everyone was dressed in rags or in sacks. They had no clothes, and the families we met were preparing the roots of trees and leaves from wild plants as their only food. They had had no cereals for some time. Others showed us the kernels of mango seeds they were eating as their main diet. Difficult to know when they had last had cereals, but we gathered that it was about 6 weeks before. Many of the children were showing all the symptoms of malnutrition.

The people have no tools or seeds so they can't make a start. It seems that the guerrillas have taken their tools away. We discussed bringing in food and we had a very faint hope of doing so from the north. That hope vanished when we saw from the air that two spans of the bridge over the Zambesi were down. We also learned how intense the fighting is in the Zambesi area, and it will be some time before that route is open. So some sort of air lift will have to be arranged. One problem is that the grass strip is short. We went in in a single-engined Piper, and I don't think anything much bigger than a DC3 could land there.

It's a situation that can suddenly become very serious, quickly, in that I think people can go on like that for a certain amount of time.

But after that, they've got no physical reserves left and they die very quickly. I think there were people dying when we were there. We asked how many children had died but we got no answer. The interpreter told us they didn't want to discuss it.

There must be many communities like Inhaminga, cut off by the fighting and suffering extreme deprivation from lack of food, lack of clothes, and soap, lack of seeds and tools. They need a lot of help, but it is difficult to get a clear picture of what is going on, and how much help is needed. Short of visiting places from the air, it is not possible to travel to them. Even travelling by air is quite dangerous. A Red Cross plane was shot up not so long ago. And once you get to these places, you usually aren't allowed to stay more than a couple of hours because of the security risk.

There are even bigger populations further north in the Zambesi area who are cut off. We don't know whether they've been able to grow any crops. [Simkin smiled sadly.] Well, it's probably good from the point of view of soil erosion and overgrazing, and of natural re-generation. And honestly, that's what is happening in Mozambique. I went to one town the Zimbabwe border, just 8 kms inside Mozambique, and two of the roads leading out, further into the province, were totally covered in bushes. They haven't been used in years.

4

DESERTIFICATION, DEGRADATION ANDDROUGHT

Africa has grave environmental problems in many areas, but perhaps the gravest problems lie in that transitional zone between the southern limits of the Sahara and the northern limits of the tropical rain forests. It is known as the Sahel and the Sudan. Both are words derived from Arabic. *Sahil* meaning "coast" or "shore" and *bilad as-sud*, meaning "land of the black people". The Sudan as a geographical term goes back to the 12th century. The names have been used differently by various vegetation classification systems applied to Africa. There is no agreed definition of the two, though most classifications seem to consider Sahel more arid than the Sudan.

It is now usual to lump the two terms together and call the area the "Sudano-Sahelian Zone". Some definitions say that the zone stretches from the Atlantic Ocean to the Red Sea, while others stop it at the mountains of Ethiopia. It is an enormous tract of the world however you care to define it. On average it stretches about 600 kms in the north–south axis; in the east–west axis, it is about 5,500 kilometres long if you limit it at the mountains of Ethiopia, and about 6,300 kilometres long if you consider that it extends to the Red Sea.

Although of course it is not part of the Sudano-Sahelian

Plate 5   Western Chad – a village being engulfed by the desert. The constantly shifting sand often covers complete villages and their fields.   (Colin Fraser)

belt, an extension of it, with similar rainfall and vegetation, loops south through the eastern part of Africa. It involves parts of Kenya, Uganda, and Tanzania, and then sweeps back across the Continent through such countries as Zambia, Zimbabwe, Zaire and Angola to the Atlantic. It leaves the tropical rain forests of central Africa to the north and the Kalahari Desert to the south. Although not as much at risk from drought as the area immediately to the south of the Sahara, this part of Africa has also been badly hit in recent years, and is suffering environmental degradation.

Much of these vast stretches of Africa are savannahs, expanses of grassland and open woodland of varying degrees of usefulness to man according to the rainfall. In the so-called sub-humid areas with 600–1200 mm of rain a year, which falls in rainy seasons totalling about 4–8 months, there will usually be abundant grass cover and a wealth of trees such as acacias. Cereals can be grown in these areas: maize where the rainfall is nearer the higher end of the range for sub-humid zones, and sorghum where it is nearer the lower end of the range.

Where the rainfall is around or below 600 mm a year, the area is considered semi-arid. As you progress from sub-humid to semi-arid, the vegetation gradually changes from the spreading, verdant acacias to the thorny ones, to scrub, and to sparse grass cover. In these areas, only finger millet can be grown as a food crop with little risk of failure.

In these drier areas, livestock production is the mainstay of the economy, provided that there are no tsetse flies to spread trypanosomiasis and so endanger animals. However, the tsetse is predominantly in the moister areas, where there is enough rainfall to support dense bush. The tsetse fly is a serious handicap because it hinders the integration of farming with livestock production. The symbiosis between the two has been the foundation for prosperous agriculture in many parts of the world. But in Africa this is not a possibility, unless or until the tsetse fly is eliminated.

★　　　★　　　★

Over the millenia, African peasants used farming methods

that were well attuned to their environment. As is usual anywhere in the world when there is plenty of available space, shifting cultivation was practised; and it still is in much of Africa. A farmer would clear the bush from a piece of land by cutting and burning, and farm it for as long as it was producing a fair crop. In most cases, this would mean 2–3 cropping years, and then he would move on and clear another piece of land.

As long as there were long rest periods, or fallows, in between periods of cultivation, the land would regenerate its fertility through the rest period as vegetation, bacteria and rain did their work. This method was perfectly suited to African conditions for thousands of years, when the fallow periods could be anything up to 20 years or more.

In recent history, however, things have changed drastically. The increasing human and animal population, and the need for countries to produce cash crops, has meant that less land is easily available for food production. The result has been that the fallow periods have been getting shorter and shorter. In some of the most densely populated countries, the fallow has almost ceased to exist.

Short, or non-existent, fallows can only lead to increasing impoverishment of the land, and this is what is happening in Africa. A study on Africa published by FAO in 1986 identifies declining soil fertility in 38 countries out of 46 south of the Sahara. Some of the 8 countries that are not suffering the problem are mainly desert already, for example Djibouti, or have such acute internal strife going on that farming is severely limited, for example Mozambique.

Fertility will continue to decline unless there are radical changes in the way African farmers go about their production. Essentially, shifting cultivation is a form of agriculture without inputs except for seed and labour. It relies on nature to restore fertility to the land during the rest period. Once the fallow is short or non-existent, or in other words, once a farmer becomes sedentary on one piece of land, he must actively ensure the maintenance, and even improvement, of fertility on that plot. That means taking a number of measures, an obvious one of which is the use of fertilizers to provide plant nutrients. But there are further aspects: there is an even greater need to protect the soil from erosion if it is being tilled most years. Soil conservation measures and the judicious integration of trees into farming, known as agro-forestry, are urgent.

Crop rotations are also needed; they will help to keep in check the pests and diseases that tend to build up during monoculture, and they will also help to ensure a balanced use and replenishment of soil nutrients.

In general terms, this is a key element of what has gone wrong with African agriculture: farmers have not had the support they need to come to terms with the new set of circumstances they are facing. How can farmers change their methods and improve productivity if the price they get for their produce barely allows them to survive, let alone have some cash to invest in improvements and inputs such as fertilizer?

The World Bank has some interesting figures on fertilizer use in many countries which are expressed here in kilograms of plant nutrient per arable hectare for the year 1984. Central African Republic used O.2; Chad used O.6; Ethiopia 3.5; Mali 7.5; Niger O.5; Burkina Faso 5.O; Ivory Coast 9.5; Ghana 7.7; Kenya 37.6, and so on. To put these fertilizer consumption figures into perspective, China used 18O.6; Egypt 363.9, while the highest consumption in the world was in New Zealand with an almost incredible 1,146.8 kilograms.

The biggest fertilizer user in sub-Saharan Africa is Zimbabwe with 57.9 kilograms of nutrients per arable hectare. This is an element in the dramatic transformation of Zimbabwe's maize production among black farmers. Maize output from this sector more than trebled in the seven years following independence. The experience in that country provides living proof of what can be done when a government gets its priorities right in favour of small farmers, providing them with support in terms of extension, credit, applied research, and availability of inputs at the right time.

However, we must also come to terms with a serious error made by many agricultural experts who have been advising Africa. These experts did not like the apparently disordered way that peasants grew their crops in many parts of the continent. There was seldom a single plot of any one crop; everything was mixed together. It was a far cry from the rational, single-crop fields of the industrialized world, and therefore, the advisors insisted on some order and pursued farmers until they were shaping up properly. Then, quite recently, some more open-minded and inquisitive researchers discovered that mixed crops, or intercropping as it has been practised by peasants in many parts of Africa since time immemorial, often gives the best results under many of the conditions found there, and certainly reduces risk.

If I may be permitted a digression to Latin America, a similar situation existed among the Andean Indians in an area of the Altiplano of Peru. They would grow two rows of potatoes in one place, and another two rows many hundreds of metres away, and the same with their cereal crops. They stubbornly resisted the advice of extension workers who pointed out the convenience for planting, husbandry, and harvesting if all the potatoes were together, and the cereals together, and so on. Finally, an extensionist who was less autocratic than some, and who was genuinely interested to know what was behind the apparent stubbornness towards this "rational" approach, managed to establish proper communication with a group of peasants, and they told him.

"Well, we don't really know," they said. "But crops have always been grown here like we grow them, and it seems to us that we have less problems with pests and diseases when we grow a few rows here and a few rows there."

He was absolutely right, of course, because even if pests struck one patch of a couple of rows, they might not travel as far as the next patch. The peasants had a "rationality" that was quite different from that of the "experts" and one which probably had greater validity in the circumstances. In fact, the enormous pest and disease problems of highly-developed agriculture, which call for all manner of interventions with chemicals, only really became problems when we put large areas of the same crop together, thus providing a feast and a perfect multiplication ground for pests.

However, let us return to Africa, even if peasants the world over are similar. For they share a rationality imbued by struggling with their environment, and by having learnt to survive against what, at times, seem long odds. Indeed, in those marginal areas on the border of the Sahara, one wonders how people do survive. Everything appears so drab and delapidated, and the natural surroundings are harsh beyond belief. People are, in fact, miserably poor but they possess a fortitude denied to those of us born in industrialized countries. Most of us would throw in the sponge if we had to put up with the hardships and rigours of life that are routine to the people living in these marginal areas.

But there are surprising pockets of wealth in this apparent poverty, paradoxes that can only leave one bemused. For example, Gao in eastern Mali appears as a rundown, fly-blown agglomeration of mud-coloured buildings. There are no streets as such, only sandy areas between the houses.

Gao is in the outskirts of nowhere, or to be more precise, it is in the southern fringes of the Sahara. Before the rainy season, it is hotter than Hades; everything you touch seems to burn in the 46°C. shade temperature. The water and electricity services are unserviceable most of the time. There are tents and improvised shelters scattered among the houses and in the outskirts. Nomads who lost everything during the 1984–85 drought are living as best they can as squatters. Everything seems to be dust and despair.

But one hot night in Gao, we sat drinking tea on the rooftop of the mud house of an elderly white-haired merchant. He sat on his bed, for it is so hot before the rains that most people sleep outside on their roofs. Not that he was leaving a luxurious house to do so; the inner courtyard was just an open area of sand, and we had made our way up a rudimentary staircase to reach the roof, in the dark because the town's generator was out of order for the umpteenth time that night.

The merchant's wife sat against a wall in the corner wrapped in voluminous robes. After greeting us, she did not say another word. The only illumination came from a single gas lamp and the stars; in this dim scene, and if you had not been told it was a person, you would have to be forgiven if you mistook the dear lady for a bundle of laundry piled against the wall. Two chatty daughters in their early twenties joined us. One had her small son with her, a grandson much doted upon by the merchant.

It was pleasant as relative cool descended after the broiling day, with a *harmattan* that had felt like the breath of a blast furnace. The elderly merchant was a charming host, and we were having an easy and informative conversation. He spoke excellent French, though our conversation was interrupted every few seconds for further doting on grandson, in Arabic. It was a perfectly normal family scene; charming, country people who were happy to socialize with others over a cup of tea.

I asked the merchant whether he had always lived in Gao. He said that he had spent four or five years in Cotonou building up an office there, but apart from that, yes, he had always lived in Gao. He went on to volunteer that the hub of his empire was an office in Geneva run by a staff of Europeans and Maliens. He mentioned that he went there quite frequently to attend to his affairs and to his health. He had a Swiss doctor who knew how to treat his malaria. Two years earlier he had taken his daughters with him to Geneva. They had had a good time during two weeks of skiing at Crans-Montana!

As in the case of this merchant, when there is real family wealth in this part of the world, it often had its origins in livestock. In these semi-arid areas, and provided that there are no droughts, only livestock can make anything of the difficult conditions of scrub, sandy wastes and thin grass.

And clearly, except during and immediately after the rainy season, when these areas can be quite verdant, there is never enough grazing in one place to allow flock owners to establish themselves there for long periods of time. They have to move out with their flocks in search of forage and water.

Pastoral nomadism probably began about A.D. 1,000 to 1,500. It may have been started when much of the best land was already being tilled, but it seems more likely that its origins were connected to tribal warfare: the mobility of nomads gave them a military advantage. Perhaps the first nomads were groups of people driven out of settlements by conflict, who then found that their mobility was a distinct advantage, allowing them to raid settlements with little chance of being caught or found later.

Pastoral nomadism is sometimes talked about as if it were a primitive and undesirable element in a nation's social make-up. It is also blamed on occasion for causing environmental degradation. On the other hand, when countries have vast areas of rangeland, but not of a richness that will allow for its exploitation by sedentary livestock populations, nomadism is the only rational way to make use of the range resource, and therefore nomads become an important element in the economy.

The terms "nomadism" and "transhumance" are often used interchangeably, but in fact they are not exactly the same, and they relate differently to the environment. Transhumance is the regular, seasonal movement of people and their flocks according to altitude i.e. high altitude for summer grazing and lower altitude for the winter months, or according to latitude i.e. movements on a north-south axis to make the best of seasonal conditions. Transhumants usually have at least one fixed settlement from which they begin their movements. In some mountainous regions of Asia, they may have 4–5 homes at different altitudes and for each season. This is so for the Kohistanis in the Swat region of Pakistan who migrate through an altitude range of 600 to 4300 metres above sea level. Transhumants are often involved in some sedentary agriculture too.

Nomadic pastoralists do not move with the same seasonally determined linear regularity. They seldom have a base and they roam following pasture and water for their animals. But this roaming is not entirely haphazard; over the centuries, tribal groups have established their routes and rights, and they tend to follow more or less the same pattern year after year, unless drought intervenes when the social structures break down and they go wherever they think they might find grazing and water.

In the Sudano-Sahelian belt, transhumants tend to come into conflict more with sedentary farmers than do nomads. Transhumance routes are usually close to villages because the transhumants barter milk and other animal produce for cereals, salt, and sugar. However, where there are villages, there are also crops that the livestock may damage. Transhumance is less flexible in its routings than true nomadism, and if there has been a shortage of rain in a certain area, transhumants would be more likely to cause overgrazing than would nomads who would simply divert to other areas.

Zakaria Osman Ramadan is from a nomadic tribe called the Waladrachid that lives in northern Chad. He must be one of the best educated Chadians anywhere in the world, for he has degrees in agricultural engineering, in economics, and in agricultural economics that he earned in Senegal, the US and Europe. Somewhere along the way, he also picked up a diploma in rural sociology. He has lived in most of the Sahelian countries, worked for several UN agencies, and now works for WFP in Sudan. He has some interesting things to say about nomads, about the way they integrate into their environment, and about what drought and gifts of relief food do to them.

Nomad societies are very sophisticated, and they are in tune with their environment. The numbers of true nomads are very small and their mobility allows them to make the best use of resources. They can predict the date of the onset of the rainy season several weeks ahead of time. In the nomad areas, droughts kill fewer people than in the sedentary areas because nomads are used to living in marginal conditions. They have developed skills to protect themselves, to move very quickly, to forecast what is going to happen, and so on.

They also have an information gathering, or **spying system.** Each group has scouts that go around in small numbers, so as not to attract attention, looking for grazing and water. They also gather information surreptitiously in the markets.

Good or bad rainy seasons determine everything for the nomads. In a bad year, when cereals yields have been low, the quantity of animal products the nomad has to barter for a given quantity of *dura* will increase. And the rainy season also determines the type and number of animals that a nomad group decides to keep, and how far they have to go to find grazing and water.

A nomadic group will have reference points for its movements, a sort of map in everyone's mind linked to the calendar. For instance, after I was sent away to school at the age of ten, I used to rejoin my group at the end of every shool year, in June. I knew where my group would be. It might take me two or three days more or less on a camel, but I would always find them.

A nomadic group behaves like a large family. They are male-dominated societies in which the man assumes the full responsibility providing food, shelter, and protection for his family. This has important implications for when things go wrong, like during a drought, and when food is being given out by aid agencies. The men feel shamed that someone else is giving food to their families. They have failed to live up to the responsibilities, and that is humiliating. I don't suppose many aid agencies take this into account in the way they give out food. They arrive in their vehicles covered with stickers, line the people up, and hand out food for which the nomad has done nothing. For the nomad, it is like begging. It would be better if the donors found a way of involving the men in the food distribution.

In addition, when nomads need donations of food, it means that they have lost their animals, or had to sell them at a fraction of their real worth. It is often said that nomads look upon their animals as wealth. And that is true because when you are a nomad you cannot have many other possessions. But a nomad's bond with his animals goes deeper than that. Every animal is linked to an important event in a nomad's life, For example, when I was born, my father gave my mother five cows. In my father's mind, those cows and their progeny were always linked to my birth.

So, just imagine what it is like for a nomad in a feeding camp. He is no longer providing anything for his family, and in addition he has lost his livestock. He has no self-respect left. If most nomads were not Muslims, I am sure that many would commit suicide when they find themselves in those circumstances, but the Muslim faith forbids suicide.

The future of nomadism in Africa is uncertain. As we saw in Chapter 1, in some countries nomads appear to be settling down to a new lifestyle. In a few countries, programmes for nomad rehabilitation are being developed. In Mali for example, it is hoped to be able to use WFP food aid to create limited funds that would allow for the purchase of a few head of livestock to give to nomads as a nucleus for future flocks. The sad sight, however, is the many nomads who are now destitute and squatting in and around the towns. They need help either to adopt a new lifestyle or to go back to the desert with some animals. However, the whole issue of livestock pressure on the land is central to the question of desertification, a vital issue in Africa at present. It seems though that the true nomads are potentially less damaging to the environment than transhumants.

It was estimated in 1982 that about half of the African continent consisted of desert or areas that have suffered some degreee of desertification. More recently, in 1986, FAO identified 21 countries where desert encroachment is taking place with varying degrees of severity. The most dramatic aspect of "desert encroachment" is when existing deserts are seen to be spreading, as is the Sahara. However, a more insidious form of desertification is also taking place when relatively productive land, not on the fringe of an existing desert, is degenerating due to abuse and misuse. In fact, all over Africa this sort of desertification from within is

73

taking place as a result of overgrazing around water holes, unchecked erosion, increasing pressure on cropland, and the cutting of trees and shrubs.

When you talk to African farmers and pastoralists in areas that are undergoing desertification, they will all agree that it is happening. They mention the increased frequency of sand storms, the poorer grazing, and the general degradation of the vegetation. However, if you ask them what, in their opinion, is the cause, they almost invariably say that there has been less rainfall in recent years. When prompted with a leading question regarding the possible role of overgrazing, inappropriate use of the land by farmers, and the cutting of trees, most of those same people look blank and reiterate that it has not rained enough.

All peasants tend to blame negative events on causes beyond their control. This is a natural reaction for someone who has had little or no education; for it is education and knowledge that give people insights into their reality, and at the same time the confidence to set about changing it. Faced with their own isolation and limited understanding, they escape into apathy and so-called "peasant fatalism". That fatalism is too often considered an inexorable barrier to development, an erroneous notion because when peasants have access to knowledge, gain confidence, and have the right incentives, they progress as fast as anyone. Thus, their involvement in halting and reversing desertification hinges initially on communicating with them and reaching a consensus regarding the problems, their causes, and options for remedies.

However, let us revert to the question of whether the desertification problem is man-made or induced by climatic variations. Clearly, there can be no definitive answer to this issue at the present level of knowledge and with the available research data, but it is an interesting field of speculation and study.

The rains in the Sudano-Sahelian belt have monsoon characteristics. Monsoons are winds that blow from the north-east for about half the year, and from the south-west for the remainder of the year. In western Africa, the north-easterly wind is the hot, dry *harmattan* that blows out of the Sahara. It is opposed by south-westerly winds from the Atlantic. The behaviour of these two masses of air is determined by the position of what is called the Intertropical Convergence Zone in relation to the Polar Front lying to the north.

When the earth is tilted so that the southern hemisphere is closer to the sun (i.e. winter in the northern hemisphere) the south-westerly air stream reaches the coast of western Africa as a shallow, humid layer of surface air seldom more than 2,000 metres thick. It is overlain by the *harmattan* which comes gusting out of the desert, and the moist air and rain brought in by the south-westerly only makes itself felt in the coastal strips of countries such as Ghana, Togo, and Nigeria.

As the earth tilts its northern hemisphere towards the sun to bring summer, the heating effect over land and ocean changes, the Intertropical Convergence Zone moves northwards, and the Polar Front retreats. This allows the south-westerly monsoon to bring rain further into the interior of Africa. By July and August, the rains will have moved to about 17° North, which takes in the southern sectors of the Sahelian countries and also delimits the southern edge of the Sahara. Some parts of Africa north-of-the-Equator get two rainy seasons: the first takes place as the Intertropical Convergence Zone moves northwards, and the second during its retreat south again as the earth's northern hemisphere begins tilting away from the sun to bring winter. We have already seen how this effect produces the short mango rains in the Sahel and the short Belg rains in Ethiopia some months before the main rains.

The seasonal shifting of the Convergence Zone and its interplay with the Polar Front also produce a dividing line between parts of Africa north-of-the-equator in which it rains during the summer months, as we have just seen for the Sahel, and where it rains during the winter, as it does in North Africa in keeping with the Mediterranean's winter rains. That dividing line runs east–west through the middle of the Sahara, at about the level of the Tropic of Cancer which passes through southern Egypt, touches the northern-most point of Chad, and continues close to Tamanrasset in the Hoggar mountains of Southern Algeria.

This in theory is how it should all work, and it usually does, but the process is not as reliable as one would hope, hence the periodic droughts which are helping the desertification process. The Sudan has abundant information on desertification. The first alarm was raised in 1939 by a colonial officer who wrote to the Governor General. He had noticed the degradation around water holes caused by overgrazing and by the trampling of thousands of hooves. In 1944, a committee was set up to tackle the problem, and much research has since been done on the subject in the Sudan. The Institute of Environmental Studies of Khartoum University now collects the data and, supported by USAID, has published some fascinating papers.

Some of those papers try to trace rainfall patterns over the centuries to be able to put the recent droughts in Africa into some historical perspective. However, paleoclimatology, or the study of the nature of past climates, includes much guesswork, though there are some good pointers to the conditions prevailing in certain periods of history.

It seems as though, in the last 20,000 years, there have been three periods with distinct patterns of atmospheric wind circulation resulting from a different relationship between the Intertropical Convergence Zone and the Polar Front. These three patterns, according to most theories, coincide with: the climax of the last Ice Age, about 18,000 years ago; the warm period of the Holocene, 10,000 to 4,000 years ago; and the present phase, which started about 3,000 years ago.

At the climax of the Wurm Ice Age, the fourth and last in Europe, the ice was probably the most important regulating factor of climate over much of the earth. The Polar Front gained in intensity and its effect penetrated Africa, possibly covering most of the Sahara. On the one hand, the effect would have been to bring rain-bearing influences into Africa, but on the other, the cold oceans of the period would have produced less evaporation than they do at present, so there might not have been much precipitation. The Polar Front would have pushed the Intertropical Convergence Zone southward, possibly confining it to the Equatorial areas of Africa.

This would mean that most of tropical Africa north of the Equator would have had a dry climate in this period. This is confirmed by the fact that it was in this time that most of the dune fields of the Sahara and of the Sudano-Sahelian Zone were formed. Furthermore, it seems that it was a period in which nearly all the lakes of East Africa were very low, and pollen analysis from the Equatorial area show the predominance of dry savannah conditions and an absence of full forest or lush vegetation.

In this same period, the Nile probably dried to a trickle. This would have stopped it reaching the Mediterranean, and it was probably in this time that it started to form its largest inland delta, to the west of the White Nile, as revealed by satellite imagery of the area.

Then, around 12,000 years ago, glacial ice over Europe began to retreat and the climate turned warmer. By about 10,000 years before the present, most of the ice had melted. The effect of that cold melt-water was to create a strong temperature gradient between the northern and southern oceans. It is speculated that this reactivated the northwards movement of the Intertropical Convergence Zone, and also helped it to reach much further north than it does today. This would have brought to an end the arid period that had prevailed in the Sudano-Sahelian Zone. Conditions in the northern half of Africa underwent considerable change, and there is evidence to this effect. The period of greater humidity hit its peak about 6,000–4,000 years ago. Rainfall belts were about 400 kilometres north of their present levels, and it is believed that rainfall quantity was about three times that of today.

No doubt this was a period of increased life in the Sahara, as witnessed by the cave drawings found in the Sahara in recent times. Many of these drawings depict species of animals such as lions, elephants and giraffes which now live in more humid habitats.

The present phase began about 3,000 years ago. There was a steady reduction in rainfall, and more active winds began to reform the landscape by moving sand. The onset of greater aridity caused groups of people to migrate. For example, in Egypt there was active migration from the western areas towards the Nile, and there were similar movements in the Sudan.

Another feature of the present period is the irregularity of rainfall, as supported by the biblical stories of seven lean years and seven fat years. The periodic droughts and famines have continued into more recent history. In Ethiopia, there are historical records of famines, almost certainly caused by droughts, in the 16th century, in 1752 and in 1772–73. There was also a drought that produced a great famine in the years 1888–89. This same drought struck the Sudan too. Then there was also the great drought of 1913 in western Africa.

Good rainfall records in African countries go back only 60–70 years at the best. However, some interesting work has been done to reach a picture of the past rainfall patterns by building statistical models of the discharge rate of the Nile, on the hypothesis that this reflects the rainfall in the vast Nile catchment area, which of course it must.

Discharge rates of the Nile at Aswan from the year 1825 have been calculated. These show a period of low discharge between 1840–1850, followed by a steady increase to the end of the century. Since 1900, there has been a continuous decline with only minor jiggles to upset the steady downward trend.

A second model, based on the Nilometer signs at El-Roda near Cairo, reconstructs the discharge rate of the Nile back to the year AD 600. It shows that fluctuations above the mean discharge rate and below go in cycles of about 100 years, apart from the years AD 950–1200 when there were no fluctuations at all. This period without fluctuations coincided with a period of so-called "climatic optimum" in Europe during which many areas had warmer and dryer conditions than either before or after. The 100-year fluctuation cycle produced smaller variations in Nile flow before AD 950, but from AD 1250 onwards, the fluctuations became increasingly greater.

There was a major downward fluctuation in the 12th century, which coincides with a historical record in Ethiopia which mentions a curse falling upon that country in the same century, as a result of which, "famine and plague broke out in the land, and the rain would not fall on the fields".

In the 13th century, too, there was an even greater downward fluctuation in the Nile's flow. And again, Ethiopian records mention a "cruel famine" in the reign of Amde Tseyon (1314–1344). The Ethiopians did not record the cause of that famine – and many have also been caused by such pests as locusts – but putting together the period with the model showing a downward fluctuation in the Nile flow would indicate that drought must have been the cause.

The most interesting thing to emerge from these Nile discharge rates is what seems to be a 100-year pattern of fluctuations. *If*, and it is a big if, that apparent pattern is in fact a pattern, we should now be nearing the end of a downward fluctuation in the rainfall in the Nile catchment area.

On the other hand, some climatologists have recently postulated that the growing amount of carbon dioxide in the atmosphere resulting from the burning of hydrocarbon fuels – producing the so-called "greenhouse effect" – is increasing rainfall in the higher latitudes of the northern hemisphere and reducing it in the latitudes closer to the equator. If this tendency is confirmed, there are poor prospects for improvement in the main drought-stricken areas of Africa.

On a more detailed level, the Sudan has rainfall records that go back about 50 years for many areas. These reveal that in the last 10–15 years, rainfall has been about 50% of the average for the preceding years. In dry periods, winds tend to be more active in moving sand, and it has been noticed in the Sudan that old dune formations, previously considered stable, have started to move again in recent years.

There is evidence, therefore, that climatic variations are playing an important role in the desertification process, though whether they are natural fluctuations, or whether they can be attributed to precise causes, is not fully understood. However, they are certainly being aided and abetted by humans and livestock. The human population of the Sudano-Sahelian zone has almost doubled in the last 25 years, and the number of domesticated grazing animals has also increased enormously. Nobody knows for certain how many grazing animals there are in the zone, but according to the latest FAO study of 1986, there are about 159 million cattle, sheep, goats, equines and camels. Just the cattle population increased by 76% in the twenty years 1963–83.

Overgrazing not only bares and tramples the land so that it becomes more vulnerable to the elements, it also reduces the quality of the pasture. Some of the more valuable species of grasses and legumes suffer from close and frequent cropping more than do the less valuable species. Since the better species are also the most palatable, animals seek them out, and the result is that the species of lower quality flourish at the expense of the better. The natural composition of the pasture is changed beyond recognition, and completely useless plants such as *Calatropis procera* (known in local Arabic as *usher*) encroach. This spindly, woody bush about three-feet high with its large and apparently succulent green leaves is in fact mildly poisonous to animals. Since no animal eats it, and since it has little competition from other plants that have been grazed out of existence, it now infests a vast area of the Sudano-Sahelian belt, plain evidence of the maltreatment of pastures.

We have already seen how traditional African farming practices based on shifting cultivation cannot be intensified to meet the extra needs without running into serious risks of degrading the environment. In the Sudan, large-scale mechanical land clearing for cash crops has been another destructive element. High-powered crawler tractors pulling a heavy chain between them to uproot and drag away everything in their path, or pushing over trees with their front blades, may have seemed like an efficient way of doing things at the time. Only recently has the long-term damage been noticed. The improper use of deep tillage implements such as disc ploughs has not helped either. It has now become clear that the less those fragile tropical soils of semi-arid areas are worked, the less they erode and lose fertility.

The issue of water supply is also important, especially with regard to livestock. In many Sudano-Sahelian countries, in the 1940s and 1950s there were programmes to drill boreholes or to dig wells or *hafirs*. (A *hafir* is a hole dug in the ground, often lined with masonry, and placed so that it catches and stores run-off during the rainy season.) The idea was that these water points should be located in such a way that they would allow pastoralists to take advantage of grazing in areas where there had been no water in the past and in which, therefore, pasture went to waste.

Dr Yagoub Abdalla Mohamed, Director of the Institute of Environmental Studies in the Sudan, has some interesting comments to make on the provision of water points, and on how the original idea has been warped in more recent years.

After attention had been drawn to the problem of degradation around water holes, a Committee was set up in 1944 to study these matters. It produced a famous report on soil conservation, and as a result, they started a programme of water provision here in the Sudan. The idea was to reduce the pressure on the existing water points. And in areas where there was plenty of pasture, good ecological conditions, and so on, but no water, they tried to solve the problem by digging *hafirs* of various sizes that would hold water for a few months only. Then the people and their animals would move on to another area, allowing the area they had left to recover.

So, based on that programme of water provision, large numbers of *hafirs* were dug, especially in Kordofan. Tied to this programme was what they called the stock route. There was a meat-packing factory at Kosti on the White Nile, and water points were provided on the route between the main livestock areas of South Kordofan and Darfur for the animals being brought to Kosti.

When Sudan became independent, the policy of water provision continued, but the authorities didn't pay attention to the possible degradation that it could cause. Previously, there were strict criteria for water provision in an area. The potential of the area was examined, socio-economic aspects were taken into account, and the type of water supply to install was decided on the basis of *not* causing degradation. For example, *hafirs* hold a finite amount of water, and once that has been consumed, people and animals have to move on.

But with political pressure after independence, these criteria were ignored. And they began drilling boreholes and digging *hafirs* everywhere without taking into account the potential of the area. And then there was the anti-thirst campaign of the '60s. Hundreds of boreholes were drilled under that programme. More water points led to more livestock, but not to more grazing, unless new areas of grazing were being opened up by the provision of water. So pressure on the environment has been increased.

So, unplanned water provision was one of the factors that led to degradation. But still, in the Sudan, I think that the main cause of the desertification problem goes back to the practices of the people, the way they use land. The old subsistence way of life has been changing with influences from outside. Trucks go everywhere, and people have become more and more involved in the cash economy. To get more cash to satisfy their aspirations, they cultivate more land and become more commercialized without taking precautions to protect soil fertility, and cause degradation. Of course, this has led to the indiscriminate cutting of trees and the expansion of farming into areas that are not suitable for it.

It is interesting in this connection to note how the millet area in the Sudan expanded in the period 1960–75 while, at the same time, yields declined. The area under millet went from about 400,000 ha in 1960 to about 1 million ha in

1975. Yields dropped from about 6OO kg/ha in 196O to about 375 kg/ha in 1975.

Increase in water consumption in urban centres is also depleting resources in semi-arid areas and reducing the water availability for agriculture. For example, in the town of El Obeid, in Kordofan, water consumption went from 1.1 million cu. m. in 1966 to 2.5 million in 1979; in the town of Umm Ruwaba, to the south east of El Obeid, it went from 65O,OOO cu. m. in 1965 to 2.62 million cu. m. in 198O.

The problem of rural energy needs is closely linked to the environment. Worldwide, in the tropical areas, it is esti-mated that already 63 countries are short of firewood and people are burning dung and crop residues which, if they went back on the land as fertilizer, could produce an extra 14 million tons of grain a year. It is also estimated that by the year 2OOO, 2.5 billion people will be short of firewood.

In Africa south of the Sahara, 3.14 million ha of forest are being cleared each year, and only 86,OOO ha are regenerat-ing or being replanted. Cutting for fuelwood is the major use of woodland, though there is also important felling for industrial purposes, particularly in the humid areas of West and Central Africa.

In the Sudano-Sahelian zone, about 85O,OOO ha a year of forests are being lost, against a gain of only 19,OOO ha. A problem in those relatively dry areas is that, on average, a hectare of forest produces less than half a cubic metre of wood per year, compared to about 2.5 cubic metres in the humid areas.

In the Sudan, it has been calculated that in the Kordofan region, 86% of all energy needs are met by wood, charcoal and other forms of biomass. Some 13 million shrubs/trees are cut each year in that region only, far more than can regenerate. Much of the wood also goes for construction and fencing.

Much the same is happening all over Africa. The Governor of Gao Region in Mali, Lieutenant Colonel Koureissy

Aguibou Tall, an impressive, lean figure in an immaculate uniform, received us in his spacious office. It seemed to have the only functioning air conditioner in the town, so we were in no hurry to go back into the 46°C. breath of the harmattan outside. This was just as well because he had some interesting personal observations on the degradation in his area.

He remarked that man had always exploited and wasted without replenishing. He recalled going to Gao as a young officer in 1962 for military exercises in jungle warfare. The forests along the River Niger were almost inpenetrable. They concealed a whole military convoy in the dense vegetation. "But today," he concluded sadly, "the trees are so sparse down there that you couldn't even hide a camel!"

A forester in Gao, Adikarim Tour, the deputy director of the local water and forest service, also described the deforestation process in the area and added that some species of trees are dying where they stand. The water table has been dropping in recent years and leaving the trees high and dry. The area used to be rich in doum palms, a branching and rather feathery palm of medium height which, although not very impressive to look at, grows out of the most unlikely-looking sand dunes and produces nuts and timber of high value. The doum palms around Gao have been plundered unmercifully, and only recently have measures been taken to protect them and allow them to re-establish.

★　　　★　　　★

Desertification is almost certainly being caused by a combination of all the factors we have seen. Rainfall cycles seem to be playing a part, and working in conjunction with the desperate need of the burgeoning population of people and livestock for agricultural land, grazing, water and wood. These are leading to misuse and abuse of land resources.

The effects of desertification are manifest. Dr. Abdalla Ibrahim El Fadl, a soil scientist working with the Relief and Rehabilitation Commission in the Sudan, describes the change in some major wadis.

In the 195Os, Wadi Howar, which starts in Northern Darfur, Wadi El Milk, which starts in Northern Kordofan, and Wadi Mugaddam, which starts in Eastern Kordofan, used to flow into the Nile. For Howar and El Milk that meant a distance of about 5OO km. But none of those wadis has reached the Nile for years now, even when the rains are good. They are choked with sand.

As described in the first chapter, Chad is another country where the sand is taking over. We came upon some villages not far from Mao during a sandstorm. Everything was grey; the sky, the land, and the sparse vegetation all merged into that dust pall. It was like a scene from a film showing the after-effects of a nuclear war. Many of the trees were dead, stark skeletons looming in the greyness. The villages were of indescribable poverty. A few straw huts, a few mangy dogs, some goats trying to browse on God-only-knows what, a patch of millet stubble nearby, and half a dozen men, huddled against the driving dust, sitting on a tree-trunk half buried in the sand. As I looked at this appalling scene, Robert MacNamara's memorable phrase came to mind: "Poverty that is an affront to human dignity." But strangely, these hardy inhabitants of the Sudano-Sahelian zone retain enormous dignity in the face of their crushing poverty.

Later, we went to a village north of Mao. It must have been prosperous once, for it is solidly built like Mao itself; today, the sand has invaded it. Dunes have built against the up-wind side of the houses so that you can walk up the sand ramps and find yourself on the rooftops. The authorities have offered several times to help the people evacuate. So far they have refused to leave; but it cannot be long before the houses disappear forever, engulfed by the voracious sand.

★   ★   ★

Erosion is perhaps the most serious form of degradation that afflicts Africa. For the ravages it causes cannot be reversed in the same relatively short time that it takes to, say, plant trees or rehabilitate pastures. Of course, erosion is the ultimate consequence of improper land use. Cultivating on steep slopes, overgrazing and trampling by livestock, deforestation and clearing of vegetation, the harvesting of crops like groundnuts which removes the whole root system and leaves the soil loose and unprotected, declining soil fertility caused by repeated cropping without replacement of organic matter and nutrients, improper use of tillage implements – these are among the factors that leave the soil vulnerable to both the miniature bomb blasts of each tropical rain drop and to the winds that carry it away.

Erosion caused by water comes in different forms. There is sheet erosion which occurs when there is a more or less uniform removal of soil from the whole land surface. It is caused by the splashing of raindrops, and it may not be very evident. From sheet erosion, rill erosion can develop. This is when the water flowing downslope concentrates into rivulets that create small channels or rills a few centimetres deep. From these rills, gulley erosion is a natural sequel. This form of erosion, if unchecked, can cut great wounds hundreds of metres wide and tens of metres deep.

Wind erosion is the removal and the deposition of soil particles by the wind, as well as the abrasive effect of the particles as they are transported.

There is not a single country in sub-Saharan Africa that is not suffering from at least one of these sorts of erosion, and many are suffering from all three, according to the 1986 FAO study of Africa.

As mentioned earlier, the effects of erosion cannot be rectified quickly. Soil is created through the natural weathering of rocks beneath the soil, and at the surface, through decaying organic and inorganic materials and through cropping. There have been various estimates of how long it takes to create 1 cm of soil, but most of these estimates vary from 100 to 400 years, which is equivalent to 0.8 to 3 tons of new soil being created per hectare per annum. The fact that rapid erosion may easily remove over a 100 tons of soil per ha each year gives some idea of the gravity of the damage that can be done. Rates of 10–20 tons of soil loss per hectare per year are commonplace.

The country in Africa with the gravest erosion problem is Ethiopia. The Highland areas of that country harbour 88% of the population of 42 million, and they contain 95% of the regularly cropped land in the country. The highlands are stupendous, rolling expanses of open country cut by deep valleys and ravines. To travel through them when they are green after rain, with the great vault of sky made an intense blue by the high altitude, is an uplifting experience.

But those hills are being mortally ravaged by man. At the end of last century, 40% of Ethiopia was covered by forest; by the early 1950s, it was only 16% forested; and the forest cover is now reduced to 4%.

Firewood is used even more here than it is in the Sudano-Sahelian zone, for it is cold at these altitudes, and firewood has always been of crucial importance. Throughout history, the capital of Ethiopia was moved once the timber around it was exhausted. Addis Ababa was saved the fate of demotion and slow extinction at the end of the last century by the introduction of eucalyptus from Australia, a tree that does particularly well in Ethiopian high-altitude conditions. Planted around the city, it provides most of the firewood and building poles required.

The enormous pressure of population and livestock in the highlands has led to overgrazing, cultivation on steeper and steeper slopes, and the cutting of trees and shrubs for fuelwood. Erosion has become dramatic during the rain storms that sweep the highlands. They do not last long, but their intensity has to be experienced to be believed. They set up a drumming, roaring, rushing and gurgling that is almost frightening. As I lay awake, having been woken by the first of what were to be three such manifestations of nature run amok in one night in Wollo, I could not help but imagine the unprotected soil in the ploughed fields and the lashing that it was taking.

In 1986, an Ethiopian Highlands Reclamation Study was carried out by FAO with financing from the World Bank. In pinpointing the degree of degradation, the study states that half the highland area, about 270,000 sq. km, is already significantly eroded. Of this area, 140,000 sq km are seriously eroded and have only thin top-soil left, while 20,000 sq. km are so badly eroded that it is unlikely that they can sustain cropping in the future.

It is estimated by the study that 1,900 million tons of soil a year are being washed away in the Highlands, though other estimates have gone as high as 3,000 million tons. Even at the lower estimate, this is about 100 tons for every hecatare of cropped land. If the erosion continues at its present rate, the land covered by soil less than 10 cm deep, i.e. incapable of sustaining crop production, will multiply fivefold by the year 2010 and reach about 100,000 sq km. This would be no less than 18% of the whole highland area, where people are already short of crop land, for there is only about 0.8 ha per farmer.

Losses in productivity are even more important than actual tons of soil lost since erosion usually removes the most fertile parts of the soil. Even if erosion were cut by half, it is estimated that there would be a reduction in total grain production in the Highlands of about 2% per year, equivalent to about 120,000 tons in the 1980s.

In real terms, per capita income in the Highlands will be substantially lower in the coming years – perhaps as much as 30% over the next 25 years. And Ethiopians are already among the poorest of the poor.

Degradation could destroy the farmland of 10 million people by the year 2010. For today's children, over a third of the Highlands could become incapable of sustaining cropping in their lifetime, while in the same period, the population could treble.

Adding to the tribulations of the poor and stoic Ethiopians are the repeated droughts. These tend to be more localized than in the Sudano-Sahelian zone, probably because the mountainous terrain makes for more irregular rainfall patterns.

A further scourge in Ethiopia is flooding. In the Ogaden in April/May 1987, there were drought conditions that caused livestock to die and people to move towards dry watercourses in the hope of being able to find water by digging. Then, in May, heavy rains came, turning those water courses into raging rivers that caused mayhem among the people gathered near them.

The carcases of dead animals lying around were a source of infection for wells and other water points. The supply of food and medical supplies to the people was rendered impossible in many areas except by helicopter.

In summary, Africans are facing enormous problems. Some are of their own making; some have been dropped into their laps by outside forces; some have been visited upon them by nature, and much of the external help that has been given to them to resolve their problems has been improperly considered and has been faulty in concept. Africa now needs help as it never has before, and needs to stir itself for a massive assault on its agricultural and rural development problems. Otherwise, its people are going to become even poorer than they are at present.

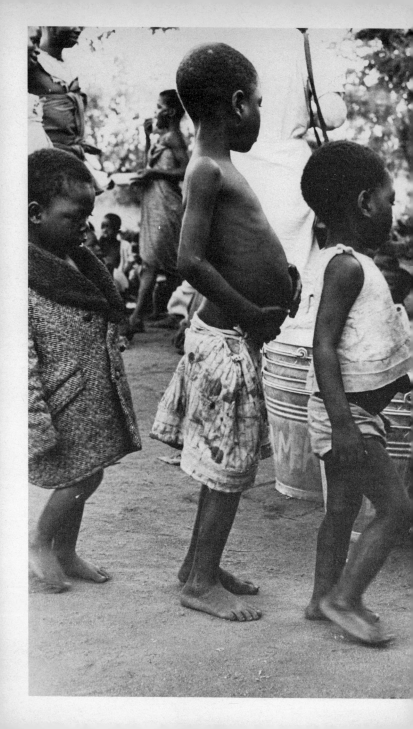

5

FOOD TO THE RESCUE?

It will be clear from what has gone before that Africa is in peril, economically and ecologically. Its people are at great risk. They have already suffered much, and they are still suffering. Aid in the form of food has been going into Africa in increasing quantities in recent years. Much of it has been donated as emergency relief, but even more goes in as economic aid. In this context, food is given to governments to substitute for imports they would otherwise have to pay for and to help them to restructure their own food markets; it may also be sold to governments on concessional terms, that is to say that they can pay for it in their own currency or get it cheaply or on credit terms in hard currency; it is used as payment to workers carrying out development activities, so called "food-for-work"; it is used in other ways for development, for example to generate cash for local development work, or another example, dried milk is used to help get a local dairy industry going; and finally, it is used in feeding programmes for school children, for nursing mothers and their infants, and for hospital patients.

No one will deny that to give food to people when they are starving, or at risk of starving, is a humanitarian act that needs no justification. On the other hand, when food is given as a form of economic aid, the issues become more

Plate 6   Mozambican children in supplementary feeding programme at camp for displaced persons, Marymount Catholic Mission, Rushinga Province in North-east Zimbabwe.   (UN Photo/Paul Heath Hoeffel)

complex. It has, in fact, become almost fashionable to criticize food aid, and some types of food aid, in some circumstances, certainly lay themselves open to criticism.

It is not within the scope and purpose of this book to attempt a definitive judgement on food aid. A clear-cut judgement is not possible. In fact, there is a vast literature covering the polemics that surround food aid. The overall criticisms in its regard are that food aid distorts local markets, discourages local production, and creates dependency on its continuing supply. Simon Maxwell, a Research Fellow at the Institute of Development Studies, of the University of Sussex, has drawn up a list of no less than 18 hypothetical scenarios of the negative effects of food aid. They cover such potential disincentives as: local market prices for food can drop because recipients of food aid sell it, or because they buy less; government sales of food aid can cause prices to fall, as can excess stocks, and as can exports from regions of a country receiving food aid to other parts of the same country; food aid can change people's tastes and thereby reduce demand for local produce; food aid can create competition for labour between food-for-work programmes and local agriculture, thereby leading to lower production; and food aid can allow governments to neglect local agriculture.

On the basis of these hypotheses, Maxwell has been studying the effects of food aid in Ethiopia and Senegal, both at the local and national level. Overall, the preliminary findings indicate that his 18 potentially negative effects of food aid in fact do exist, and the list is uncomfortably long. However, the disincentives can be avoided if food aid is planned in the context of national policy, and provided there is good and continuous monitoring. The fact that Maxwell's research is being financed by WFP is indicative of its concern over such issues.

However, in the context of the earlier chapters, it is worth looking at some aspects of food aid in Africa, at some of the problems that were encountered in administering it during the last drought, and at some of the issues facing it now and in the future, both during emergencies and as a tool for economic development. Let us begin with some background to food aid and how it is organized.

International food aid began in 1812 when the US gave food to Venezuela following an earthquake. In the last half of the 19th century, Britain bought wheat to help relieve famines in its colonies of India, the Sudan, and British Somaliland. Then, after World War I, there was a major long-term programme of food aid to Europe from the US.

During and after World War II, first under US Lend–Lease aid to its allies, and then under the Marshall Plan, food aid took on tremendous size and importance. However, these programmes of US food aid were approved by one-off laws on each occasion, as was the response to a request for food aid from India in 1951 after the monsoon rains had failed.

By the end of the 1953–54 cropping season, and after several very good farming years, the US was holding stocks of 25 million tons of wheat, an amount equivalent to the total world annual trade in wheat at the time. These surpluses, in addition to any humanitarian considerations, brought about the famous Public Law 480 under which, from then on and with several extensions of the same law, the US Government has been able to buy surplus food from its farmers and make it available on concessional terms, or as donations, to developing countries. This programme was later given the name of "Food for Peace". Hitherto, the US has provided some $40,000 million-worth of food aid and concessional sales to developing countries.

More and more food-surplus countries have since started food-aid programmes; by 1986, over 10 million tons of cereals and 908,000 tons of other food items were disbursed to developing countries. Expressed in terms of value, this represents 10.4% of all official development assistance to the Third World, and at constant 1984 prices was worth just over $3,000 million.

To set these figures in the context of world cereal production and surpluses, it is estimated that 1,845 million tons of cereals were produced in 1985–86, and that there were 399 million tons of cereals in stock, a record level, of which 271 million were held in developed countries. Thus, food aid shipments were less than 4% of the cereals in stock in developed countries.

As a proportion of all food aid in the world, sub-Saharan Africa received 15% in 1979–8O, but its share has been climbing steadily, and in 1984–85 it received 4O%. Provisional figures for 1985-86 show that it received 38% of all food aid.

Initially, all food aid was given bilaterally, that is to say from one government to another, and largely as a means of getting rid of surpluses. Then, in 1962, the UN and FAO launched the World Food Programme, for so-called multilateral food aid. WFP would accept food commodities from many donors and distribute them to Third World countries. Today, bilateral programmes still account for 75–8O% of all food aid, with the remainder going through WFP.

Most of the food provided by WFP goes for development, usually as an input to projects. For example, rations will be given to farmers and their families when they are settling into a new area and need food until their first crops are harvested; or rations will be given to people who are working in soil conservation schemes, road building, reforestation, drainage, irrigation, and so on. WFP also has school feeding programmes aimed at providing proper nutrititon in state schools and at encouraging parents to send their children to school. There are also feeding programmes for so-called vulnerable groups, that is to say pregnant and nursing mothers, infants, and the sick.

Of course, WFP also provides food during emergencies caused by natural calamities such as droughts and earthquakes, and during man-made calamities such as war and political actions that cause innocent people to become refugees.

All of this type of food aid is normally known as "project food aid" or "targeted food aid" because it is agreed upon between the recipient government and WFP according to precise parameters of how much food, for how many people, for how long, and for what purpose. A project document enshrines all the provisions agreed upon by the government and WFP. This type of food aid is in contrast with "programme food aid" which is when a donor gives or sells food on concessional terms to a government as broad-based economic assistance.

★   ★   ★

There are about 30 major donor countries providing commodities to WFP, or cash to buy commodities, and those commodities go to almost 120 recipient countries, over half of which are defined as "low-income, food deficit countries". The "low-income" criterion is the same per capita income as that used by the World Bank to decide whether a country is eligible for soft loans, i.e. loans on easy terms. In 1985, the upper limit was an annual income of $790 per capita.

Donors make their pledges to WFP on a biennial basis, and they are voluntary, unlike those for many UN organizations where members have assessed contributions which they are obliged to pay if they wish to remain members. There is a pledging conference in New York in February or March of every second year, but donors can also make pledges outside that conference, and many do. Pledges are expressed in cash terms, in the currency of the country making the pledge. According to the basic regulations, a third of the total pledge should be made available to WFP in cash to pay for transport, and administration. However, not many donors meet that proportion. The largest donors usually give less in cash. On average, and taking into account all donors, just over a quarter of the total pledge to WFP is in cash. The remaining two-thirds or more of the pledge goes to buy commodities, and it is up to WFP and the donor to work out what kind of commodities, and their quantities, are going to be supplied.

95

The person with day-to-day responsibility for matching food aid channelled through WFP with project needs in the field is Langdon Smith, a personable American in his early 5Os who has spent almost thirty years working with food aid in many parts of the world. He has a relaxed air about him, and a dry sense of humour. As he explains the management of resources, you realize that the sense of humour is an essential qualification for the job.

"Well, it's a two-pronged operation,"said Langdon Smith.

It's getting the commodities, resources, and cash, with all that that entails, and getting those commodities to the field where they belong. Part of the latter is looked after by our transport people, but getting those commodities, and allocating them where they are supposed to go, is the job of this service.

Everyone likes to think of themselves as the centre of the universe, so we are definitely the centre of the universe ... well, in a way we are the pivot point between the donor and the recipient, between the supply and the demand.

We have these 3O major donors or so that give us commodities, or cash for commodities, and we've got these hundred or so countries on the other side that have projects into which we are putting those commodities.

That supply-and-demand equation looks quite easy. You've got the commodities on one side and they are supposed to go to the other side, so just get them there! But in reality, it's a bit like being in the juggling seat at the circus, because there are so many variables that change all the time.

The problems begin because the pledges are made between February and May of the year before a biennium begins, so for the '87–'88 biennium that we are in now, they were pledging in the first part of 1986. They are trying to commit commodities a couple of years before they have even grown them or produced them.

A lot of the negotiation of commodities with donor governments is traditional because we know what they have given in the past, and they know what we need. But many things happen in donor countries over the period of time between pledging and delivery that can change the mix of commodities they want to give us. And just when you think you've got a good mix of commodities agreed with a major donor, something happens and you find out that the mix is all shot to hell! And it always seems to happen [he concluded with a wry smile].

The vast majority of the commodities handled by WFP are in fact cereals. The matching problems usually concern other and minor commodities, such as, for example, tinned fish. Taking tinned fish as a case in point, what may well happen is that a major donor, such as Holland, Japan, Norway, or Canada, telephones to advise that it intends to increase the quantity of tinned fish in its "food basket" for the year. This, in itself, may present no problem, but it frequently happens that another major donor of tinned fish has just notified that it too intends to double, or even treble, the quantity it is giving to WFP that year. Clearly, there is the need to balance the quantities of commodities between the various donors to avoid WFP having excessive supplies of certain items and not enough of others.

I asked Langdon Smith if he could refuse a commodity that was being offered in excess.

Well, you don't really refuse it – officially. You say no to them personally on the telephone and say that you'll never take them out to lunch again if they do this to you! And you ask what *you* can do for *them* as a favour? And they say that's great, and that they'll reduce the canned fish to what it was last year if you'll take 5,OOO tons of dried potatoes, the instant whip sort. You feel like saying, 'Thanks a bunch!' but you're stuck with dried potatoes and you look for every institutional feeding programme round the world that could use them! But at least you've scratched their backs and they've scratched yours. What probably happened was that the day after the fish people went to see the minister in the donor country, the potato people went to see him, and the minister wanted *something* done, and we've helped.

Week by week, and day by day, these problems develop. Suddenly there is too much rain in the western belts and the wheat crop is less than expected. Or the pulse crop has gotten some sort of a bug and you're not going to get it, or you've got too much. It's one thing after another, and we have to try to balance out the various commodities.

On the other side of the supply-demand equation, you've got the recipient projects, and those too have their problems. I mean, if a project is for four years and it is going to take a thousand tons, it doesn't mean that it will take 250 tons a year. Off-take by projects changes every time there is a flood, or a drought, or a change of government, or a change of project administration, and so you find that you originally thought you'd be a hundred thousand tons of wheat short this year and then you suddenly have a hundred thousand tons of surplus. And you don't know what to do with it, and you've got to draw it down immediately, and where shall we send it, because if we don't, the pledge lapses!

Langdon Smith rolled his eyes skyward in a comic expression of despair.

WFP is trying to improve its capacity to supply commodities which are akin to the traditional staples in certain countries. White maize, sorghums, millets and certain types of local pulses are among such commodities. This policy is a response to a number of critiques on food aid claiming that it sets out to develop markets for commodities that people do not really want. It has also been realized that it is self-defeating to provide a commodity that is unfamiliar and disliked. There is a limit to the pace of progress in this direction, however, because WFP works under the guiding rule that it must take commodities. Not to take up its pledges would be a waste of resources. Even with these constraints, however, WFP bought just under 250,000 tons of cereals from countries in sub-Saharan Africa in 1986.

The timing of deliveries is another issue that can make life difficult for Langdon Smith and his staff. Donors usually make available their commodities on a fiscal year basis, and that varies from country to country. It is usually two months or so into the donor's fiscal year before their budgets are in final form, before a provisional food basket is agreed, and before WFP can start drawing its commodities. This delay is not a serious problem in respect of most donors, but in the case of Canada, the timing can be critical. For Canada's fiscal year begins on 1 April, and it is usually late May or June before WFP can begin to ship its Canadian food. But the St

Lawrence Seaway freezes over in winter, so in effect, there are only about 6 months to draw all the commodities.

Langdon Smith humorously illustrated the sort of problems he seems to thrive on:

Then you get into the situation where everything is going fine and you are drawing, for example, vegetable oil out of Canada for those six months in which you can move things. And then you find out that every order you've sent for vegetable oil in the last month, and every one you're sending in now, is being backlogged because the can-making industry is on strike and there are no cans for the oil. And you start heading into October, and everyone starts panicking. The projects in the field are swearing at us because the commodity isn't there. You've got the big freeze coming, so it's a crisis!

Then we have some countries which all of sudden turn to us and say, 'Okay, you've got to draw down all those commodities next month'. We tell them that we can't, and they tell us we must because otherwise the funds will be withdrawn. They have just been told so by their treasury. This literally happens. One donor did it to us recently. We shipped the commodities to Singapore where they are very well organized and we can get 27 days of storage at no cost.

Most of the commodities pledged to WFP are for development projects, but of course there are also emergencies. For the most part, emergencies are met from a separate resource base. It is called the International Emergency Food Reserve, or IEFR. The target for the IEFR is 500,000 tons of wheat equivalent each year. Donors pledge to the IEFR separately from their other pledges to WFP. In several recent years, WFP has exceeded the IEFR target, with the highest amount of over 700,000 tons in 1985. WFP also has access to $45 million of cash a year for emergencies. This can be spent to buy services or commodities, according to need.

In addition to the problems Langdon Smith and his contacts in donor governments encounter in their good-humoured juggling to match commodities to needs in the field, a complication arose after the Chernobyl disaster.

Naturally enough, services were set up to check on radioactivity levels of commodities that were being made available under food aid before they were shipped. However, one country refused to accept these tests and insisted on carrying out its own. But they refused to send someone to carry out the tests before the cargo was loaded in its port of departure, saying that they would test it on arrival. They thereby introduced the risk that they might reject it after a large sum of money had been spent on getting it to them.

During the African crisis of 1984–85, WFP found that when it called forward commodities pledged under the IEFR, there was no significant shortening of the waiting period over that for commodities going to *routine* development projects. This has been a source of concern, and WFP was only able to expedite emergency deliveries to some countries by borrowing and diverting commodities destined for development use.

Overall, even if delays were a problem, finding food to meet the 1985 African crisis was not difficult. As we have already seen, the aid effort began late in many countries for a variety of reasons, but once it did get under way, there was no lack of generosity towards "starving Africa". Once pressure from the public built up after the BBC TV coverage, and as a result too of the stunning feat of fundraising launched by the Irish pop star, Bob Geldof, under his Band Aid and Live Aid initiatives, donors found it easy to get their treasuries to commit funds. Where WFP was concerned, some donors were pushing commodities in its direction, often specifying the recipient country and a time for delivery only a few weeks hence.

On occasion, WFP was forced to state that the food was not required in that country at that time because ships were already backed up waiting to unload. WFP would suggest another country in need where the shipment could be unloaded. When the donor insisted on its original country of destination and the timing (usually for political reasons), WFP would often divert a ship destined there to another country in order to make room for the new donation, at the same time trying to satisfy the needs elsewhere. "Juggling" is certainly an apt word to describe these operations.

6
FOOD ACROSS THE OCEANS

People invariably give generously to relieve the suffering of famine victims, once they are aware of the situation, but they seldom know what is involved in mounting the logistic chain to get the food where it is needed. This and the next few chapters will be looking at the logistics of moving food, with special reference to Africa, both in times of emergency and in more normal times. Let us begin with shipping.

Shipping of food aid is a major and complex industry. It is difficult to imagine quantities like 10 million tons, the amount of food aid shipped each year in the world. However, if it were all together in one place, and if it were all cereals in bags, and they were piled on a hectare of land, they would reach over 3,000 metres into the sky. Or if you preferred to pile them on an acre, they would reach over 25,000 feet. WFP shipped almost a quarter of this monstrous pile in 1986. Their reputation for expertise in food shipments is so good that other donors often commission them to ship on their behalf, so not all of the food they ship is actually theirs. During the last African emergency, WFP was more or less involved with the movement of about 6 million of the approximately 10 million tons that went into Africa.

Shipping is critical for food aid. It is interesting to

Plate 7   Mozambique – unloading food aid from the Cinq Juin, the low-draught coastal vessel chartered by WFP.   (WFP/Frances Vieta) examine some of the problems faced during the last African famine, and to see also how more routine shipping operations are organized.

When Per Ivarsen, a charming and helpful Norwegian, arrived at WFP in 1966 to work in the shipping operation only about 2OO,OOO tons of food were being shipped annually. Now Ivarsen is the head of the operation and it is shipping well over 2 million tons a year. At any one time, WFP will normally have 25–3O ships on charter. In 1986, WFP chartered 126 vessels, making it one of the world's main charterers. In terms of volume, the oil and grain trading companies are larger charterers, but probably none are as complex as WFP in terms of the number of ports of call and the number of shipments.

A charter means that the whole vessel is taken up by the charterer for a specific voyage, but liners are used too. Liners are vessels that ply regular routes and take on cargo for different customers. WFP also used 1,559 liners in 1986.

Charters are cheaper than liners for shipping food. The average charter load for WFP is about 13,OOO tons, whereas the average liner shipment is only 328 tons. The average cost per ton in 1986 for charter shipment was $23, whereas it was $95 per ton on liners. WFP's largest single cargo to date was 11O,OOO tons of grain from Portland, Oregon, to Bangladesh. The shipping cost was $5.2 million.

In the early days, Per Ivarsen recalls that much of the food was shipped in bags, and this is still the case for commodities such as dried skim milk. Nowadays, however, cereals are usually shipped in bulk because it results in a saving of about US$4O per ton over bagged cargoes.

In the early days of bulk shipments, bagging on arrival was often done by hand in the hold of the vessel, but this was very time consuming. Even with modern bagging equipment on the quayside, it usually takes 1O days or more to offload a cargo of, say, 15–2O,OOO tons of grain. Imagine how it must have been inside the hull of a ship in a port such as Assab, the main entry point for Ethiopia, with an outside shade temperature of 45°C. and with a relative humidity of

90%. The rate of work can hardly have been electrifying when bagging by hand in those conditions.

In fact, the bagging process was often a bottleneck in the rate of food cargo off-take in ports. In Africa, many of the ports are small. To get ships in, unloaded, and out again in quick succession is crucial for meeting an emergency. Furthermore, a 15–20,000-ton vessel – rather small in terms of today's bulk carriers – is about the maximum size that can be docked in most of Africa.

The port of Assab has only two jetties and berthing space for four ships a time. A week after the BBC TV coverage of Ethiopia, Per Ivarsen led a mission there to look into the logistics for moving large quantities of food into the country. Assab was bound to be the key port, for although Massawa in Eritrea is an efficient – if small – port, the road from it to the main famine areas passes through country which is under constant guerrilla activity. Djibouti, the tiny country on the coast south of Assab, has a good port, and a railway line from it to Addis Ababa. However, for Ethiopia to use that entry point involves payments to Djibouti in foreign currency, a commodity of which there is a chronic dearth in Ethiopia. In addition, it is known that moving food through another country is seldom as reliable as bringing it in direct because the transit country gives priority to its own transportation needs.

Per Ivarsen and his mission recognized that unloading and bagging was a limiting factor in the port of Assab. There was bulk handling equipment in the port but not enough of it, and it was mainly for use with fertilizers. They calculated that the throughput of the port could be 75,000 tons a month, *if* extra bulk handling and bag-stitching machines were brought in. Rather than proposing sophisticated pneumatic unloading systems, which need space and spare parts, they recommended simple grabs and hoppers. The grabs were to be specially made for grain in that they would close completely when full to prevent grain being blown away by wind. They would lift the grain out of the holds and unload it into hoppers on the quayside. Bagging could be done below the hoppers, or the hoppers could be bulk discharged into dumper trucks passing below them and taking the grain away to a warehouse for bagging. The Netherlands financed eight grabs and six hoppers and Britain supplied 1O dumper trucks. The whole system was delivered, installed and running in about 4 months. The grabs and hoppers, which cost less than $1 million to supply, turned out to be a crucial input. Port throughput was never a limiting factor thereafter. Trucking away from the port is another story, as we shall see later.

Ship charter is a world unto itself. There are two basic types of charter used for food shipments: time charter and voyage charter. As the terms imply, voyage charters are arranged on the basis of shipment from port of loading to port of discharge for a price per ton. The total price also includes an estimated and agreed time for loading and discharging, known as lay time. Time charter, on the other hand, is a rate per day or per month for the ship and its crew, with all other expenses met by the charterer. Charter-able cargoes range from a minimum of 5OO to a maximum of 13O,OOO tons of food. For a charter, the ship owner is "free of the cost of loading and unloading", whereas in the case of liners, the ship owner pays for them.

Inevitably, variations creep in, and that is where the problems begin. For example, when a ship on voyage charter has to anchor offshore and wait to unload, demur-rage is charged if the pre-agreed lay time is exceeded. Demurrage runs to about US$4,OOO per day for an average grain carrier of about 15–2O,OOO tons. On the other hand, if a ship on a voyage charter unloads in less than the foreseen time, dispatch is paid to the charterer. Dispatch is normally half the rate of demurrage for that particular ship, so a refund of US$2,OOO might arise. Time is a highly sensitive issue in chartering operations: calculations for demurrage and dispatch payments are based on a minimum accounting period of one minute!

Peter French, a young chartering officer, is one of only two handling the work for WFP. He has commercial ship chartering experience in his native Sydney, in London , and in the US. He finds the humanitarian aspects of his work with WFP particularly rewarding.

According to French, a few African countries manage to earn dispatch in normal times through fast unloading. During an emergency, no country would be likely to do so.

"About 70% of our charters end up with us paying some demurrage," French said.

We try to chase recipient countries to pay the demurrage as a way of putting pressure on them to improve their port handling and to make them give us the same priority they give to commercial cargoes. But it isn't easy. Many recipient countries are so poor anyway, and our representatives in the countries get tired of the hassle. Of course, during an emergency, demurrage becomes a major factor. It's quite common in such circumstances to have waiting periods of 20 or 30 days, so in round figures, you're talking about $100,000 of demurrage per shipment.

We probably know more than anyone about conditions in developing country ports all over the world, so we usually come up with a fairly accurate assessment of lay time. But then we have problems with some countries that want to give us a lower daily discharge rate than they have for their commercial cargoes. For example, one far Eastern country has a discharge rate of 3,000 tons a day for commercial cargo, whereas the initial rate they agreed with us was for only 1,500 tons a day. It took a visit there to persuade them to give us the same discharge rate that they give to commercial cargo.

About 95% of our charters end up in discussions, not to say disputes, with ship owners. It is a legal condition that they get paid 90% of the charter fee on loading, but it's the remaining 10% plus demurrage or minus dispatch, and other odds and ends, that causes the problems. There is an arbitration system based in London, and that is where disputes go when the parties concerned can't settle them. We have a couple of cases a year that go to arbitration.

One of our main concerns is bankruptcies. The shipping industry has been having a hard time in recent years. If a ship owner goes bust with one of our cargoes on board, it's a real problem. It happened not so long ago with a Greek ship. It went into Piraeus because the Greek courts try people *in absentia*. The crew stayed on the ship because they saw the value of the cargo as the only power they had to get their several months of back pay. They tried to keep people off the ship at gunpoint and the whole thing was blocked for months. The commodities on the ship were needed at their destination, so we had to call forward other commodities to replace them. A bankruptcy like that can cost us half a million dollars, as that one did, so we try very hard to find out who is *not* going bankrupt before we fix a charter! Our brokers are supposed to know, but a couple of years ago we had two bankruptcies in one year, including the Greek one.

There are about 75,000 merchant ships in the world, and a complex system of brokerage exists for chartering them. There are owners' brokers who are trying to find charters for the owners of vessels they represent, and there are charterers' brokers who try to find vessels for people with cargoes to move. The normal commission rate is one and a quarter per cent.

WFP uses 13 charterers' brokers scattered around the globe. When they have a cargo of food to ship, for which they know full details concerning its time of availability, characteristics, port of loading, and so on, an identical telex goes out to each of the 13 brokers asking for quotations. These telexes are sent as simultaneously as the capacity of four telex machines allows. It is rare for all of the brokers to reply with an offer, but 8–10 usually do within a day. Their telexes specify the ship that they can offer, and its cost, and often the offers are valid for as short a period as 30 minutes! Seldom is the deadline more than two hours.

Such a take-it-or-leave-it-in-30-minutes offer occurred for a cargo of Canadian wheat destined for China in early 1987. The rate seemed good, but Ivarsen and his staff decided not be be rushed because they felt sure that they would receive a better offer. In particular, they were hoping that a broker would offer a Chinese ship. The Chinese usually quote highly competitive rates, but unfortunately they often take longer than others to make their offer.

On this occasion, no better offer arrived and they lost the original one. In the meantime, ocean freight rates were soaring, and in fact they increased 60% in six weeks. By the time a ship had been found, it cost WFP a lot more than the ship they had turned down.

During the 1984–85 African crisis, there was one particularly harassing period for the whole of the WFP logistics team. Chad, the most landlocked country in Africa, was receiving food through two ports: Apapa, the port of Lagos in Nigeria, and Douala in Cameroon. From Apapa, food was being trucked 2,200 kilometers (almost 1,400 miles) to N'Djamena, whereas from Douala, it was going by rail to Ngaoundéré, and from there by truck to N'Djamena, a total distance of 1,800 kms (1,125 miles). Although the overland distance from Douala was slightly shorter, there was the major disadvantage of extra handling between rail and road transport compared to Apapa which involved road transport only.

In the early months of 1985, it had been calculated that Chad needed about 120,000 tons of food to see its people through the year. But that food had to be in the country and distributed before June; after that, every track and so-called road would be made impassable by the rainy season.

Everything was nicely on schedule in February. The offtake from Apapa was about 25,000 tons a month, and from Douala, about 5,000 tons a month, for a total of 30,000 tons. The four months available should have given exactly the required tonnage before the rains hit Chad. Then, on 6 March, the MV Daphne, a German ship, arrived in Apapa with 7,000 tons of wheat to be divided between Chad and Niger. Days passed. There was no sign that the Nigerians were going to unload the cargo. The port authorities never clearly said whether the Daphne, or any other food ships, would be allowed to unload. Day after day, they told WFP that they would make a decision tomorrow. From other sources, it was learned that Nigeria might, in effect, be closing Apapa for food cargoes destined for the landlocked countries to the north. It was a bombshell.

Differing explanations have been put forward for why the Nigerians took this apparently inhumane step. One version is that the northern parts of Nigeria were suffering food shortages because of drought, and that food trucks roaring through to destinations further inland were causing unrest among the people.

Another version concerns an event that is alleged to have taken place in 1984. Agricultural prices in Nigeria tend to be lower than they are in the neighbouring and drier countries to the north, such as Niger. Therefore, there is a natural desire on the part of Nigerian farmers to smuggle out their produce and sell it in neighbouring countries. This had happened with some Nigerian sorghum in 1984. Then, so the story goes, the EEC bought this same sorghum to distribute it as food aid in Chad, knowing full well its origins. To add insult to injury, the EEC transported it through Nigeria on its way to Chad. The Nigerians were understandably peeved, but it would have been better to take issue with the EEC rather than punish their fellow-Africans to the north.

Tun Myat, a Burmese who trained in London for a masters degree in maritime law and also became a chartered insurer there, has worked in WFP transport operations for almost 10 years. He has a phenomenal memory for detail and clearly remembers those days when it was becoming clear that Apapa was being closed.

We waited three weeks. It seemed to go on and on. By March 29th, we knew we had a serious problem and we couldn't wait any longer. The Daphne was still laden, and there was no decision from the Nigerians. So we had to make one. There were millions of people in Niger and Chad at risk. It was a panicky situation, aggravated by the fact that we had two more ships on their way into Apapa. The Madura was a Canadian ship carrying wheat for Niger and Chad and she was due in Apapa on March 31st. The other was the Flora C, a ship carrying 10,000 tons of US sorghum for Chad and Niger too, and due to dock on April 4th.

Friday, March 29th was a fateful day. One doesn't like to divert ships because it creates all sorts of complications and expenses, but we took a long hard look at things and decided to divert the Madura to Cotonou and the Flora C to Douala. We left the Daphne in Apapa, not to force the issue but at least to make a point that transit states have to have respect for the rights of landlocked countries. If there is a cargo which is transitting through their country in a normal commercial manner, paying port dues and charges, then there is no valid reason why transit rights should be denied. It was a month before Nigeria let us unload the Daphne – but at Port Harcourt, not Apapa.

The Madura and the Flora C were carrying their grain in bulk. We decided that the whole of the Madura cargo would go to Niger via Cotonou, and the whole of the Flora C cargo would go to Chad. But we had to get bagging equipment into Cotonou rapidly. Luckily we knew a company in Lome that had equipment available and we had them move it to Cotonou by road over the weekend and set it up.

The situation with the Flora C was a bit more complicated. She belongs to a big company called the Nigerian Flour Mills Ltd. and run by a Greek in Lagos. They regularly bring in grain from North America, mill it in Lagos and bag the flour. So our contract arrangement with them was that they would load bulk sorghum for us in the US and deliver it to us, bagged, in Lagos for road transport into the landlocked countries. Since they couldn't go into Apapa and use their own bagging plant there, we had to arrange for bagging in Douala instead. We did that by having the Flora C pick up bagging equipment in Abidjan on her way into Douala.

Two diversions in one day, with all the complications that go with them, are fortunately not commonplace, though diversions *per se* are not rare. During the early days of emergencies, ships may be diverted *into* ports of critically affected countries. The first shipment of WFP food to reach Assab was diverted from China. Later in the emergency, ports may become jammed, and quick decisions have to be taken. WFP diverted several ships away from Assab, including a British one that went to Pakistan.

Another complication of diversions is that the onward overland transit may become overburdened. In effect, when Apapa closed, the only way of getting the required food into Chad before the rains was by increasing the off-take from Douala via the railway from 5,000 tons per month to about 30,000 tons per month. We shall see how that was done in a later chapter.

The African crisis of 1984–85 provoked month after month of unremitting pressure on WFP's transport staff. The head of the operation at the time was a Dane called Erik Moller. He was a bulldozer second to none, a tough task-master who drove others as hard as he drove himself. For him, 18-hour days, and 7-day weeks were the norm during that period. No detail was too small to be unworthy of his attention, and he would often be seen holding a telephone to each ear as he wrestled with logistics problems on a global scale. His staff were also doing 14–15 hour days. Moller was suffering from cancer and there can be no doubt that his hard-driving style shortened his life.

In May 1986, not long before Moller's death, US Vice President George Bush wrote him a letter of personal thanks for his work during the African emergency. Parts of that letter run as follows:

On behalf of the President of the United States of America and the American people, I would like to personally commend you for the outstanding work you performed in the recent African food emergency....

You were instrumental in solving transportation problems and bottlenecks that threatened to bring to a halt the shipment of grain and other commodities to those who were in such desperate need of assistance. Of particular importance to the United States was the role that WFP assumed under your direction in coordinating donor food aid shipments and in publicizing and disseminating information regarding port conditions....

Your unselfish and tireless work enabled the donations of the US and other countries to reach their destinations – and saved thousands of lives. Your efforts and successes stand out in the tremendous undertaking we have been involved in. We are deeply grateful to you.

★　　　★　　　★

There was a fascinating sequel to the Apapa saga in late 1986 and early 1987, 21 months or so after the infamous closing of the port in 1985. The events demonstrate the importance in the shipping industry of making decisions to meet changing circumstances, and they also illustrate the economic importance of such decisions.

After the closing of Apapa in March 1985, food for Chad continued to pass through Douala. However, as 1986 progressed, the shipping staff in WFP noted that the port handling and railway transportation costs involved in shipping through Douala were rising in dollar terms, because the dollar was weakening while the CFA Franc, the currency in which the costs of transit through Douala had to be met, was holding up well. On the other hand, the Nigerian Naira had weakened along with the dollar, so in dollar terms, it would be cheaper to ship through Apapa again, at least in theory.

Japan had donated 9,800 tons of Thai rice to Chad, and the idea of sending it through Apapa was mooted. But there had been no contact with the Apapa port authorities since the events of 21 months earlier. WFP put out feelers through its forwarding agent in Lagos to find out whether a cargo destined for Chad would be unloaded. The answer was not clearcut, but there were indications that the Nigerian authorities might cooperate.

So a calculated risk was taken; it was decided to send the ship to Apapa, even though it was known that if the gamble went the wrong way, considerable extra costs would be involved.

The ship arrived in Apapa with its 9,800 tons of rice. There was an agonizing delay of 6 days while the Nigerian port authorities kept a stony silence. Per Ivarsen and his staff in Rome were chewing their nails. They knew that if the ship was not unloaded, ridicule and scorn would be poured down upon them from a great height. Everyone would be quick to call them idiots for having tried to transit a shipment through a port that had turned away food cargoes and taken none in almost two years.

However, their advance information proved correct; without comment, the Nigerians unloaded the rice, and it was duly trucked the 2,2OO kms to N'Djamena. The saving made by passing though Nigeria instead of Cameroon was significant – in round figures, a cool US$1 million. In other words $1 million saved from the Japanese pledge. There-fore, $1 million-worth of extra food to send to countries in need.

★   ★   ★

Let us return to the question of the throughput of ports. The issue of cargo-handling equipment has been men-tioned in connection with the grabs and hoppers for Assab, but many less obvious factors play a vital role when every ounce of food that is unloaded and trucked away to those in need counts. It is literally a matter of life and death.

For example, when the emergency operation for Ethiopia was in full swing, congestion in the port of Assab was an overriding problem. There was the obvious issue of bring-ing ships into berths and unloading them. In that connec-tion, there was the well-publicized case of an Australian ship laden with food that was forced to lie off and wait many days for a berth because armaments were being unloaded in the port. Less well-publicized was the fact that, at the request of the Australian Embassy in Addis Ababa, Kurt Jansson, the UN-appointed coordinator for the whole relief operation, went to see Chairman Mengistu about it. The very next day, the Australian ship docked.

However, the less obvious issues concerned even such details as how food was stacked in the limited areas available after it had been unloaded from ships and was awaiting trucks to take it into the interior. There was a Japanese team in Assab for most of the period of the emergency doing nothing but advise on stacking methods to make the best use of the available space.

The port of Assab came under the spotlight because of the central role it played in getting food to the starving millions in Ethiopia. Less well-known was the role of Cotonou in the west African country of Benin. Cotonou was the major entry port for the landlocked country of Niger to the north. There is a railway that runs from Cotonou to Parakou, about a third of the way to Niamey, the capital of Niger, and from the Parakou railhead, food was trucked onwards.

Benin was marginally affected by the drought compared to the Sahelian countries, so the WFP man in Cotonou spent much of his time working in the interests of Niger. He was Piet Winnubst, a Dutchman, who now works in Chad. Winnubst is in his 50s, tall and white-haired, and wears glasses. He has a modest and measured manner, and a few minutes of conversation with him are enough to appreciate his quiet qualities of human warmth and of concern for others. He spent many years working for religious voluntary relief agencies, work that got him into such holocausts as the Biafran war. Apart from having a background in journalism and communication, he has training in the field of management, which, with his fluent command of Dutch, English, German, and French would make him an asset to any relief and development organization.

Winnubst recognized that the throughput of the Port of Cotonou could be improved and so, in agreement with the government of Benin, he asked WFP headquarters to send him a logistics specialist who could help the port and railway authorities improve their performance. So Giles Vallette arrived from France. He was a man with a military background, self confident and correct. At the same time he could be friendly, in an austere way, and he commanded natural respect.

Vallette spent hours in the harbour, casting his eye over everything. The harbour was well-endowed with physical infrastructure of wharfs and storage space; they had been built with funds from Germany not so long before. However, the monthly offtake seldom exceeded 3,000 tons. Vallette soon saw that the problems were essentially ones of organization. There were good people in charge in the customs service, in the port authority, and in the railways, but they did not work as a team and coordinate their activities properly. So, for example, the customs documentation was still awaited when a train was loaded and ready to leave; or cargo was ready for loading but the railway wagons were late or insufficient in number. There were also problems because the use of space in the warehouses was not being properly planned, and because there were some items of equipment that were unserviceable for want of a minor spare part.

Vallette was constantly touring the harbour facilities, talking to people on the job and in their offices. He wrote memoranda to all concerned making specific and clear suggestions for improvement. He called regular meetings to discuss problems and their solutions. In this way, he managed to break down the watertight compartments in which people had been working. He promoted an information exchange so that they began to work as a team with a common purpose. (Incidentally, the purpose of improving the port offtake was evident to all, and it was not only humanitarian; the more food aid that went through Cotonou, the greater the revenue to the country from port dues, handling charges, and rail freight.)

The throughput of Cotonou harbour began to rise rapidly and it doubled within weeks. Vallette's meticulous attention to detail covered everthing, even to the way vehicles and equipment were moved and parked for loading and unloading. His was a firmly persuasive presence, always courteous, but brooking no nonsense.

Piet Winnubst recounted the following anecdote that tells us much about Vallette:

Vallette and I went down to the harbour together one day and as we walked around, he spotted a vehicle that was not parked according to his precise instructions. It was partly loaded and the driver was nowhere in sight. While we were looking at it, one of the port authority managers came around the corner. Vallette called him over and asked politely whether he had not made it clear how such vehicles should be parked, and whether the manager had not passed on the instructions to the staff concerned, and finally, where was the driver of the vehicle in question?

The manager launched into a lengthy explanation of how difficult everything was because workers in the port came under various authorities, and they all had different chains of command, and the railway people had a different union, and you couldn't just push the people around, and in any case they didn't listen, and you couldn't just give orders directly without going through the proper channels, because this was a Marxist-Leninist state, and even if he wanted to give direct instruction, he couldn't because everything had to be discussed at weekly meetings.

Vallette listened very carefully and courteously, without comment, and when the man had finished, he said, 'Yes, I quite understand. So where is the fellow in charge of this truck?'

Such was Vallette's style, at all levels. In meetings, people would raise objections as to why certain things could not be improved. He always listened, and then forged ahead as if he had not heard. Sometimes it was almost as if he had not understood, even though he most certainly had, because he was very intelligent. He even dealt with ministers in the same way, but he always just managed to avoid reaching the point where people might get angry and tell him to leave them alone.

Vallette's effectiveness was considerable. Under a few months of his meticulous attention to detail, the throughput of Cotonou multiplied sixfold, and it became one of the fastest ports for unloading in West Africa. All he really did was to mobilize and organize the existing resources. The only important material inputs were some spare parts and a few tyres.

Many of the logistical problems of shipping and distributing food during an emergency can be avoided with the proper scheduling of ship arrivals. At the beginning of an emergency, clearly there is a need for ships to arrive with the utmost urgency, but once the ball is rolling, the opposite may be true if bunching is to be avoided. When bunching does occur, it is costly in demurrage and creates enormous dilemmas for logistics advisors. Robert Pearson, a Briton who was WFP logistical coordinator in Somalia in 1980 following very severe floods there, recalled waking up one morning, looking out to sea from his hotel window in Mogadiscio, and counting eighteen ships lying at anchor waiting for a berth in the harbour. "A nightmare", he remarked.

However, experience has shown that to persuade a donor to delay a shipment may be very difficult. Once public pressure had forced many governments to react to the Ethiopian need at the end of 1984, those governments wanted to be seen to have done something. Many donors looked to WFP as the natural leader for coordinating shipping and for providing information and statistics on arrivals, port offtake, distribution, and so on. But on several occasions, when WFP pleaded with donors to delay a shipment or divert it elsewhere and replace it later, the response was that a minister had already made a statement in parliament or to the press to the effect that a shipment was leaving, and they could not delay it. On some of those occasions, it was WFP, which has fewer political constraints and is less in the public eye than governments, that was able to divert one of its cargoes to make space for another which was to arrive amid public fanfare.

Though hardly fitting the title of this chapter – food across the oceans – there is an interesting seaborne operation that has been in progress in Mozambique since late October 1983.

The internal war that has been going on for years in Mozambique has made overland transportation almost impossible in many parts of the country, as we saw in Chapter 3 when describing the situation in Inhaminga. Moreover, Mozambique was seriously hit by a drought which began in 1981. Famine conditions began to develop by 1982, especially in the areas of Gaza and Inhambane.

The combination of civil strife and drought proved disastrous. Mozambique's Director of Natural Calamities estimated that at least 100,000 people starved to death in Gaza and Inhambane as the drought intensified in 1982 and 1983. At Vilanculos, where it had not rained for two years, people were even breaking open anthills in the hope of finding some kernels of maize.

The problem was how to reach people with food aid in these war-torn areas and with limited road transport capacity. UNDRO and WFP jointly instituted a plan to use a shallow-draught landing craft that could navigate the coastal waters, in which there are many sandbars and shoals, and come close enough inshore to unload easily.

WFP's transport specialists found a landing craft with a capacity of 350 tons that was being offered for sale on the London market for US$1 million. She was in the Seychelles and bore the name "Cinq Juin", the date the ex-French colony became independent. She had been a gift from France to commemorate that occasion, but she was not suited to the high seas of the monsoon season. Hence, she was up for sale. She would be perfect for the conditions along the coast of Mozambique, and WFP managed to negotiate a time charter for her at $1,700 per day. (UNDRO had raised the funds to start the operation, which was later turned over to WFP.)

When the "Cinq Juin" arrived at the end of October 1983, relief supplies were piling up in the ports of Beira and Maputo while people continued to starve. Quite soon, however, the constant trips along the coast by the "Cinq Juin" to unload supplies at strategic points began to transform the situation for the people. The worst of their suffering was relieved.

Operating the "Cinq Juin" is not without its problems. The quickest way to unload her cargo is to bring her in to the beach, when the sea and other conditions permit, but this is often risky because of guerrilla activity. For this reason, unloading is more usually carried out by transferring cargo to a small barge which the "Cinq Juin" carries on deck, or to other barges or small fishing boats that ferry the food to the beach or to some derelict wharf. Most of the food is then moved inland a few kilometres to where there are resettlement camps for those displaced by strife or drought.

It is not only direct guerrilla activity that makes the operation dangerous, however. Not long ago, it was heard that the area around Chinde in the Zambesi delta was desperately short of food. No cargo vessels had been into Chinde for a long time because of the turmoil in the area. It was decided to send in the "Cinq Juin", but there was a communication breakdown, and it was not known that she was coming. The locals almost opened fire on her before they realized she was friendly.

More recently, and in view of the success of the coastal operations with the "Cinq Juin", a Kenyan freighter called the "Idun" has been taken on charter. The Netherlands government has given five barges for transportation of relief food. The "Idun", with a capacity of 7OO tons, lies offshore and the barges ferry the food to the coast.

The "Cinq Juin" has become such an important factor in the lives of the people of Mozambique who live in destitution near the coast and depend on food aid for their survival that she has been nicknamed "Moanize", the Portuguese for "saviour". Marxist government or not, it seems that many people have not given up Christianity completely.

7

FOOD OVERLAND

In the final analysis, the succes of relief operations depends upon transportation. The difficulties, and the life-or-death nature of the matter, are summed up in the following incident that happened in Chad in 1985.

Jato Tcha-Tokey, a volunteer from Togo who has worked with WFP in Chad for several years, was returning after dark to his home in Mongo, about 400 km east of N'Djamena. It was an evening in early April, at the height of the dry season. As the headlights of his vehicle swept an open area in the village, they lit up a small child sitting on the ground, alone, and with a tin can in his hands. Jato stopped and went to the child. In the bottom of the can were a few seeds of millet mixed with grains of sand. The child reached into the can and put some of this mixture into its mouth.

The child was pitifully malnourished, with a swollen belly and a dazed expression. Jato lifted him into his vehicle and took him home, where he gave the child some left-over rice, and tried to talk to him. But the child spoke no French, and Jato speaks no Arabic. After a while the child made motions to leave, and Jato followed him. He went about two hundred metres down the road to where an improvised lean-to of mats and straw had been erected.

There, Jato found the child's mother with another, older child. She spoke a little French and was able to explain that

Plate 8   Somalia – fleets of trucks take food from the ports inland to distribution centres.   (WFP/Cristian La Ruffa)

the younger child was called Bechir. He was four years old. The children's father had left them to go to look for work or for food, and she had not seen him for several months.

Jato told her to send Bechir to him for meals, which she seemed reluctant to do. However, over the coming days, Jato regularly went and fetched Bechir and took him home to eat, and also arranged for the mother and older child, who was not so malnourished, to receive food.

As the weeks passed, Bechir began to recover. Jato took him to the doctor to check on his progress. Gradually, the light returned to his eyes and his symptoms of malnutrition waned. He became an engaging, happy child.

There were many people like Bechir and his mother and sister surviving as best they could in Mongo, and as the rains approached, the authorities decided to provide them with food, seeds and tools and settle them near a village called Katalogue, about 66 kms away, where there was land available for cultivation. So after the first rains had fallen, about a hundred people climbed onto trucks, with a month's supply of food, seeds and tools, and were taken to Katalogue. They were to receive rations every month to tide them over until they harvested their own crops. Jato and Bechir had grown close, and Jato was sad as he embraced the departing child.

Not long after the people had left for Katalogue, the rains arrived with ferocious, tropical intensity. Towards the end of the first month, the next month's rations were loaded onto a truck and it set out for Katalogue. The crew of the truck struggled for hours in the mud and water, but just 30 kms short of their destination, they could go no further. They tried repeatedly at intervals over the following weeks to get through, but each time, they were repelled by the quagmire.

Finally, when the rains let up after almost three months, Jato got through to Katalogue in a Land Cruiser. He made his way to the settlement area, and soon found Bechir's mother.

"When she saw me, she began to weep," he said, "and for a long time she could say nothing. Then she told me that Bechir was dead. So were most of the other small children, and many of the older people. They had gone through hell. She was skin and bones herself. Yet there was plenty of relief food in Mongo. We had been blocked by 3O kms of mud, and of course they had no way of telling us what was happening. By the time they were really in trouble, no one was strong enough to make that 66 km journey to Mongo."

★   ★   ★

In industrialized countries, trucking is not usually thought of as an occupation calling for exceptional skills of management and for clockwork organization. But trucking in Africa calls for these in abundance, allied with flexibility; and it also calls for courage because trucking in Africa, apart from being a continual challenge, is often highly dangerous.

Let us just consider Chad for a moment. It is a country twice the size of France, yet it has less than 1OO kilometres of asphalted roads, and most of these are in N'Djamena. And it is not as if the non-asphalted "roads" were dirt roads in the sense they are known in many other parts of the world, that is to say graded and gravelled regularly. Vast tracts of desert and semi-desert in Chad have no roads of any sort. There are merely meandering wheel marks in the sand that go in a general direction, seem to branch off for no apparent reason, dodge in and around the scrub, and criss-cross the dunes.

Drivers who know the direction they should be going, or have a good guide, give their individuality full rein, each making his own path, sometimes as much as a kilometre or more from other wheelmarks. Sometimes the only sign that a vehicle has ever passed that way is a crankshaft or back-axle housing lying in the scrub. This is testimony to the amazing ability of African mechanics to carry out major repairs in conditions which most European mechanics would declare impossible.

In Chad during April 1987, food was required urgently near Zouar, about 1,OOO kilometres to the North. While the Chadian army had been driving out the Libyans in a series of battles that had gone on for weeks, many of the local people had fled from the fighting. Then, following the Libyan defeat, they came flocking out of the hills in desperate need of food, and so a convoy of 10 laden trucks set out from N'Djamena.

They were blue-painted Renaults, with six wheels of which four were driving, known as "six-by-fours" among truck specialists. They had 240 HP turbocharged diesel engines, and their chassis and clutches had been reinforced to cater for the tough conditions. Such trucks cost over $100,000 each.

Each of these behemoths has a trailer and the total capacity is 30 tons – under normal conditions. But in Chad, conditions are far from normal: with the sand and totally untamed terrain that has to be crossed, the load can seldom exceed 20 tons, and even then, when the trucks leave the hardtop road just a few kilometres out of N'Djamena, the drivers have to reduce their tyre pressures for extra floatation in the sand.

Each truck carries a driver and two helpers for digging out and placing sand ladders when they get stuck. They also carry no less than 3 tons of water, food and extra fuel. This fuel is carried in 600-litre tanks specially fitted under the trailer. Many trucking operations can carry their spare fuel in drums on top of the load, but when trucking food under such rough conditions, the diesel oil in the drums would invariably leak and cause spoilage.

One of the ten trucks is a mobile workshop carrying 3,000 litres of extra fuel, a generator, a welding plant, spare parts, and a two-way radio to be able to communicate with the radio operations room in the UN building in N'Djamena. Real Metivier, the Canadian who has spent a lifetime in military and private trucking and who set up and runs this 200-truck fleet in Chad, speaks in glowing terms of the mechanic and his two helpers in this truck. "They perform miracles in the desert," Metivier said. "That mechanic is very special. He's the type of guy that is never stuck. He'll always find a way of getting a truck moving again. He's worth a lot of money, a guy like that." In fact he gets a salary of about $800 a month, which for Chad is considerable.

The crews often have to leave their trailer in the desert when things get really difficult. One of the helpers stays to guard it, while the truck and the rest of the crew continue to the destination. Once there they unload, then they return to the trailer, transload from the trailer into the truck, and go back to destination a second time. The costs of trucking under such conditions are enormous. Hauling a 35-ton load of food from N'Djamena to Faya Largeau, a distance of about 1,000 kilometres each way, costs about $9,000; and this is a relatively easy and cheap route because there is a sort of track that is harder than ordinary desert sand. This permits the use of large Mercedes 40-ton semi-trailer trucks.

Transport operations in Chad, when they involve going into the remote north, are like setting out on an ocean voyage. Convoys will be away at least a month, if not 6 weeks. The trucks of the convoy do not normally follow in line astern, partly because the sand kicked up by their passage may make it difficult to see, but mainly because the drivers are experienced in picking their way over the firmest terrain. They judge where to go by the colour of the sand – and there are some who never seem to get stuck – but no driver trusts the judgement of another to keep him on firm ground, so each prefers to make his own track.

They fan out over square miles of desert, each crew struggling ahead, but staying in visual contact with the lead truck. As evening approaches, they come together again, park, have their evening meal, and go to sleep under their trucks.

The navigation is left to guides the convoy picks up at various stages of its journey. These guides are desert people and the good ones have an uncanny knack of finding their way. I asked Zakaria Osman Ramadan (the ex-nomad mentioned in Chapter 3 who used to set off into the desert on a camel at the end of each school year to find his tribe) how he and his people navigate. He chided me gently, in his courteous manner.

"You can't ask a question like that", he said. "It's based in western rationality and science. Things just don't work that way for us. From childhood we are brought up in the desert, watching, observing, listening to our elders and the way they function. I can't really analyse in your terms the culture which has become part of our way of life over centuries. If I tried to, I suppose I would say that when we travel we take into account the direction of the wind in relation to the time of year, the sun, and of course the stars at night, the type of shrubs and brush and their colour, the shape of the dunes and the way they are oriented, the colour of the sand, and the way the grass lies and what it looks like, and probably a number of other things. But we are never conscious of these factors and of taking them into account. Our senses must take them in, but all we know is the certainty that we have to go in this or that direction and roughly the number of days the journey will take."

I had heard that the guides in the desert in Chad would normally know the terrain within a radius of about 200 kilometres from their base, so I asked Zakaria if this was true, and again I was made to feel slightly foolish by his reply.

"There is no answer to that question", he said. "Look at it this way. If you are a guide in a village, you'll know the terrain as far as a water hole which is a convenient travelling time away, assuming that there are several of them on the route. If there are very few on the route, you'll know the terrain as far as the nearest one. And since you will wait at the water hole where you leave your customer for another customer going back towards your home, the more travelled the route, the less terrain you will be familiar with."

A week after its departure from N'Djamena, it was known from the daily radio calls that the convoy was about 600 kilometres to the north, close to the Niger border. On the map of that area, there is no track or village shown, only an expanse of yellow signifying desert. While the convoy was there, a sandstorm started. The convoy was totally blocked for 4 days and nights before it could move northwards again.

Sandstorms, apart from being extremely unpleasant, can also be rather frightening. We had a guide with us on our trip to Mao, which should have been via Bol on Lake Chad. We picked up the guide in the outskirts of N'Djamena at dawn and he assured us that he knew the way to Bol. He was a man of about 55 who said not a word as he sat next to the driver, constantly chewing a twig, the African toothbrush. He made peremptory gestures with his hands to signify left, right, straight on, and various gradations in between as we bucketed among the thorn bushes, over the dunes, and in and out of wadis.

I was impressed by his seemingly unerring feel for the route to Bol. I had not yet met Zakaria and I asked a Western-culture question regarding what reference points he was using in what, to me at any rate, was a featureless wilderness. I got no meaningful answer.

About three hours later, when we should have been arriving in Bol, having been dug in up to the axles in sand twice, and in a blinding sandstorm that had slowly developed, we chanced upon a few poor huts. Someone told us more or less where we were; we were about 4O kms to the east of our track.

Undaunted, our guide led us off again. An hour later, we were in a wadi with no way to go but back because of the dense vegetation. Exasperated, the driver turned to me. "He's dropped us in the shit!" he said. "He has no idea where he is."

We were lost. We had no compass, and the sandstorm was so dense we could not locate the sun. The driver and the guide shouted at each other in Arabic. Then we started back. We groped about for a tense hour. We tried to retrace our tracks, but they had been almost obliterated by the sandstorm. Luckily, we again chanced upon the same group of huts, and luckier still found someone who could guide us to a point on the route for Mao. We abandoned the idea of going to Bol without regret. We were too relieved to have found *anywhere* in that awesome world of driving sand and featureless terrain.

Our toothbrush-chewing guide had neither Zakaria's cross-cultural awareness that would have allowed him to give me a lecture about asking silly Western-culture questions, nor did he have Zakaria's acumen for finding his way. He certainly would never have reached the echelons of the best educated Chadians, as did Zakaria, because he would have died of thirst or hunger looking for his tribe after his first year at school!

So there are guides and guides. Presumably the truck convoys pick better ones.

★   ★   ★

To be lost or stuck in a sandstorm is a relatively minor hazard in trucking in Africa. Flash floods are far more serious. When the rains do arrive in these desert areas they can send a wall of water metres high down a dry wadi in seconds. In Chad a completely loaded food truck in a fleet being operated by FAO was caught by one, rolled over and buried, never to be recovered. There was a similar accident in the Sudan, but the top of the truck remained visible after the water subsided and it was eventually dug free.

Greater hazards still are posed by military mishaps. Mines placed by guerrillas have caused much damage to trucks moving food in Africa. In 1985, near Abéché in Chad, a truck carrying food detonated a mine. There was considerable damage, but fortunately no one was hurt on that occasion. Other drivers have been less lucky. In Chad and Ethiopia they have lost their legs completely, or had them shattered by mines exploding under the cab. In Chad in 1984, one of the trucks of the UN-run fleet was caught in a battle between Chad and Libya and the crew of three was killed.

One of the most dangerous trucking operations in Africa at the time of writing is hauling emergency food and supplies into southern Sudan from Kenya and Uganda to the south. Speedways Transafrica, a company based in Nairobi, does a lot of trucking for the UN and for WFP. They go into areas where the protracted war between the Sudan People's Liberation Army and the national troops of the Khartoum government is causing much hardship.

An Italian, Carlo Gola, who used to work for FAO and for the EEC as an agricultural adviser in the field, is the principal of the trucking company. It seems to be doing quite well out of the contract, but not without risk. Gola recounted some of the problems his operations face.

In just under a year, we've trucked 5,700 tons of food from Kitale to Juba. Some has gone to Yambio too, which is even more difficult to reach. I have twenty-five trucks of my own, and then I hire in others when necessary. I have had to modify the trucks so that each has a 2,000-litre fuel tank because you can't get fuel along the road to Juba and back. And you can't get anything else either, so the crews leave with everything they are going to need for the trip, which can last anything up to two-and-a-half months, though 6–8 weeks is more usual.

Before the Sudanese government starting closing off roads, we used to be able to do the round trip between Nairobi and Juba in 2–3 weeks, but now we have to make a long diversion from Kitale through Uganda and up into Sudan. This puts costs up a lot. We're talking about 4,000 Kenyan Shillings a ton – about $250 – now, and that's double what it was a year ago. And commercial cargoes may go as high as 5,000 Shillings a ton.

The problem with the route through Uganda is not just the distance, and the roads are not too bad either ... no, it's the fact of the civil war there. There is a stretch that has to be done under military escort. We go from Kitale through Kampala and up towards the Kabalega National Park without any problem. But when we get to a village called Karuma Falls, we have to pick up the escort to take us to Pakwatch, on the Nile just below Lake Mobuto. The escort usually consists of 200–300 troops and of course, they only mobilize when they have enough trucks waiting to make it worthwhile. I have had trucks wait for an escort for almost a month in Karuma. But it's a bit better now, and I must say, the

Ugandan troops are always very correct and courteous. As a matter of fact, since they are government people, they are more at risk from the rebels than my trucks are.

Even so, last year I had two road tankers taking fuel up to Juba for UNDP. They were rocketed on that stretch and they burned out. Worse was that the two crews of three in each truck were burned to death. My contract with UNDP stipulated that the cargo was my responsibility, so what with compensation to the six families, and the value of the fuel and the trucks, that cost me almost 3 million Shillings, about $200,000.

I had another truck come home with 43 bullet holes in it. I left it in the garage unrepaired for a bit, and when people complained about the high rates per ton, I took them to the garage and showed them the damage!

These attacks on trucks have had a secondary effect. I've got first-rate Somali drivers, who are courageous and know Fiat trucks, but now they are so scared on that stretch that when they are going through it, they bunch up one behind the other, imagining they'll be safer that way, I suppose.

But of course, when one brakes, the one behind runs into him. Last month I had three radiators stoved in. Then it gets dramatic because the truck is immobilized and the escort won't stay with it. We have to get a new radiator from Nairobi, take it up there and wait for for an escort to take us to the truck and guard us while we do the repairs. At least the food in the trucks was never stolen, though I now have a different arrangement with the UN and with WFP: they take responsibility for the cargo, and I take responsibility for the trucks and crews.

The troubles are not completely over once we get past Pakwatch and into so-called safe territory. The road we have to use from Arua in northern Uganda to Yei in southern Sudan is a secondary one. The main one has been closed by the government. There are some steep hills on the road we use and we have to couple two trucks to one trailer for the climb, and then go back again for the next trailer, and so on. Luckily I've got Fiat 682s. They're often called the workhorse of Africa. Tough, rough and reliable. Glorious things they are! Someone tried to get a more modern American Mack Truck semi-trailer over that road to Yei a few months ago. They didn't make it because you can't couple semi-trailer rigs together like you can the old-style truck.

Our Fiat 682s with their trailers take loads of up to 30 tons, and they easily last 10-15 years, doing 70,000 kms a year. We've made engine changes out on the road, they're so simple to work on. Unfortunately, we are not allowed to use radios in Uganda so we can't keep in touch with our trucks should they break down, so we lose a lot of time before a message gets back to us.

So it's not easy, as you'll understand, but there has been one improvement in recent months – the Ugandans don't make us load and unload the trucks two or three times en route like they often used to. And once they sent a truck back 570 kilometres from the Sudan border to Kampala to have some papers verified!

Situations such as those surrounding trucking into southern Sudan at the time of writing lead to all manner of abuse: for example, although the risks and costs certainly are high, they tend to be exaggerated to justify even higher trucking costs, and few people really know what the risks are. Furthermore, donors have been competing against each other to obtain the limited trucking services available in order to ensure that *their* food and relief supplies get to their destination. The result is spiralling trucking costs.

In March–April 1987, WFP took an important initiative in this connection. It sent Andrew Toh, a senior logistics officer, to Karuma Falls to talk to the military authorities. He was to ascertain the real level of risk and look into ways of speeding up the escort operation. He was also to explore the possibility of other routes that would avoid the rebel-infested area of the Kabalega Park. Toh, a humorous and hard-working Singaporian, claims to be a coward and to have been scared witless all the time he was at Karuma Falls.

Fortunately, no one shot at him, and after he left Uganda, he organized a meeting in Nairobi of donors to South Sudan. The purpose was to try to coordinate and order the procurement of trucking services so donors would not compete and prices could be stabilized. There was general relief among the donors that someone was willing to try to put an end to the madhouse situation. At the time of writing, attempts are being made to arrange for large convoys of 3O–5O trucks bearing relief supplies from various donors to leave at once under international convoy leaders. Clearly, the freight rates for such large convoys could be standardized, and just as important, negotiated down to the bone.

Donors sometimes refuse supplies because they doubt whether they can be delivered. This was the case for South Sudan in 1987. The WFP staff in Juba estimated a need of 4O,OOO tons of food, but for a long time only 2O,OOO tons were pledged because donors knew of the chaotic trucking situation. It is therefore vital to improve transportation as a prerequisite for food to be offered.

In the Sudan recently, a truck with 11 illicit passengers on it overturned killing 6 of them. In countries such as Chad and the Sudan, with enormous distances and little transport, there is always the problem of people, usually whole families, trying to hitch a ride. Doubtless, truck crews get extra revenue from this, and so it is difficult to stop. Accidents such as the one in the Sudan raise problems of claims and liabilities that cause strained relations, even when there is no legal responsibility.

We have seen some of the details of trucking in Africa, but what happens when widespread catastrophe strikes, as it did in so many countries of Africa in 1984–85? Hundreds of thousands of tons of food have to be moved and distributed with utmost urgency. How is the operation organized?

Usually, there is long-haul trucking from the nearest port or railhead, which may be many hundreds of kilometres distant, to depots within the country. From there, distribution to camps and communities is done by smaller trucks.

In some countries, numerous private trucking groups or individuals can be mobilized to transport relief food. In Mali, for example, Francis Valere Gille, the WFP chief of operations, stated that the government created the only real transport problem by offering rates that were inferior to normal commercial trucking rates. Few trucks were offered by their owners until Valere Gille interceded with the government. Once they started paying normal rates there was no lack of availability, and in fact many trucks came in from neighbouring countries.

Mali was one of the luckier countries because it has a reasonable road network running through the southern part of the country, as well as a railway from Senegal to the west. Many other countries were less well-served. The Sudan, for example, had no shortage of commercial trucking for the main routes, but there were almost no four-wheel drive trucks for final distribution into the remotest areas. Ethiopia, at the beginning of the crisis, is believed to have had a total of more than a thousand trucks for relief work but half of these were out of order at any one time. Chad had quite different problems connected with the closing of Apapa port by Nigeria at a critical time when food was being brought into Chad before the rains, compounded by problems of getting trucks across the River Chari into N'Djamena. The particularly interesting ways in which these problems were solved will be covered in some detail in the next chapter.

In fact, in many countries during the 1984-86 period, very efficient logistics operations were ultimately built up with outside help. Some were directly run by UN Agencies, and at the time of writing some still are. Many of the staff involved in logistics with the UN agencies are ex-military. Alan Jones is such a person. He now works for one of the large grain trading companies and is based in Nairobi, but before that he worked for WFP for a number of years and carried out assignments in Nigeria, in the Sahel, and in Ethiopia. He worked for the Save the Children Fund and for the International Red Cross in Biafra organizing the movement of relief supplies during the war there, and this together with his experience in doing the same type of work during the Sahelian crisis of the early 1970s, and in Ethiopia for several years from 1973, must make Jones one of the most experienced logistics people anywhere. In

Ethiopia, he also helped to set up the RRC, when it had just 6 people, compared to the many thousands it now employs.

Alan Jones is of medium height, in his 40s, slender and clean-cut. He has a brisk and decisive manner, probably a legacy of his training at Sandhurst and his 7 years in the British Army. WFP sent him to the Sudan in early 1985 to tackle the enormous logistics problems that were brewing to the point of boiling over. When Jones arrived, there were very few people in the international aid community with solid experience of mounting a relief operation. And everyone, except the US, had started late because of the unwillingness of Nimeiry to call for help.

In mounting any relief operation, enormous inertia must be overcome before things start to roll. Furthermore, the Sudan had some of the greatest distances to cover – hardly surprising because it is the largest country in Africa. The food ships were arriving in Port Sudan which is at the opposite side of of the country from the areas of Darfur and Kordofan that were famine stricken.

It is roughly 1,200 kilometres by road from Port Sudan to Khartoum or to Kosti on the Nile. This stretch is served both by a railway and an asphalt road, but westwards from Khartoum, the conditions are similar to those described in Chad. The distance westward from the Nile before reaching the main famine areas in Darfur and Kordofan was another 1,200 kilometres. Once inside those areas, enormous transportation problems remained, however. Darfur alone is the size of Spain, without a road worthy of the term – except perhaps for two stretches totalling 600 kms from Nyala to El Fasher and from Nyala to Zalingei.

In fact there *is* a railway going west as far as Nyala in Southern Darfur, and thereto hangs a sad tale. The Americans drew up a contract with the Sudanese Railways to carry 250,000 tons of sorghum to Nyala. From there, it would be trucked the relatively short distances into the main famine areas. About 1,800 tons of food a day needed to go by rail from Kosti, south of Khartoum, to Nyala if Darfur were to have food to see its people through the rainy season due to begin around the month of July 1985.

The confidence of the Americans in the capacity of the railway turned out to be totally misplaced. Its inefficiency was so monumental that, on average, less than a quarter of the agreed amount was transported per day. According to some reports, priority was given to items such as sugar during Ramadan; wagons that should have been full of grain travelled empty because they had been reserved for merchants; and grain disappeared *en route*. Then, once the rainy season began, there were washouts of the track and derailments.

For the Americans, who had assumed the responsibility for meeting the crisis in western Sudan, and who wanted to show the rest of the world how they could organize relief operations for their friends, it was a major setback. It took them a long time to extricate themselves from their contract with the railways, and they had to ship in more trucks and use helicopters for local distribution. Perhaps less hurtful than the extra expense was the failure to deliver as promised. They learned the hard way about the inefficiency of Sudanese Railways and the problems that seem endemic to Africa.

When Alan Jones arrived in Khartoum, the donor community was still in disarray. It was being widely predicted that millions of people were going to starve to death. No one seemed to know how to come to grips with the problems, and there was no shortage of infighting and personality conflicts. The US had not yet met its Waterloo on the Nyala railway and the head of the USAID team in Khartoum, a very strong personality, was taking the stance that he and his team were going to handle everything for the west and needed no help from anyone.

It may sound obvious, [said Alan Jones,] but the problem in a food emergency is simply delivering the food. Too many people take their eyes off that fact and say they'll provide medicines and put in water wells, and that's all very important. But when people are hungry, the first priority is to get food to them, and it's a matter of logistics. Can you deliver it from where you've got it to where the people are? In the Sudan, as everywhere else, it's mainly a matter of logistics from the port. Because the world is perfectly capable of delivering to the nearest port. Your real problems always start once you get there. That simple fact is something that often seems to get overlooked.

Your problems are both material– getting the equipment there – and financial. Take the Sudan as a very good example. If you want to move a million tons in the Sudan, where the average cost ranges from $125-150 per ton, you need about $150 million. Unless you've got amounts of money on that scale, you're never going to move it, and that's where the problem lies. I mean, there is no point in delivering to Port Sudan or Massawa or Djibouti or wherever and telling the government to take it from there. In those circumstances, governments are even more stretched than they normally are.

So money for food movement is the key, but donors often seem reluctant to put up cassh for trucking. Aid agencies always seem to want to compete for prestige and credit through inputs that are more glamorous than money to hire trucks!

The first shipment of 4,000 tons of food – excluding the food that the US had given prior to the Sudan's official call for help – arrived in Port Sudan three months after that call, about par for the course, for unless ships carrying less-urgently required food can be diverted from other destinations, 3–4 months is about the normal time lag. The 4,000 tons were WFP food, and the arrangement had been that the Sudanese Food and Nutrition Administration (FANA) would transport that food to where it was needed. But they did not, or could not. This, and other food began to pile up in the port. For this reason, WFP contemplated setting up a logistics operation in the Sudan, and finally decided to do so.

However, that decision was not taken easily, for WFP itself was divided in those days regarding whether to get involved in actual internal transport operations. Those in favour pointed out that if people had begun to starve, the local infrastructure and management had already shown that it was incapable of responding adequately to a growing crisis, and that it certainly would not be able to handle the now urgent and massive food transportation and distribution required if millions were not to die. The more traditional elements argued that the governments should take responsibility for food once it reached their ports, as per the basic regulations of food aid. But faced with the irrefutable fact that the lives of millions were at stake, those in favour of taking direct action won the day.

As a matter of fact, there had been some pressure from within the Sudan for WFP to get into logistics. The previous year, when the crisis was still in its infancy, the Government of the Netherlands sent a small team of logistics specialists to work in the Sudan. The team was from a Dutch transport concern, Van Gend and Loos, a household name in Holland and a company that runs about 850 vans and 450 long-haul trucks in Europe.

The head of the Van Gend and Loos team in the Sudan was Fred Van Ginkel. He told me that when things began to become hectic in the early months of 1985, there was almost no coordination between the multitude of donors, whether governmental or private.

"So there was a tendency to look towards WFP, as the UN food aid agency, to take a lead," Van Ginkel said. "In fact," and his blue eyes twinkled in his mustached, suntanned face as he went on, "we forced WFP into taking the lead!"

WFP set up its Road Transport Operation in the Sudan and sent Nils Enqvist, their most experienced trucking specialist, to supervise its start up. Enqvist, also an ex-army man, had experience in Biafra and other war-torn areas such as Karamoja where, in 1980, he had the dubious honour of leading a relief convoy and being shot at. He was working in Juba, Southern Sudan, when he was called to start the trucking in the north.

Slowly, the donors began to pull as a team. A number of voluntary agencies put their people to work with WFP, and the Dutch team from Van Gend and Loos also came under the WFP umbrella to form a group known as the Management and Logistics Team (MALT). At the peak of the operation, the Netherlands provided 24 people to work in MALT and made a cash contribution of $5 million towards trucking costs. The World University Services of Canada, who were also involved in transportation, seconded one of their people, Rudy Rodrigues, to work in the WFP team, and another, Frank Dyke, to run the telecommunication system.

Italy gave a hundred four-wheel drive trucks for final distribution in the road-less areas of the west. They were BM 9O military vehicles, rather sophisticated perhaps but excellent performers in the conditions. They had a payload of 5 tons. Other donors such as OPEC and Sweden provided 7–8 tonners made by Magirus Deutz and Mercedes, until a fleet of about 2OO trucks were plying around the most remote areas of Darfur and Kordofan. The long-haul trucking was being done by private truckers.

USA for Africa, the fund-raising group of American singers and actors of which Harry Belafonte was a main personality, gave radio communication equipment that would allow contact to be maintained between logistics bases and between them and truck convoys. Since telephones and telexes are often broken down in the Sudan, the UN brought in a mobile telex van from their peace-keeping force in the Middle East. Strangely, it was hardly plugged into the Sudanese system, in a locked yard, before it was burned out.

In the context of telecommunications, it is interesting to record that the Hotel Acropole in Khartoum played a key role. It is far from being a luxury hotel; in fact it is a very modest establishment, set in a dishevelled side street. Since it is cheap, the majority of voluntary agencies made it their headquarters when in Khartoum. George, the very helpful Greek who runs it, somehow managed to have two international telephone lines open every night, whereas calling from the better hotels is often well-nigh impossible. His contribution to the relief operation, by arranging for those in the field to contact their headquarters, was fundamental. It is not well-known, however, and so it is a pleasure to record it here on behalf of all who benefitted.

Rudy Rodrigues is Kenyan-born, of Goan extraction, with Canadian nationality. He spent several years in the Kenyan army before becoming involved with World University Services of Canada in the Sudan and being seconded to work with WFP. He recalls that before the donors began to get their act together in the Sudan, there were 40 ships at anchor in the Red Sea waiting to unload, and hundreds of thousands of tons of food filling every warehouse in Port Sudan and piled on the wharfs.

The Italian trucks arrived rather soon on a roll-on-roll-off ferry. A problem was that they arrived on the major holiday at the end of Ramadan. Rodrigues and his team managed to persuade the authorities to open the port and to have all the officials on hand and ready to deal with the paperwork and the registration of the trucks. They also had the drivers ready, and had arranged with the local Shell depot to be open to fuel the trucks.

The ship was due to dock at 8.30 in the evening, but in fact only entered harbour after midnight. It was docked and unloading by 3 a.m. In less than 14 hours, all the trucks had been cleared, registered, fuelled, and were on their way to Darfur.

The Italians were as good as their word regarding the excellent trucks and mobile workshops to service them, but they were seriously remiss in providing the promised finance for their operation. A hundred drivers and their assistants had to be recruited, fuel purchased, and so on, but the Italian cash did not arrive until almost six months after the trucks. Fortunately, WFP had access to funds and was able to step into the breach.

The Road Transport Operation, later known by the acronym WTOS, became a model of cooperation between aid agencies. Voluntary groups such as Save the Children Fund, CARE, Oxfam, World Vision, International Christian Aid, and many local ones such as Red Crescent, all tied in with WTOS to help provide information from the field and to assist with final distribution.

In the first year, WFP raised about $12 million to help meet operating costs, and a further $1.5 million per month in the second year. With EEC financing and aircraft, WTOS also organized airlifts of food into western Sudan. Airlifting is hugely expensive, and it has been said that when airlifting is resorted to, it means grave mistakes were made earlier. On average, air transport costs are 10 times those of road transport, which in turn are 2–4 times those of rail transport – provided the railways function and have not been allowed to fall into disrepair as have those in the Sudan.

The subject of railways raises another interesting aspect of relief transportation during the 1984–85 crisis in Africa. With funds donated to its African Task Force, WFP put rolling stock in order on the railway that runs from Dakar to Kayes and Bamako. There are a number of downhill stretches on that railway, and owing to defective braking systems on the wagons, derailments were frequent as the unbraked wagons pushed against the locomotive, or against the first wagon ahead of them that was braking properly. A derailment not only results in losses of cargo, but may also block the track for days at a time. So WFP arranged to buy spare parts for the braking systems and have them installed. They also renovated other wagons that were out of service for want of items such as wheel bearings, with the result that, as the crisis deepened and ever more food arrived in Senegal to be moved into Mali, the railway functioned regularly and at high capacity.

Similar forethought was shown in the Sudan. The normal route west from the area around Kosti and Khartoum goes through El Obeid and El Fasher. However, it was expected that this southerly route might become impassable once the rains started. Taking this into consideration, WTOS decided that they needed a route further to the north where the rainfall would be less. That route, passing through Sodiri, would have to cross many wadis. So it was decided, ahead of time, to send a grader across the desert to smooth the wadi entries and exits. The operation cost about $100,000. Hundreds of trucks passed that way later as the southern route became more and more difficult, probably saving two weeks or so on the round trip.

WTOS was a considerable success. At the peak, it had 45 expatriates and over 500 Sudanese working with it. It was operating over 200 trucks, to hundreds of distribution points in Sudan, doing an average of 900,000 kilometres a month. Those four-wheel-drive trucks took over all the local distribution work in the remote areas. In addition, the MALT unit of WTOS was hiring and organizing the work of hundreds of private truckers.

WTOS was even running an aircraft provided by International Christian Aid to help in the management of the operation, for to send a manager overland to look into a situation could easily take a journey of a week out and a week back for 2 hours on site.

At one point, diesel fuel began to run short in the Sudan. The urgency was enormous, and so WFP headquarters bought a total 10,000 tons of it at sea and had it delivered to Port Sudan. WTOS regularly organized for fuel to be trucked to points all over western Sudan.

It is true that WTOS started late, as did all assistance to the Sudan during the crisis. And there were also criticisms that food-laden trucks were roaring through the Red Sea Hills just inland from Port Sudan ignoring people starving along the roadside. But that food was American sorghum destined for western Sudan, and once the aid agencies had got themselves coordinated, the people in the Red Sea Hills were looked after too.

WTOS moved hundreds of thousands of tons of food. Just as important, however, as the amount of food moved by its own fleet of trucks was the way it helped to regulate the private truckers. Its operations, which were commercial in that it charged normal economic rates to donors whose food it was moving, provided competition for the private truckers. And since WTOS was fully operational itself, it knew about operating costs in the Sudan and could drive hard bargains when negotiating trucking contracts. Even so, and despite their best efforts, freight rates doubled in 1985.

However, Fred Van Ginkel said, "There was never even a rumour of food going missing while it was being trucked. The private contractors had to put money down before they got the job and were fined three times the value of any missing cargo." The engaging twinkle came back into his eye as he said, "Sure, we had bank accounts opened all over the place for the donations we were receiving, and when a WFP auditor came down to have a look, he was frightened out of his mind. WFP's systems are too tight when you have to run an emergency operation like that. But Alan Jones was flexible. He just didn't tell Rome what was going on!"

Alan Jones commented: "We were getting out and doing things. Trying to pull the voluntary agencies together and generally getting food moving. In a crisis like that, with millions that could easily starve to death, donors rush to support people who are already in action. So we got millions donated from various sources, mainly through the Khartoum embassies of major donor countries. But there were no rules in the WFP book for handling the cash and in-kind contributions we were getting, so we just did the obvious – opened bank accounts and got on with it!"

In point of fact, the better UN organizations realize that their normal procedures – all established with the best intentions of making graft and corruption impossible – are far too cumbersome for rapid operations in the field. If the leaders of these organizations are action-oriented, as is James Ingram of WFP, they may actively encourage key staff to take short-cuts in time of need. Ingram's sense of urgency and his personal interest and involvement were such that he supported the bending of the rules by Jones, Moller, and others whose decisions were crucial in getting food to the starving.

Returning to the Sudan situation, Jones drew some interesting general conclusions in summing up the operation.

"We all worked together well, private agencies, government agencies, and so on. We pooled our resources and our expertise. If there is ever another crisis like that, the various organizations should cooperate as they did in the Sudan. Despite the predictions that millions would die, the worst didn't happen. We made mistakes...." He trailed off, looking thoughtful. Then he added, "It's a lonely and hazardous business running relief operations. You never get it all right. What's more, relief operations always start too late, get too big, and go on for too long."

That clipped and bare statement from a man with so much experience in the field of organizing relief operations is noteworthy. We shall come back to it later.

As a postscript, the Blue Nile Brewery just outside Khartoum is worth a mention. It has not been permitted to make beer since the days in which Nimeiry decided that his country should return to the path of Moslem purity, to the chagrin of many expatriates, and to plenty of Sudanese too. However, the brewery has at least served a useful function as HQ for WTOS operations and fleet maintenance.

At the time of writing, much food is still being transported by the remnants of the WTOS operation. Most of that food consists of locally grown cereals, especially dura, that have been bought with EEC and WFP money and are being transported from surplus to deficit areas. WTOS has also transported large quantities of seed shortly before planting seasons.

In Ethiopia there is also a large trucking operation run by WFP and known as World Food Programme Transport Operation in Ethiopia, or WTOE for short. The need for external assistance for transportation had been clear from the start of the crisis. Many of the thousand or so trucks belonging to the Relief and Rehabilitation Commission were ancient. Some had been donated to the country during the famine of 1974. I saw one of them thirteen years later, struggling up a hill in Wollo, belching black smoke, and with such a permanent list to starboard that it seemed bound to topple into the ditch at any moment. It was a miracle it was running at all.

It is estimated that about half of all the RRC trucks were unserviceable at any given time in early 1985. In this connection, it will be remembered that it was precisely the issue of logistics, and how much food it was thought could actually be distributed, that began the fatal reduction in the amount of food actually requested by the country to less than half of its real needs of over 9OO,OOO tons.

It was never actually WFP's intention to run a logistics operation in Ethiopia. It happened because, faced with the real problems, many donors decided that the best contribution they could make would be trucks. The Italian Government promised some, and so did USAID and Band Aid, among others. There was some talk of a private American entrepreneur running part of this fleet, but few thought this desirable. The special Office for Emergency Operations in Africa of the UN suggested that WFP should manage the fleet. Ingram immediately dispatched his deputy, a gently persuasive Bangladeshi called Salahuddin Ahmed, to Addis Ababa. He was accompanied by a team that included Erik Moller and Per Ivarsen. They were to negotiate with the Ethiopian Government, USAID, Band Aid and Kurt Jansson's office and draw up the outline of an agreement.

There were certain misgivings in taking on the responsibility, but Moller in particular was never one to turn down a challenge. The main problem was that he and his staff had no real say in the type of trucks that they were to operate; there was absolutely no infrastructure in Assab to use as a base; and the donors had given little thought to the complex matters of spares, maintenance, driver training, and the numerous other details necessary to run a truck fleet successfully.

The first gift of trucks, and money to run them, was from Band Aid, the charity started by the Irish pop musician Bob Geldof. The work of Geldof and of the Buerk/Amin team from the BBC probably did more than anything to arouse public awareness of the tragedy that was unfolding in Africa. From a background of being a school dropout, and after a turbulent and rebellious adolescence, Geldof had found his way into pop music and had started a relatively successful group, "The Boomtown Rats". By chance, he saw the Buerk/Amin TV coverage.

Shocked and moved by the horror of famine, Geldof dedicated himself night and day for months on end to doing something practical and concrete to help. He convinced many of the most famous pop musicians to donate their time, firstly to make a long-playing record. The sales from this record went to create Band Aid. He followed this by laying on an internationally-relayed marathon concert, Live Aid.

Geldof and his fellow musicians undertook considerable expense and lost revenue in these two initiatives. From Geldof, it was also a tour-de-force in terms of organization, drive, sheer personal commitment, and persuasive powers. Some have commented that the $100 million that were raised was a pittance compared to the overall cost of the whole African relief operation. What a short-sighted comment! The efforts of Geldof and his colleagues mobilized millions of people to care about what was happening in Africa, and to make whatever contribution they could. The money raised came from individuals. It may have been a small amount compared to the total cost of $3.8,000 million, but most of that came from government sources. We should not be overawed by that amount either. Certainly it was generous, but to put the amount into perspective, the cost of replacing the ill-fated space shuttle that blew up is over $3,000 million. And anyone who cares about their fellow humans should also be grateful to the irrepressible, funny, and irreverent Geldof for the blunt and uncompromising stance that he took while talking to many world figures and important bureaucrats. Unintimidated, he told them bluntly and with a refreshing disregard for protocol about Africa and where humanitarian duty lay.

The first 54 Band Aid trucks were Magirus Deutz bought second-hand in Saudi Arabia, in the hope that it would be quicker to get them operating in Ethiopia if they did not have to be shipped a long distance. However, it still took until November 1985 before they could be put to work, even though they had been in the country some time before that. The second batch of 46 Band Aid trucks were also Magirus Deutz, but new ones from an assembly plant in Kuwait, and they began operating almost a year later. They had been driving around the Arabian peninsula for some time before being shipped to Ethiopia because of some disagreement between the Kuwaitis and the Saudis.

USAID provided 150 DAF and Fiat Iveco trucks through World Vision, a large US voluntary agency. The first of these also became operational in November 1985. The total WTOE fleet consists of 250 trucks and 76 trailers, but it was as late as October 1986 before they were all in commission.

There was considerable initial criticism of WTOE for being slow in getting the trucks moving. It is easy to overlook, however, that it takes more than trucks alone to start a road transport operation and there was much to be done. For example, in Assab, there were no maintenance workshops or tools, and no office space or living quarters for a logistics team. Starting from scratch, WTOE used 8 truck semi-trailers as "buildings", and layed on water and electricity. They put up tents as temporary workshops. They had to find mechanics and drivers and train them, order equipment and spare parts, and they also had to plan the routes and bases in the interior.

Then, when the trucks began to arrive in large numbers, new problems were encountered. Many of these were a direct result of WTOE having been presented with a *fait accompli* and not having had a chance to plan the complete operation from the beginning and order the trucks. To cite a few examples: the Band Aid Magirus trucks bought secondhand in Saudi Arabia arrived with their tyres badly damaged by exposure to the sun, so WTOE had to arrange to fly in new tyres; no less than thirty of the Fiat Ivecos arrived without the cables to connect the tractor to semi-trailer, and they were blocked for a month before the cables could be delivered; the DAFs were built to European specifications, and did not have spare wheel carriers; and the second batch of Band Aid trucks assembled in Kuwait arrived with drawbars that were too weak for the trailers supplied with them.

Unfortunately, such problems have been very common in mounting emergency operations in the past. Many of the trucks that Italy sent to Ethiopia were painted in military colours. Since Ethiopia is a country with several civil wars going on, they all had to be resprayed to offer them minimum assurance of not being attacked. In Chad, many trucks arrived with air-filters that sucked in air from *underneath* the engine – for a desert country without roads! Some van-type vehicles arrived with radial tyres, which, though good for traction, have side-walls that are easily penetrated by thorns, of which there are plenty in the desert. Furthermore, these vans had less than 2O cms ground clearance and were two-wheel drive only. And politics interfered in the provision of trucks to Chad: obviously, four-wheel drive is an enormous advantage in such a country, but some donors would only give two-wheel drive trucks because they thought that they might be used in the war against Libya, or that even if they were not, the donor's relations with Libya might suffer.

The reason for these stupid errors – the technical rather than the political ones – is that everyone is in a rush. Certainly, many of the trucks that manufacturers have immediately available for delivery may be built to specifications for industrialized countries. But surely, it would be much quicker to modify them at the factory, with all the facilities and parts available there, rather than have to do so in the country of destination, cobbling up parts and improvising, often in appallingly difficult conditions.

An interesting example of a flexible operation took place in 1985 when the British government gave a batch of Leyland Landmaster trucks to the Save the Children Fund in the Sudan. They were fitted at the factory with twin tyres at the rear. When they were about to be loaded aboard the ship to Port Sudan, it was realized that the tyre sizes fitted were not available in the Sudan, and that the twin tyres would pick up stones between them in the desert. So wheels and tyres of the right size were also loaded aboard, and mechanics modified the trucks at sea before they reached Port Sudan.

In Ethiopia, there were bureaucratic as well as technical hitches. The initial idea was to clear the trucks through Assab according to UN diplomatic procedures, since they were destined for a UN/RRC project. However, it then emerged that clearing under that system would involve some port charges totalling about $500,000. Protracted negotiations had to take place before the right formula was found for bringing them in free of cost.

The first WTOE trucks left Assab for Addis Ababa on 25 November 1985. In the next 17 months, WTOE transported 279,000 tons of relief cargo, over 90% of it food. Overall, in 1986, WTOE lifted 23% of all relief cargo from the ports, and in the early part of 1987, it was lifting 39%. It has worked for 30 clients, most of them voluntary agencies.

WTOE is run as a commercial operation, as was WTOS, charging normal transport rates. Of course, it was started up with donations and loans. These totalled about $6 million and were from the US, Band Aid, EEC, Australia, Canada, UK, and Switzerland. Other inputs have come from Switzerland in the form of engineering specialists, and from Sweden in the form of driving instructors.

One major advantage of this UN fleet, until recently, was its ability to function in areas where other fleets were unable, or unwilling, to go because of guerrillas. (Few African governments care to draw attention to the existence of internal political opposition, so they usually term these hostile and armed people "bandits". With greater linguistic subtlety, they might even be called "miscreants"!)

For all practical purposes, the civil strife in Ethiopia divides the country in two: Eritrea and Tigray in the north, and the rest of the country further south. Of course, the situation is in constant flux, but in general terms, the Tigray stretch of the main road which leads up the backbone of the country from Addis Ababa to Asmara in Eritrea is under constant threat of attack from Tigrean forces. This stretch is some 200 kms long and lies more or less between Maychew in the south, and Adigrat in the north.

The rub is that many drought and famine areas can only be serviced from this stretch of road, and Makelle is a key point that needs to be supplied. WTOE keeps about 40 of its trucks in Asmara for offtake of relief food and supplies from the port of Massawa, and transport within Eritrea itself is seldom a security problem. When supplies are needed in Tigray, however, WTOE fills the warehouses in Adigrat, the furthest point south that they can safely go, and waits for the army to declare the road open. When and if it does, convoys shuttle back and forth as fast as possible to supply the areas in need.

In early 1987, the government undertook to open the road for 10 days each month, but they have not been able to do so. It may remain closed for weeks at a time, and when it is opened, it is only between 0800 hours and 1700 hours. The convoys that then set out, with government artillery on the surrounding hills to guard them, are only those of the Red Cross and the UN. Each truck, which is painted white and has enormous identification letters painted on it, also flies a large flag. The convoys take great care to disassociate themselves from the escorting military vehicles which travel in front and behind by insisting on a 2-3 km gap to emphasize their neutrality.

Not a single UN truck was attacked in Ethiopia in almost two years of operations. Indeed, there were a number of UN people who believed that they could operate in that sensitive area of Tigray without government troops opening the road and placing artillery on the hills. There had been an incident that seemed to confirm this view: a mixed convoy of six trucks was stopped, probably by genuine miscreants, not far from Kombolcha, an important road junction in Wollo. They were all carrying food; three were private, two were from World Vision, and the other belonged to WTOE. The group that had stopped the convoy started nosing around, waving their weapons menacingly, and asking questions about the cargoes. The WTOE driver explained that his was a UN truck carrying food. He was told to get back into his truck and drive on. The other five trucks were set alight and burnt out.

It is sad to relate that WTOE's safety privilege came to an end in October 1987. One morning, government troops checked the road south of Adigrat, and a convoy of sixteen WTOE trucks set out later. They came under rocket attack from the Eritrean rebel forces. A driver was killed, and the trucks and food were set ablaze. No comment on such wanton destruction when innocent people are in need could be adequate.

The Ethiopian government has shown reluctance to take over the WTOE operation. Perhaps the earlier security offered by the UN label was a reason for this reluctance. As things stand at the time of writing, WFP will continue to run the fleet until June 1989.

Trucking conditions in Ethiopia are not easy, but the problems do not match those of the Sudan or Chad. At least there are roads of sorts, many of them left behind by the Italians after their few years of colonization. In fact the network of main roads was built by them. They are equivalent to third-class road in Italy today, for they are narrow and twist through the wild terrain, as do the roads of the same epoch in the hinterland of Italy's mountain areas. But they are graded and laid out with all the unique flair of the Italians for civil engineering.

According to the RRC, Ethiopia has 16,400 kms of roads, of which 4,300 kms are paved. This may make it sound like a truckers' paradise compared to Sudan, Chad, and similar desert countries where digging out of sand, or out of mud in the rainy season, can consume hours of each day. However, there are still plenty of difficulties in Ethiopia. The 30-ton semi-trailer trucks that are a normal sight in industrialized countries as they trundle down our wide and gently curving highways become juggernauts as they negotiate those roads. Even if they were beautifully engineered all those years ago, they were laid out to take vehicles which were tiny by comparison. Come around a corner in those majestic Ethiopian highlands, and find yourself face to face with a monstrous truck whose driver is swinging wide so that his trailer, with its rear wheels following many yards behind, will not clip the verge as he returns to his side of the road, and you will wonder how it is that WTOE has only written off twelve of its trucks in accidents. The trucks are quite simply outsized for the conditions. And when it rains, they slide and slither all over the roads.

The WTOE trucks only carry one driver, and the fact that there is only one assistant for every three trucks gives some idea of the relative ease of the conditions compared to many other parts of Africa. But as in any vast country, break-downs far from base can involve weeks of lost time. WTOE has evolved a system to avoid these in so far as possible.

Firstly, to avoid breakdowns in the first place, the truck fleet is run like an airline. There is a network of mainte-nance bases, of which the most important is the enormous one at Kombolcha. This base is strategically situated on the main trucking routes between Assab and the interior. It has almost $2 million worth of spare parts and workshops which, even if some of them are in tents, clearly operate with clockwork precision.

Just as in airline operations, preventive maintenance is carried out. Components are replaced at pre-determined operating distances, rather than have, say, a clutch burn out when a truck is in some remote corner of the interior. The only problem with the system is that the drivers have a bonus scheme based on the numbers of trips they make. A computerized record service coupled with rigid enforce-ment are the only basis for ensuring that drivers bring their trucks into the Kombolcha base for the routine periodic checks and maintenance required.

However, if despite the preventive maintenance, there are breakdowns on the road, the loss of time is reduced to a minimum by a system similar to that of road patrols in industrialized countries. There are seven Land Cruisers, with two-way radios, provided by USA for Africa, constantly on patrol in pre-determined areas. Each convoy has a radio transceiver in the first and last truck and can call in the patrolling vehicle in case of need. If the crew of that vehicle cannot handle the problem, they in turn can call in the mobile workshop, which is fully equipped to deal with any type of mechanical failure. In practice, however, there are few breakdowns, thanks to the preventive maintenance programme.

An idea of the extent to which WTOE has become part of the Ethiopian scene is given by events in May 1987. The rains arrived early, several weeks before they were expected, and the Ministry of Agriculture was deeply concerned by the urgent need to move large quantities of seed and fertilizers into the remote parts of the interior. They called on WTOE to carry out the task. It involved a total re-organization of routes and scheduling, as well as temporary re-location of workshops and spare parts to support the fleet while it operated in areas outside its normal remit. The WTOE management was wrestling with these problems at the time of my visit.

WTOE is the largest trucking operation ever run by the UN. It certainly encountered criticisms in its early days, but it has vindicated itself since. Above all, it has helped to bring to light a series of basic problems concerning the setting up of such operations in the future. Logistics consist basically of common sense, and the only problem with common sense is that it is not really as common as the term might lead one to believe. On the basis of the logistics experience during the 1984–85 crisis in Africa, a number of people are trying to draw up guidelines for the start up of emergency operations. Nils Enqvist is one of them. He has gained his experience the hard way and is convinced that the greatest lack when an emergency relief operation has to be launched is people with practical experience. The people exist, but since emergencies in the past have not cropped up that often, they tend to scatter to the four corners of the earth and cannot always be found, or are not available, when their services are needed. However, the increased frequency with which emergencies seem to be occurring is also increasing the number of people experienced in handling them.

As has been seen, the costs of internal transport are enormous in Africa. In theory, recipient governments are supposed to assume the cost of moving food from the port of arrival. In practice, however, they seldom can. During a crisis, it is probably true to say that they almost never can, for if they had the means, there probably would not be a crisis in the first place. Even in normal times, when the food aid is mainly food-for-work, school feeding programmes, and the like, many countries cannot afford the transport costs. The result has been the introduction of an Internal Transport and Handling Subsidy (ITHS) by WFP.

In principle, the ITHS is provided only for Least Developed Countries. Normally it covers half of the costs of internal transport and storage. However, in exceptional cases, particularly for some emergencies, it may be increased to cover 100% of the cost. Food donors such as WFP often need to find other donors to help provide the ITHS during an emergency. In this connection, we should remember the comment made by Alan Jones: all that really counts in getting an emergency operation moving is money to hire transportation, but few donors find such an input appealing.

8

THE CHAD SAGA

The most complex and dramatic logistics operation of the 1984–85 African crisis was that for Chad. It became a saga, and since it illustrates so well the problems of getting food to people in Africa when there is a disaster, and how those problems can be overcome, it warrants a chapter on its own.

The vast distances from the ports of Apapa and Douala, 2,200 kms and 1,800 respectively, have already been mentioned. Distance, however, was only part of the problem, and the most serious obstacle of all was the River Chari that runs alongside N'Djamena and forms the border with Cameroon. Every single truck, whether it was coming from Nigeria or from Ngaoundéré, the northernmost point reached by the Cameroonian railways, had to cross that river. In the dry season, the Chari runs sluggishly at the bottom of steep banks and is about 250-metres wide. During a normal rainy season, it may rise many metres and also become much wider. At the beginning of the relief operation, there was a single pontoon-ferry available that could carry one 30-ton truck at a time.

By 1982–83, Chad already had serious food shortages as the drought set in. The country received about 30,000 tons of emergency food aid that year. By the time 1983 was running into 1984, it was clear that much more food would be required. In fact, in 1983–84, 77,000 tons were

---

Plate 9   Chad – wells in the desert serve as a focal point for people and animals.   (WFP/André Girod)

brought in, and it was in bringing in that quantity that the River Chari crossing first showed itself to be a serious bottleneck.

In the last weeks of 1983, as the intense period of food transportation got under way to ensure that Chad would have what it needed before the rains began in June, there were over 2OO laden trucks waiting to use the single ferry. Kousséri, the small town on the Cameroon side of the Chari, was inundated by them, and their bored crews were causing problems in the town, quite apart from any consideration of lost time and delayed food deliveries.

There were a number of factors determining the rate at which the ferry could bring food trucks over the Chari. Some were economic, and some were technical. On the economic front, the ferry belonged to the Chamber of Commerce of Chad, the head of which was a powerful ex-ambassador. The ferry was an important source of income for the Chamber of Commerce, because every commercial truck that came across paid the equivalent of about $9O for the trip. Indeed, so important was the revenue that the Chamber of Commerce was one of only three buildings in N'Djamena that were usually repaired rather quickly after being damaged by the constant warring in the town; the other two, so it was said, were the mosque and the brewery!

However, the agreement was that food trucks should not pay any ferry dues. This represented a serious loss of revenue to the Chamber of Commerce, and of course, Chad did need some commercial goods as well as food. So the Chamber of Commerce decided it would alternate food trucks with commercial trucks.

The technical problems of the ferry concerned the loading of trucks onto it without them falling into the river. Many of the trucks, especially the Nigerian ones, had poor brakes and were old and underpowered. As they came down the quite steep incline of the bank, they would need a certain momentum to get themselves up the loading ramp and on to the flat deck. To stop them on the deck, there would often be a boy to fling wooden chocks under the advancing wheels at the critical moment. If he missed, or had to jump aside to save his own neck and could not place the chocks, the truck would simply trundle ahead and over the other end of the ferry into the river. Many trucks fell into the water in this way, and operations were held up while they were retrieved.

In sum, on good days no more than 10 food trucks would come across the Chari, 300 tons of food in all. In addition, there was demurrage to be paid for the hundreds of trucks waiting in Kousséri, at an average of about $150 per day per truck.

Something had to be done, and there was a formidable team of people concerned with emergency food aid in Chad at the time to do it. On the government side, a Ministry of Natural Disaster Relief had been created in 1982. This Ministry was headed by a remarkably competent and prestigious man who had access to the president himself. That Minister, or a member of his senior staff, met with donors every Friday morning in the so-called Action Committee, to discuss the relief programme and take decisions. The calibre of those who attended these meetings was such that *everything* could be discussed, even issues such as corruption and inefficiency. There were frequent and major arguments in those meetings, with occasional table-thumping, but at the end of the day, decisions had been taken and everyone had had the chance to have their say.

This open decision-making process between government and donors was very valuable, for it led to coordinated actions that all had approved. This was not the case in every African country receiving emergency food aid. Too often, donors would meet among themselves because they felt that they could not settle certain issues if government people were present; and sometimes there was a lot of behind-the-back criticism and recrimination going on as well.

Among the donors, WFP was playing a major role, for about two-thirds of all the food aid was coming through WFP. The

WFP Representative, and also the UN Resident Coordinator, was Wali-Shah Wali, nominally from Saudi Arabia because he held a Saudi passport, but in fact a member of the old Afghan royal family. Wali was extremely effective, combining good organization with dynamism and an ability to get on well with people. His WFP chief of operations was a young American called Jamie Wickens from New Hampshire. Wickens is a smallish, energetic man with a mop of straight hair and steel-rimmed pebble glasses. He is open, articulate, and very much to the point. He has spent much of his working life in West Africa, and he plainly enjoyed being in the storm centre of the Chad logistic operation.

By January 1984, the Chari ferry problem had become critical. Wickens had been to see almost everybody that he could about the Chamber of Commerce ferry, but the general reaction was that WFP should negotiate a price to use it, and that donors would just have to take the extra cost into account. Wickens pointed out that, in effect, this would mean that less food would be available, but the power of the head of the Chamber of Commerce was such that none of the people Wickens was talking to was ready to take up the issue.

Finally, Wali-Shah Wali and Wickens went to see the Secretary-General to the Presidency, the equivalent of the prime minister, to explain the ferry problem. They had seen a small army pontoon-ferry that was only used occasionally, and they offered to resurrect it and run it exclusively to transport food trucks, with WFP assuming all the costs. The offer was accepted, but it did not prove too easy to get the ferry running because there were no people with the required experience. Wickens put his driver, who was also a mechanic, to the task of getting a team together, and he did. Within a week, the ferry, which was driven by two outboard motors and just had room for one 30-ton truck, was making 20 river crossings a day, operating from dawn to dusk.

This ferry brought the monthly tonnage crossing the Chari to 18,000 and was sufficient to bring in the 77,000 tons for that year. However, as 1984 progressed, and there was no rain, it was clear that even more food would be required to see the country through until the harvest after the rainy season of 1985.

A request for another ferry was put out, and in July 1984, Sweden offered a ferry to Chad. But it was huge – 52 metres long! It had originally been destined for the Nile, but the agreement with the Sudan had fallen through, and so the Swedes were suggesting that Chad take it. However the Chari is not the Nile, and there was no possibility of using it. Therefore Chad and WFP sent their regrets and asked for something smaller.

The Swedish response was magnificent. They loaded a modular military pontoon-ferry into three C13O Hercules and flew it to N'Djamena. It arrived in August. With the help of a Swedish major to oversee the operation, and the French army providing cranes and transporters to move the components from the airport to the river, the ferry was assembled and running in under a week. The Swedish major had also trained the crew.

Thereafter, with the two ferries running and up to 4O trucks a day being brought across the Chari, the capacity of 1,OOO-1,2OO tons a day was finally sufficient for the prospective needs in 1985.

★   ★   ★

Some of the more imaginative in the donor community in Chad had for some time been mooting the idea of a bridge. Among those promoting the idea were Wali-Shah Wali and Wickens, but obviously this would be a longer term project. Neverthless, Wali-Shah Wali was able to take a first step by bringing in two Dutch army engineers for two weeks in June 1984 to look for a possible site and to advise on suitable types of bridge.

During the mission of the Dutch engineers, Wickens was trying to make a case for a bridge based on the inefficiency of the ferries, and although the Dutch engineers located a suitable site, they seemed unconvinced of the need for a bridge.

"On their very last day," Wickens relates,

they asked me to take them down to the river again because they wanted to do some photography. We were standing on the bank and they were taking all sorts of pictures of the Chamber of Commerce ferry, and one of these Nigerian lorries drove up onto the ferry, couldn't stop, went clean across the ferry, and ... plonk! ... nosedived straight into the water. Those Dutch accused me of setting the thing up to make my point about the ferries!

Anyway, I took them back to the Chari Hotel, which is on the river, with the idea of picking up their bags and taking them to the airport. But I called the airport and the plane was late, so I suggested we have a drink on the terrace that overlooks the river. From there we could see the other Chamber of Commerce ferry that does nothing but bring fuel tankers across, because fuel was a big priority too. We were drinking a beer as a tanker truck rolled down the bank and up onto the ferry ... and it went into the river too! They just couldn't believe it. Two within half an hour or so. Anyway, that was the end of our problems in justifying a bridge. Those incidents were written up in their report.

In this way, the issue of a bridge was officially brought under discussion, but at least $1 million would be needed. And there was a political problem connected to a bridge that also had to be resolved. It was not the first time in history that the idea of a bridge between Chad and Cameroon had been raised, but Cameron had never wanted one. To be more precise, the Sultan of Kousséri did not want one because he had a monopoly on the dug-out canoes that carry people and their small livestock back and forth across the river. It was a profitable trade, and the sultan was influential with the government in Yaoundé.

The president of Chad, Hissan Habré, was convinced of the need for a bridge, so with a briefing for him put together by staff of the UN in Chad, covering the economics of the bridge and its potential advantages to Cameroon too, Habré set off for Yaoundé on 14 August 1984. He discussed the matter with Paul Biya, the president of Cameroon, and came back with a signed agreement for a bridge to be built.

The financing was still not secured, and Wali-Shah Wali was putting pressure on the UNDP in New York to find a solution. Finally, the UNDP Emergency Fund agreed, but the $1 million was actually advanced after Wali-Shah Wali negotiated with the FAO Representative in Chad, Philippe Mengin, and they agreed to divert $1 million already allocated by UNDP to the agricultural development programme in the country, against replenishment later.

★   ★   ★

While the bridge proposal was going steadily ahead, the ferries were running equally steadily towards trouble. Even in the 1983–84 dry season, which had not been as severe as the coming one promised to be, the river went so low as the season progressed that the ferries were beginning to bottom. That year of 1984–85, with Chad in the grip of the worst drought in recorded history, with almost half of the country's population at real risk of starvation, it looked as though the Chari would dry out so much that the ferries would not be able to operate. And there was no chance that a bridge could be built in time.

One day in November 1984, Real Metivier, the Canadian who runs the UN truck fleet in Chad and who was mentioned earlier, and Jamie Wickens went down to the river to see how things were going with the ferries. While they were there, Metivier thought of the solution to the problem. They would build a temporary causeway and floating bridge!

Metivier had seen three old and very rusty barges lying as scrap in the backyard of a government agency. He had them taken away and carefully welded with steel plates to stop them leaking. Then as the river shrank, and with financing drummed up from the EEC, earthmoving equipment began working on the banks of the river to create a dyke or causeway. Obviously, a channel for water had to be left open, and in this the three barges were anchored. Planks were fixed to them to create a floating bridge.

On 9 February, 1985, when the river was so low that the ferries would have to cease operations any day, the causeway and floating bridge were ready and brought into use. Between that day and the end of June, when the rains washed away the causeway, no less than 75,000 tons of food was trucked across it, a high proportion of the 200,000 tons that Chad needed, and got, to feed its people in 1984–85. Without that causeway, there would have been a total lack of supply for several months.

★   ★   ★

Just after the causeway was opened, the Nigerians dropped their bombshell – the closing of the port of Apapa described in the last chapter. It will be remembered that of the 30,000 tons of food coming into Chad each month, about 25,000 tons were coming though Apapa, and only about 5,000 tons through Douala. The flow of 30,000 tons a month had to continue to provide the 120,000 tons required in Chad in the four months before the rains began in June.

Jamie Wickens was in Geneva for a donor meeting when Erik Moller told him that Apapa was closed. Wickens was thunderstruck. Even if the Nigerians were to allow Port Harcourt or Calabar to be used, neither of these ports had the capacity of Apapa, for they did not have modern cargo-handling systems.

Wickens was convinced that the Chadian relief operation was finished, and that many people would be doomed to starvation. When the decision was taken to divert about 100,000 tons of food aid from Apapa to Douala, there was absolutely no guarantee that it could be forwarded north to Chad at the required rate of 30,000 tons a month, compared to the previous rate of about 5,000 tons.

Prior to these events, delays on the route via Douala and the railway to Ngaoundéré had been causing concern, and for this reason it had been decided late in 1984 to post a logistics coordinator in Douala. Tun Myat proposed Ramiro Lopez da Silva for the job. Da Silva, of Portuguese descent but born in Mozambique, had been the regional director of the Beira railway, with responsibility for both the port and the railway operations. Better experience for trying to improve the performance of Douala port and Cameroon Railways could hardly have been found, and da Silva had been in Douala several weeks already when Apapa was closed.

When Wickens got back to N'Djamena after his attendance at the donor conference in Geneva, he and Wali-Shah Wali decided that he should go to Cameroon to talk with the authorities, and especially with the management of the railways. By fortunate coincidence, Wali-Shah Wali had worked in Camerooon and was a friend of the director of the railways, a man by the name of Moudouki. Wali-Shah Wali gave Wickens a personal letter for Moudouki, and armed with this he set out for Douala.

Moudouki had the reputation of being busy and therefore difficult to see. Indeed, Wickens, da Silva, and Martin Mock, the WFP man in Cameroon, had no success in trying to fix an appointment, so they presented themselves in the outer office, where a secretary tried to ward them off. But Wickens produced the personal letter and Moudouki immediately had them ushered in.

Wickens explained the problem of moving food into Chad now that Apapa had been closed, and produced a schedule for the next three months of all the ships due to unload their food destined for Chad in Douala. He stressed the humanitarian problem, the prestige that would accrue to Cameroon if they could take over the role that Nigeria had refused, and he also mentioned the enormous revenue that the Port of Douala and the railways could generate by increasing their offtake and onforwarding of food from 5,OOO to 3O,OOO tons a month.

Moudouki was a man of imagination and action. Then and there, he summoned the port authorities, the customs, the police, and some of his own senior staff of the railways. He explained the problem to them and said, at the end: "We are going to make this commitment to onforward 3O,OOO tons a month of food for Chad, for humanitarian and economic reasons."

On the practical level, the order went out that every available wagon in Cameroon should be mobilized in order to provide the wagons required by WFP, and to keep normal commercial freight moving in Cameroon at the same time.

Da Silva is an electrical engineer by training, but he has spent his entire working life in transport and logistics. (He went on from Douala to Ethiopia to run the WTOE operation described in the last chapter, and at the time of writing he is still doing so.) Tun Myat had been right about him. He turned out to be one of the best among the 17 logistics advisors that WFP moved into Africa during the crisis. As a railway and port expert, he spoke the same language as those he was dealing with in Douala. But as an outsider, he was neutral and could intercede to make the forwarding agents, the port authorities, and the railways pull together. He was in constant touch with them all to cajole, explain, advise, coordinate and encourage – and to bang a few heads together when necessary.

When da Silva arrived in Douala in late January 1985, Per Ivarsen in Rome had told him that his target was to move 6,000 tons of food per month through Douala. In January, only 3,800 tons were moved, and da Silva discovered that one problem was wagons going astray on the run to Ngaoundéré. It was difficult to monitor the food wagons when they were only a few spread among others in a long goods train, and many food wagons got forgotten in sidings after shunting operations, uncoupling and recoupling, and so on.

So da Silva's first move was to propose that the railways make up a so-called block train each day which consisted only of wagons filled with food, and all going to the same destination.

He soon discovered that another important limitation to the offtake and forwarding capacity of Douala was a lack of coordination between the various donors and their fowarding agents, and between the railways and the road transport system at Ngaoundéré. Every morning at 7.00 there was a meeting in the port at which railway wagons were allocated to different forwarding agents. This was done on an *ad hoc* basis and the forwarding agents with the most "influence" got the lion's share of the wagons. Moudouki immediately agreed that this system should stop. All wagons would be allocated to WFP, to da Silva in person, and he would assign them to forwarding agents on the basis of what food cargo they were holding for Chad. In effect, this meant that da Silva was arranging for all food being transported, irrespective of the donor. The daily block train began operating in the last week of February, and this and the new wagon allocation system raised the food moved to 12,000 tons in March.

In early April, da Silva was making his way back to Douala after a visit to Ngaoundéré and was in Yaoundé when he received a telephone call from Tun Myat in Rome. Tun Myat told him that the port of Apapa had just been closed and that, henceforth, he had to move 30,000 tons a month. He was not as shocked as one might have expected because he had confidence in the railways by then, but he was very concerned about the road transport from Ngaoundéré into Chad. There was a formal agreement between Chad and Cameroon that 45% of all the road transport on that route would be done by Cameroonian trucks, and the remaining 55% by Chadian trucks, and this might complicate the issue of finding enough trucks.

They would need to move about 1,200 tons per day arriving in two block trains, each carrying 600 tons in 15 wagons. That tonnage would call for 40 trucks of 30-ton capacity each. However, since the round-trip time between Ngaoundéré and N'Djamena would be about 10 days, a total of 400 trucks would be required, a large number by any standard.

A related, but smaller, problem was that the forwarding and warehousing business at the railhead in Ngaoundéré was in the hands of a few elderly Frenchmen whose main interest was to make sure that all rail freight was unloaded and stocked in their warehouses for a few days before it was reloaded for its ultimate destination by truck. Theirs was not an arduous existence, and they could go off in good time for their pastis and game of cards. They had to be convinced that emergency food was a different matter and that it would be unloaded from the rail wagons directly into road trucks. Furthermore, double working shifts would be needed.

Wickens unearthed 5O of the 4OO trucks that were needed from Cotton Tchad, the state cotton corporation. Others were made available from the Chadian Transport Cooperative, an official cooperative of truckers who were already doing sterling service transporting food within Chad.

★   ★   ★

From his side in Cameroon, da Silva had visited the Minister of Transport who had shown his concern and promised all possible support. Since trucking in Cameroon is in the hands of many small private operators, it could have proven difficult to contact enough of them to find the required trucks. The Minister himself charged the National Road Transport Syndicate to mobilize trucks from all over the country.

So the logistics chain was complete: ships unloading in Douala; two block trains a day; 4O road trucks a day, and the causeway across the Chari. But there were still doubts in many quarters as to whether the required tonnage could be moved. The USAID mission in Chad sent a long telex to WFP in Rome saying that in the light of previous experience in West Africa, it was an impossible undertaking, and implying that if da Silva thought it could be done, he did not know what he was up against.

However, the operation went remarkably well, so well in fact that they never hit their targeted 3O,OOO tons per month – they reached 28,OOO tons – because they ran out of stocks in Douala! They were fortunate that there had been no accumulation of stocks in Douala. This was because, just prior to the diversion of the ships from Apapa in early April, da Silva's efforts and the resulting 12,000 tons moved in March, had emptied the warehouses.

Bagging of the bulk cargoes was being done by hand in the holds when da Silva first arrived in Douala, and that too was reorganized. One of the biggest forwarding agents was persuaded to invest in quayside bagging equipment. Later, arrangements were made with a company operating throughout West Africa for ships on their way into Douala to pick up bagging equipment at sea. It was packed in three containers, and had a crew of four people to assemble and run it. They worked non-stop, day and night, and could unload and bag a cargo of 10,000 tons in 3 days.

The trans-loading from railway wagons to road trucks was a potential bottleneck. Wickens based a Swiss Disaster Relief Unit man, Jean Michel Jordan, in Ngaoundéré to organize the work. In gangs of ten, and paid on a per ton basis, the workers would transload 40 tons in 45 minutes.

A fundamental need was for instant communication to keep track of the operations and direct them. Since telephones in Africa are seldom instant, even when they do function, a radio link was set up between Douala, N'Djamena, and Ngaoundéré. In N'Djamena, the UN complex had a walkie-talkie system for reasons of security. Wali-Shah Wali agreed that it be used for logistics, and in this way it was possible to keep contact between the ferries, the WFP office, the warehouses, and the customs in Kousséri. These radio links were instrumental in keeping the food flowing smoothly and in avoiding lost time for trucks.

Pilferage in the port of Douala has always been a serious problem. The port management staff have the habit of a leisurely lunch break. Somnolent after a good meal and a glass of wine, or two, they take a short siesta before returning to the port. The pilferers know this well, and one day, when there were three food ships in harbour, da Silva

was on board one of them when he saw about 60 people
hard at work pilfering on another that was carrying USAID
food. Edible oil and other high value items were their main
target. Da Silva went to the US consul in Douala, and
arrangements were soon made to alert the local governor
before a food ship was due to dock. He provided an army
guard for food ships while in port.

★   ★   ★

Once the food aid began reaching N'Djamena at a rate of
1,200 tons per day, the problem of storage arose. There
was a central storage complex of 9 buildings put up during
the drought of the early 1970s and situated in Chaguoua, in
the outskirts of the town. When the relief operation began,
this complex had a nominal capacity of 13,000 tons, but
the buildings had been badly damaged by the strife and had
to be renovated. Additional pre-fabricated buildings given
by the US and by Switzerland were erected. But even these
were not enough during the build up to the peak of the
operation in 1985.

Wickens organized the building of temporary roofs over
the space between the buildings, and Norway gave
numerous Rubb Hall tents. These arrived in a Hercules and
the Norwegian manufacturer's representative trained
Wickens' ex-driver, of ferry fame, in their erection. These
large tents each held about 800 tons of food and were an
excellent speedy solution to the problem. They are still
being used in many parts of Africa.

From the Chaguoua store complex, food was taken to
four regional sub-depots throughout the country from
where final distribution could be made. These sub-depots,
or Regional Logistics Bases as they were called, each had a
WFP person to manage it and to train local staff as
warehouse keepers and so on. The bases also had workshops to handle truck maintenance.

A fleet totalling 300 trucks was being run by UN
agencies. FAO had 125 trucks donated by Italy; WFP had
100; and UNDP had 75. WFP handed over its trucks to be

run with those of UNDP under the management of Real Metivier, rather than duplicate administrative costs. Other internal transport was being done by the Chadian Transport Cooperative.

Distribution plans were drawn up for a month at a time on the basis of information received from all over the country concerning the needs. There were private organizations and government agencies providing this information. A Monitoring and Surveillance Committee, set up by the Action Committee which grouped donors and government and met each Friday, made a synthesis of the needs in the third week in each month for the following month. This formed the basis for the detailed distribution plan which specified regions and districts, and quantities for each. Once the Action Committee had approved, and the Minister for Natural Disaster Relief had signed it off, a copy of the distribution plan was sent to all concerned.

When Chaguoua was full, even with its capacity expanded to 25,000 tons, the decision was taken to truck directly from Ngaoundéré to two of the sub-depots in southern Chad, those at Sarh and Moundou. Compared to the route to N'Djamena, which is asphalted, this was a difficult undertaking from the point of the terrain and lack of roads, and it was also hazardous because of rebels operating in the south. The Cameroonian truckers were very reluctant to make the run to Sarh or Moundou, but da Silva had an answer for them. They were making good and relatively easy money on the N'Djamena run, so he simply told them that if they did not go to Sarh or Moundou, they would get no more traffic to N'Djamena. There was some weeping and wailing and in the end a compromise was struck: for every trip to Sarh or Moundou, they would be given two trips to N'Djamena.

★   ★   ★

Finally, we must return to the story of the bridge. After the $1 million had been allocated by UNDP, the first time the UN had financed a bridge, the search began for a secondhand bridge with a span length of 220 metres. One was found in the Middle-East, and a German construction company, which was resurfacing roads in northern Cameroon and had a base in Kousséri, transported it in, built a series of reinforced concrete piles for it in the river, and erected the whole assembly in less than five months. The cost was $960,000.

The fact that a German contracting company had been engaged to build the bridge had a useful spin-off. Wali-Shah Wali and Wickens explained to the German Ambassador that access roads would be required for the bridge and asked whether it might be possible for the German government to finance them, since a German company, already on the spot, was installing the bridge. The upshot was that the German government indeed financed the access roads at a cost of $1.5 million.

When the rains of June 1985 washed out the causeway, the two ferries were brought back into use until, at the end of July, the bridge was inaugurated. It was a major moment. At the ceremony, the USAID man who had sent the telex to Rome to say that the 30,000 tons a month via Douala were impossible met with da Silva for the first time. In shaking his hand, he said: "Listen, if you say in future that you can do a hundred thousand tons, I'll give you the benefit of the doubt!"

When I saw this "Bridge of Life" in April 1987, one of its piers had been damaged by a man who had floated down the river in a boat, and placed explosives against it. He blew himself up in the process.

Unlike the situation in so many other countries, relief operations in Chad began in time to avert major disaster. They were successful despite numerous difficulties, and misgivings all round as to the feasibility of what needed to be done. Quite apart from USAID's point of view, an FAO/WFP Crop Assessment Mission that had worked in Chad in October 1984 – when the port of Apapa was still open – had stated that it would be impossible to get more than 100,000 tons of food into the country. In fact 200,000 tons were brought in, and 130,000 of those tons came in *after* Apapa was closed.

Certainly people died of hunger in Chad, but there was no mass starvation even if almost half of the population of 4.5 million required food aid to survive. The success was certainly due to the excellent Natural Disaster Relief Ministry whose staff worked so well, in a frank and open way, with relief agencies. And the staff of the relief agencies were caught up in a great humanitarian cause which was a challenge to their ingenuity. They worked exhaustingly long hours, 7 days a week, knowing that their efforts were for the benefit of so many people.

9
FOOD FROM THE SKY

There may be situations during an emergency when the only satisfactory way to move food is by air. More often than not, however, resorting to such an expensive mode of transport is the result of poor planning and logistics earlier in the operation. In fact, it was because of the late beginning of the relief operations in the Sudan and Ethiopia that a number of donors provided air transportation of food in those countries. The US, the Soviet Union, UK, Poland, Australia, West Germany, East Germany, Belgium, Denmark, France, Italy, Libya, and the EEC were among those involved at various stages and in various ways.

Most of the aviation input was for airlifting of food, that is to say, loading food at one airport and landing at another to unload it. This is distinct from airdropping, when food is dropped to people from a low-flying aircraft. Airlifting and airdropping may well be the only way to get food to people who are isolated by floods, features of terrain, or security risks that make surface transport impossible.

The first air-transport operations got under way in Ethiopia in November 1984, within weeks of the general public becoming aware of what was happening there. The aircraft were lifting food between Assab, Addis Ababa, and Asmara. Owing to the security problem on the road from Addis Ababa to Asmara, that route might have been

Plate 10   Ethiopia – after the airdrop there is a rush to collect grain that may have fallen from broken sacks.   (WFP/Frances Vieta)

economically justifiable until such time as food ships could arrive in sufficient numbers in Massawa, the port in the north close to Asmara. The Assab–Addis route could be served more economically by trucks, but donors felt that their air operations were a high-profile way of showing that they were taking action.

Much changed, however, with the arrival in Addis Ababa at Christmas 1984 of Staffan de Mistura. De Mistura is a 40-year-old Swedish-Italian who at the time was desk-bound in a high-level administrative job at FAO in Rome. However, he had a background in emergency relief work, and in particular, he had done a course in airdropping with the Swedish Air Force. He decided to use his holiday, and later some leave of absence from FAO, to see what he could do to help in Ethiopia.

De Mistura dresses immaculately and has a suave manner, so much so that it has been remarked that he appears as a person who would be most at home on the cocktail-party circuit. It so happened, however, that his practical experience coupled with his diplomatic ways, allowed him to trigger a truly international airdropping operation that saw military personnel from Warsaw Pact and Nato countries working and flying together for the first, and so far the only, time in history.

Although there were millions of people in Ethiopia receiving food in camps or through food distribution points scattered around the country, there were large numbers of people isolated in the mountains, probably more than 50 km from the nearest road. The terrain is so rugged, with high plateaux deeply fissured by valleys, that the only way they could be reached was on foot, and similarly, their only way of escape would be on foot. But hundreds of thousands were so weak from deprivation that it was impossible for them to undertake the walk to where they might receive food.

De Mistura realized that the only means of helping these people was by airdrops of food that would allow them to gather their strength for the journey to the nearest road.

From there, they could be helped to reach feeding centres. De Mistura's first port of call was the British Embassy in Addis Ababa.

"Mr Ambassador," he said, "I believe the two Royal Air Force Hercules that are running a taxi service for food between Addis and Asmara could be used to better effect. It's a boring job for such competent crews, and any charter company could do it. May I suggest that you do something more worthwhile, something that will be more interesting and motivating for your crews? Why don't you try to drop food on the high altitude plateaux where people are dying and are too weak to come down?"

The ambassador said that it was a good idea but that the budget for air transportion provided by the Disaster Unit of the Overseas Development Administration (ODA) was almost exhausted.

Then de Mistura came up with an ingenious proposal. "Look," he said, "the RAF must have an enormous training budget in the UK, some of which is for airdropping. Instead of practising airdrops on golf courses or wherever in England, why don't you do your practising here in Ethiopia? It would be more realistic training, and you'd earn prestige and the gratitude of all."

The ambassador telephoned London and obtained agreement that the Ministry of Defence would share the cost – over $2 million a month – with ODA. Airdropping would begin in a week or so.

De Mistura then visited the German Embassy and began to tell the ambassador that the RAF would be starting airdrops to people beleaguered on the high plateaux the next week. The ambassador was immediately interested and said that the Luftwaffe knew how to do it better than anyone. He requested that Bonn send down a second Transall to join the one already airlifting food in Ethiopia, forty extra people, pallets, and the other equipment required.

The Ethiopian authorities, in the form of the Relief and Rehabilitation Commission, were pleased with the idea but told de Mistura that the Russians would have to be in agreement.

De Mistura thought out his tactics carefully before he went to see the Russian ambassador. When he did, he let him understand that this initiative by the RAF and the Luftwaffe in a country allied to the Soviet Union might look strange unless the Soviet Union were also involved. Specifically, he asked that the Soviets make available two of their flight of 23 Mig 19 helicopters to support the airdrops. They would survey the drop-zones and fly in the ground crews to make the preparations. He told the Russian that he would say publicly that the drops would not have been possible without this support, which was true. The ambassador consulted Moscow, and obtained approval for the use of the two Mig 19s, but on condition that Polish pilots flew them, rather than Russian.

De Mistura had given the name "Operation St. Bernard" to his initiative, in honour of the Swiss dog. The Russians were suspicious, however, thinking that it was in honour of the saint who had founded mountain rescue. Even when they had been assured that it was in honour of the rescue dog rather than the saint, they insisted on a more neutral name. So "Operation Tesfa" was chosen. (Tesfa means "hope" in Amharic.)

There were some amusing moments as "Operation Tesfa" got into its stride. De Mistura remembers that at the first meeting to plan the operations there was a suspicious atmosphere between the Russian general, the German and the Ethiopian colonels, and the British wing-commander. All the conversation passed through de Mistura who sat on a table in the middle of the room. De Mistura had to ask the wing-commander what time he planned to take-off, and then ask the Russian whether they could take off an hour earlier, and then ask the German whether they could follow a few minutes after the RAF, and so on, with no one speaking directly to each other.

In the end, it was the technical aspects of the work that drew them all together. For example, in deciding what radio frequency to use for their communications that day, the Russian general might mention one, and the RAF wing-commander might ask him why that one and not another. The Russian would appear not to want to answer directly, but as the days passed, he was forced to participate as these professionals discussed their work. After only a few weeks, the aircrews were drinking tea together in a tent down at the airfield. It was commonplace for a Russian Mig 19 helicopter to be flown by a Polish pilot, with an RAF co-pilot, and a German navigator, carrying Italian doctors who would examine people in the planned drop zones. And it was Canadian wheat given to WFP that would be dropped. This really was the UN at its best. No other body could have pulled such disparate elements together for the benefit of the poor Ethiopians.

The first step before deciding on an airdrop was for the Polish-piloted helicopters, and a Swiss one that also helped out, to take the Italian doctors into those isolated highlands to check on the levels of malnutrition and decide on the priority areas. They would also reconnoitre potential dropping zones. Once a drop was planned, a helicopter would take in the ground crew who would make all the preparations. The local population had to be organized so that the people were out of the dropping zone, seated, calm, and understanding that they were not to move until authorized to do so. Once this was done, a smoke flare could be lit to help the pilot of the Hercules or Transall as he made his first trial run. Lining up for the drop-zone often called for precision flying of the highest order, hopping over ridges and hauling around hill tops until the aircraft could make its run in. It had to pass over the drop-zone at not more than 25 feet above the ground and at the lowest possible speed.

The food was in double bags on pallets in the hold. The pallets were especially arranged on slides that allowed them to be pushed quickly out of the rear cargo doors by the crew inside, who were clipped to wires to prevent them going with it. The lower and slower the giant aircraft could overfly the drop zone, the less risk there would be of the bags bursting as they hit the ground.

It was a dramatic sight to watch a Hercules as it roared in over the drop zone, flaps extended, and often with its landing gear down too. At a signal from the pilot, the crew in the hold pushed a pallet out. The pallet and its bags would hit the ground travelling at almost the same speed as the aircraft; the bags would bounce and roll in a cloud of dust and wheat from the few bags that had burst.

It was a critical moment for the pilot as the pallet left the rear of the aircraft, for the change in weight distribution would cause the aircraft to pitch suddenly. That was why some of the pilots who were trying to get as close as possible to the ground had their wheels down: were they to touch ground by mistake, they might have the luck to bounce off again. As soon as the pallet had gone and the sudden pitch change been corrected, the pilot would pour on the power, climb away to a safer height and manoeuvre for his next run.

When all the pallets had been discharged, the unbroken bags would be collected by a gang appointed to the task while the rest of the people still sat, expectantly waiting. When all the unbroken bags had been gathered, a signal was given, and the hundreds of spectators were free to come and collect the scattered grain.

They plunged forward and ran with the urgency of life and death, but their emaciated bodies and stick legs gave them little speed. Many were pitiful to watch in their unsteady progress towards where they sank to their knees and gleaned every single grain from among the dust.

There was much rivalry among the aircrews engaged in airdropping. The RAF turned out to be the best at it, showing a degree of precision flying that none could match. But all showed a degree of dedication to the work that was admirable, never wanting to take any time off, including on Christmas day.

The official records at RRC show that a total of 43,380 tons of food were transported by air from November 1984 onwards, but those records do not differentiate between airlifting and airdropping. However, of the total moved by air, the RAF accounted for the most with 11,207 tons, the Soviet Union next with 10,920 tons, then the US with 7,913 tons, and then West Germany with 5,837 tons. The also-rans made up the remainder. Clearly, when the RRC presents the information in this way it throws the best possible light on the fraternal efforts of the Soviet Union. However, it is much easier and faster to airlift food than to airdrop it, and the Soviet Union did none of the latter.

It is estimated that almost a million people were reached with airdrops by the RAF and the Luftwaffe. Their work drew a lot of media attention, but in fact, the amount of food moved by air was paltry compared to that moved overland.

Certainly, there is glamour attached to air operations, and the 70 or so RAF staff who lived in the Hilton Hotel in Addis Ababa – the only Hilton in the world with neon signs on the roof proclaiming international peace and friendship and other Marxist-style messages – were a focus of admiration for their derring-do. In the best tradition of the RAF, they launched at least their fair share of carousing, but it did not seem to affect their professional performance the next day.

This glamour that is attached to aviation arouses a certain amount of ire among the earth- and seabound truckers and shippers who claim, rightly, that the attention claimed by these operations is out of all proportion to the amount of food they move. They also claim, and again rightly, that the cost is enormous, and that while the prestige attached to aviation often guarantees its financing, they are scratching around for small sums of money which, in comparison, would enable them to move far more food.

This would probably be an unfair stance vis-à-vis the airdrops in the Ethiopian highlands, for there was no other way of getting food to those starving people. On the other hand, in 1985 in Mali, almost at the end of the crisis, a donor airlifted food from Bamako to Gao when there was a reasonably good asphalt road covering the 1200 km and allowing the journey to be done easily in two days. (I did it in one day in a Land Cruiser.) That particular airlift aroused a storm of criticism. There is one stretch of the asphalt road that badly needs some resurfacing, and many pointed out that the same sum of money spent on that could have been of more lasting benefit.

★   ★   ★

Airlifting has been a feature of the relief operations for South Sudan. The civil war in the Sudan, with the Sudan People's Liberation Army (SPLA) fighting the Khartoum government has created havoc. In addition, the situation is complicated by tribal tensions, and everyone seems to be armed. Occasionally news leaks out that there have been massacres of and between tribal groups, presumably to level old scores.

It has been impossible to know exactly what is happening in South Sudan with regard to food requirements, though it was estimated that for the first half of 1987, 71,000 tons of relief food would be required. This estimate was largely guesswork because the security problem is such that it is difficult to move around and see what the agricultural production patterns are, let alone to carry out nutritional surveys. Some private relief agencies such as Oxfam are doing sterling work, and they are the main sources of information.

What is certain, however, is that in towns such as Juba, and Wau, there are recurrent and sometimes severe shortages of food and other essentials. As we saw in the chapter concerned with trucking, food comes in from Kenya via Uganda, but with great difficulty at the best of times. At the worst of times, the borders are closed and no traffic at all can enter the Sudan from the south. This happened in September 1986 as the result of increased security problems in Uganda.

A natural response would have been to organize an airlift to Juba and Wau, but all the airports in the south were closed after the shooting down of an aircraft on 16 August near Malakal. The aircraft was a Sudan Airways internal flight with 60 people aboard. It had just taken off from Malakal to head north when it was downed, with the loss of all lives. The SPLA boasted about the feat and made it clear that they had deliberately and knowingly shot down a civil flight.

With all the airports closed in the south, and with the Uganda route blocked too, there was almost no way of moving food into Juba and other towns in the area. By this time Staffan de Mistura was working for WFP in the Sudan, and with his aggressive attitude in favour of the hungry, he did not want people to be actually starving before making a move. Prevention was the key, rather than waiting for the BBC to announce a tragedy, as he said.

De Mistura called a meeting of representatives of the major donor countries' embassies in Khartoum and proposed the pooling of resources to mount an international airlift. There was the usual concern about donor visibility and credit, so de Mistura suggested calling the initiative "Operation Rainbow". Thus, every participant's colours would be included in the special identity of an international consortium which, while not belonging to any one donor, would belong to all. From that point on, the donors were enthusiastic and the idea began to snowball.

However, from the government and the SPLA's viewpoint, there were many difficulties to be resolved. Both sides seemed to agree in principle, but each wanted flights to different places. In point of fact, the SPLA were less interested than the government because the most serious food shortages were developing in towns which were government controlled garrisons. The less food these towns had, the better for the SPLA. Therefore, as the publicity for Operation Rainbow began to mount, the SPLA announced no less than eight times in one day that they intended to shoot down the aircraft.

In the meantime, WFP was hunting for a Hercules to charter but was finding it difficult when there was such a potentially dangerous mission in view. Ultimately, the Indonesian government offered one and it flew to Khartoum. Once there, it was painted with rainbow stripes to help identify it, and government and private donors began to pull together to prepare the operation.

In view of the repeated threats by the SPLA to shoot down the flight, contact had to be made with them. Winston Prattley, the New Zealander who had been appointed by the Secretary General of the UN as his special representative to run the relief operations in the Sudan, authorized de Mistura to go to Addis Ababa for this purpose, for Addis is the international base for the SPLA leadership.

A meeting was arranged in the gardens of the Hilton Hotel. De Mistura had no trouble recognizing the three SPLA representatives since they were very tall Dinkas. They wanted to know why he had come to see them, and he explained that he wanted them to know that the Rainbow flight would be leaving in three days time, as already reported by the BBC. He had come to see them to avoid any possible misunderstanding regarding the flight, its date and time of departure, its destination, and its humanitarian purpose. If anything happened to it, the SPLA could not claim that they had assumed it to be a hostile mission.

The SPLA representatives responded to the effect that the flight was only a test by the government of their resolve and their capabilities. They would shoot down the aircraft to show that they meant business and to prevent food reaching the government-held towns.

De Mistura remonstrated with them about the implications of their plans to shoot down an international relief aircraft carrying food; food that would be distributed under careful control to children and others in dire need, to the people whose rights the SPLA claimed to be fighting for; food that had been given by countries that one day might help South Sudan.

The SPLA people were unimpressed and repeated that they would shoot down the flight. De Mistura replied that in that case he was sorry that their pleasant intercourse would never be repeated because he intended to be on the Hercules. They laughed and accused him of wanting to end up like Dag Hammerskjold.

On this unpromising note the meeting ended. A few hours later, however, they called de Mistura to say that they had thought about it: if the flight landed first at Yirol, a town under SPLA control, and offloaded some food, it could then continue to a town under government control. De Mistura replied that if there were people in Yirol who were really in need, he would have no objection, for the flight had been planned in the humanitarian spirit of bringing relief food to anyone in need, regardless of their faction. However, he would have to talk to the government in Khartoum about the proposal.

At this point, the SPLA committed a breach of faith: they told the BBC of the conditions they were imposing for the flight before de Mistura had a chance to return to Khartoum and discuss the proposal, evidencing at the same time their will that the Operation Rainbow should not take place. The SPLA request might discreetly have been catered for, but once it had become known world-wide, there was no possibility that the government could lose face by acceding to it. Indeed, de Mistura was told by the government that the flight could only go into secure areas in its control.

The publicity which Operation Rainbow was generating, and the risks involved in flying into the south under threat of being shot down, caused the insurers of the Indonesian Hercules to ask for an extra premium of $2 million to cover the aircraft, clearly a request that could not be met.

By now a game of poker was enjoined. The Hercules was loaded and readied for take-off while WFP in Rome hurriedly looked for a second aircraft. They found a French charter company called SF Air which had a DC8 that had total insurance cover, even for war zones. It arrived in Khartoum with its ex-French Air Force crew. This crew was briefed in respect of evasion tactics such as coming out of the sun, changing arrival and departure routes for every flight, making steep, spiralling departures and arrivals overhead the airfield, and so on.

On 11 October, amid much fanfare, the Hercules took off from Khartoum fully laden. It headed south, but it did not go to Juba: it went to Isiro in Zaire. From there, trucks moved the food it had been carrying into South Sudan over the following days.

Immediately after the Hercules had rumbled into the sky, the SF Air DC8, also painted with Rainbow stripes, followed. Ostensibly, it was en route for Entebbe in Uganda, but instead it spiralled out of the sky and landed unharmed in Juba. Over the next 5 days, it made nine successful flights into Juba, delivering about 250 tons of food.

SF Air had a prior commitment for the DC8 immediately after those first nine flights and therefore had to withdraw it for a few days. It resumed flights to Juba on October 23rd and made two more trips. However, at that point, Winston Prattley, who had gone to New York, instructed his deputy to tell de Mistura to stop the operation.

Operation Rainbow was surrounded by much controversy. It is a matter of record that Winston Prattley was declared *persona non grata* by the Sudanese government shortly after the events described above, and possibly in connection with them. Today, talking to UN people in Khartoum and elsewhere leads to the impression that there are many who consider Operation Rainbow as a debacle, and as an embarrassing skeleton in the cupboard. Perhaps they are being oversensitive. It is true that relations between the government and some UN agencies operating in the Sudan have since been strained; but at least it showed that the UN can take the initiative in responding to a disaster in the making and not end up being criticized for arriving on the scene too late, as it often is.

Operation Rainbow, though curtailed, also had an important after-effect. It had proven that airlifting food into the south was a feasible proposition, even with the SPLA making threatening noises. In the early part of 1987, WFP signed a contract with a Sudanese charter company called

Nile Safaris to fly 3,OOO tons of EEC and WFP cereals into
Juba in 58 days of operations. The cereals are locally grown
and are being purchased in Gedaref from where they are
being trucked to Khartoum airport. Two Nile Safaris
Boeing 7O7s have been shuttling to and fro between
Khartoum and Juba, but at the time of writing, the SPLA
have again threatened hostile action.

The record of the SPLA in respect of shooting down
aircraft leaves serious doubts regarding their moral values.
More recently, they downed a Cessna 4O4 belonging to a
Sudanese charter company called SASCO. The pilot was a
49-year-old Dutchman called Ed Folman, and his co-pilot
was 32-year-old Theo Coelen, also Dutch. Folman was the
only charter pilot operating into and all over the south, and
he was much in demand by relief agencies. He was courageous to a fault, always the first pilot into a dangerous place,
and the last out, and always joking.

There is some mystery surrounding the crash of the
SASCO Cessna 4O4, in which Folman, Coelen and their
passengers died. The SPLA claimed to have shot it down
near Malakal. Only a week before, Marius Fortman of the
WFP office in Khartoum had carried out a series of flights in
the south with Folman. He remembers that between Aweil
and Wau, in the heart of SPLA territory, Folman cruised
along confidently at about a thousand feet. When Fortman
asked him why he was flying so low, he replied that there was
no problem because the SPLA would not shoot at him. Then
he buzzed around Wau at a hundred feet to announce his
arrival. Again Fortman asked him what he was doing that
low, and again Folman made it quite clear that the SPLA
would not shoot. Nor, it seems, did he ever bother with the
standard safety measure of climbing, or letting down, in
tight circles over the airfield to avoid low flying over terrain
that might hold hostile and missile-toting elements. And he
never was shot at by the SPLA, unless it was on that last flight
to Malakal. On the other hand, the Sudanese government
troops shot at him several times in cases of mistaken
identity!

Fortman feels that Folman had an understanding with the SPLA, or he would not have taken what appeared to be wild risks, and that in fact he may not have been shot down at Malakel. The army unit that claimed that they went to the wreckage reported that all the bodies were burned beyond recognition and that they had buried them. They brought back no detailed evidence or personal items such as rings. Only a week before, Folman had been having problems with an engine. Since he quite often flew overloaded, perhaps this and an engine failure confirmed the aviation adage that, although there are old pilots, and although there are bold pilots, there are few old bold ones.

Whether the SPLA shot the SASCO Cessna down or not, the fact that they *claimed* to have done so when the aircraft was engaged solely in humanitarian missions proves their ruthless and uncaring attitude. With this in mind, there can be little doubt that airlifting of food would have to stop if the SPLA could hold positions close enough to airfields to hit aircraft with normal weapons, or if they were ever equipped with modern ground-to-air missiles.

With such risks, airlifting food into South Sudan is bound to be expensive. The first Rainbow contract for the Indonesian Hercules worked out at the astronomic price of US$12 per kilogram transported. The SF Air price was much lower, and the average for Operation Rainbow was about $5 a kilogram. The Nile Safaris contract was negotiated hard and is only costing 37.5 US cents a kilogram, a very good price considering the circumstances, but still expensive compared to what it would cost by truck, were trucks able to get through.

Airlifting and airdropping creates welcome publicity for relief operations. There are circumstances when they are indispensable and play a crucial role, as they did in Ethiopia. However, we should not be hoodwinked by media coverage into thinking that the "daring young men" of the air forces are doing the lion's share of the work. Almost all of that is done by the unsung heroes manning the trucks that slog through mud or sand, or grind along the appalling African roads.

10
FOOD FOR "GREENING"

Much of the first part of this book has been devoted to describing the situation in sub-Saharan Africa, and we have seen what happens there when the delicate balance is tipped towards disaster and food has to be brought in and distributed for famine relief. But what about those basic problems that make Africa so vulnerable? What about the environmental degradation and the failure of food production to keep pace with population growth? Until such time as these underlying problems can be eradicated, the future for Africa will remain bleak.

In 1985, under the aegis of the Organization of African Unity, heads of African states adopted *Africa's Priority Programme for Economic Recovery – 1986-1990*. If it is followed through energetically, and with sufficient help from outside the continent, much could be achieved. The Programme puts appropriate emphasis on agricultural and rural development and on fighting drought and desertification.

The Programme foresees activities with high labour requirements. For example, for the building of small bridges, access and service roads, small dams and other irrigation structures, fish ponds, food stores, etc., and also for such works as protection of the vegetative cover, reforestation, sand-dune fixation, and soil conservation.

Plate 11   Mao, Western Chad – preparing young trees for use in sand dune stabilization and reforestation work.   (Colin Fraser)

And there are more general activities foreseen such as improving the amenities in rural areas to avoid the exodus of skilled manpower and young people. These will involve, for example, the building of health and community centres, creating rural water supplies, and so on. All of these activities, and many others too, lend themselves to food-for-work programmes.

The concept of food-for-work is an outgrowth from ideas that were originally embodied in the Indian Famine Code. This Code was drawn up by the British administration in India in 1892, and subsequently modified in 1913. It was designed to pre-empt and counter famines by delegating authority, and funds, to local colonial officers to launch public works in areas affected by scarcity; these works would provide employment, and thus income to buy food. A provision of the Famine Code were so-called Test Relief Works. In order to find out what degree of scarcity and hardship really existed in a given area, the District Officer would offer *half* of the normal daily rate for casual labour to the population to come and work on some public project or maintenance activity. The number of people who turned up for only half of the normal salary would be a good indication of the degree of hardship they were suffering or were anticipating.

The Famine Code was applied rather successfully over the whole of the Indian sub-continent, and it was in that same region that the world's largest food-for-work programme was later launched. This happened in the mid-197Os in Bangladesh after disastrous floods followed by severe famine left the country destitute and with an enormous rehabilitation and development job to be done. There was no cash to pay the million or more people who were to become involved in the works, but food aid was made available from world surpluses to pay people in the form of rations.

Just as in the case of Bangladesh, most African countries are suffering such hardship that it is quite impossible for them to finance public works and the building of infrastructures in rural areas on the scale required to reverse the African decline of recent years. The opponents of food aid often say that people should be mobilized to carry out self-help programmes without the inducement of food rations. This is fine in theory, but among the really poor and emarginated, and these make up most of Africa's rural population today, this may be a utopistic viewpoint.

I was personally involved in evaluating a project in the Sudan which provides an interesting example of the practical difficulties that may be encountered in self-help programmes. The project was financed by Sweden through the UN Sudano-Sahelian Organization (UNSO). UNSO is primarily concerned with projects for environmental protection and rehabilitation, and this particular project was in a seriously degraded area around the small town of El Odaya in Kordofan. The project was implemented by FAO.

El Odaya has good sources of water the year round with the result that, as the dry season progresses, all the resident livestock within a radius of about 30 kms depend increasingly on El Odaya. People bring their cattle in from the surrounding villages at least every other day to water them. In addition, towards the end of the dry season, nomads move also towards El Odaya. The result in recent years has been the degradation of the rangeland around El Odaya and a tendency towards desertification that is so severe that it is evident in satellite photographs.

In the main, the UNSO project set out to mobilize the local population to fence off large enclosures near El Odaya so that the rangeland could recuperate, and later, be grazed under properly controlled conditions as pasture got scarcer before the rains. The project also aimed at encouraging people in surrounding villages to dig wells and *hafirs* by hand so that, once villages had their own water supplies, the pressure on El Odaya would be reduced. The project was to provide the fencing materials, as well as building materials for lining the wells and *hafirs*.

All the labour was to be voluntary. This meant that people would have to be mobilized through information and education to understand the problems of the degradation around El Odaya, and the practical solutions to those problems, so that they would volunteer their labour.

There were numerous hitches and delays with the supply of the materials required, but they do not need to concern us here. What is of interest is that the people were indeed motivated to do the work. Village leaders were taken to an area not far to the north where a whole community was being engulfed by sand. Seeing this with their own eyes, and hearing from the project staff about the causes of the degradation in their own area and what they could do to rehabilitate it, had a marked impact.

So people began to lend their labour, but progress was slow. Especially during the dry season, when it could have been expected that labour would be more freely available because there were no crops to tend, there was a shortage of able-bodied men. It transpired that many of the men routinely left the area during the dry season to seek work in irrigated areas near the Nile. There was not enough for them and their families to eat and they had to earn money to be able to buy food. They simply could not afford to stay at home and carry out voluntary self-help work.

The original project had not included any food-for-work, but WFP was able to make a small allocation of 40 tons. This was instrumental in changing the situation for the following dry season, for with food for themselves and their families assured, the men were able to stay at home and provide their labour for the fencing and for the well-digging. During the general evaluation of the project, it emerged clearly that the food aid element had been a crucial input, and it should have been included in the original project design.

The problems of desertification and degradation are now so enormous in many parts of Africa that they have gone far beyond the capability of governments and aid agencies alone to handle them: they require enormous inputs of effort from local populations who, in effect, must be mobilized to shoulder the responsibility and carry out the required works, but of course with technical support from government staff. And since so many of the people living in these fast-degrading and food-deficit areas are on the razor's edge of survival, food-for-work becomes a logical and highly useful input. It allows people to stand and fight the desert where they are, rather than retreating before it, continually falling back on better grazing and cropping lands because they need food to survive, and allowing the desert to follow them. This has been the pattern of the past, and it must be stopped. Food aid can be a major factor in doing so, through food-for-work programmes.

In most of the semi-arid areas, it has finally been recognized by the local people that reforestation to create barriers against the desert are necessary. In addition, the ever-increasing distances that people have to go for fire-wood, and the degradation they are causing by cutting trees, has also aroused interest in the idea of planting village wood-lots of fast-growing species.

Around Gao in eastern Mali a programme of reforesta-tion and conservation has been under way since late 1982. The programme is supported by UNSO and WFP. The basic aim is to create a green belt of over 200 ha outside of the town to stop the further encroachment of sand, to create industrial plantations in critical areas where there are moving sand-dunes which threaten cultivated areas, to create village plantations for fuel wood, and to close off the few existing areas of sparse woodland in order to let it recuperate.

A first step in any such programme is the creation of tree nurseries of suitable species. This has been successfully done and the output is now reaching its planned total of 85,000 seedlings a year.

There are hopeful signs of some impact being made by the reforestation, even if, by 1987, only 20 ha of the planned 200 ha of shelter belt outside Gao had been planted. The saplings are mainly eucalyptus on the outside of the shelter belt and native species in the centre. This is because the eucalyptus grow faster and therefore create an effect more quickly, at the same time protecting the native species as they establish themselves.

None of these trees was very impressive in 1987, for they were still small and spindly, but the effect even their undistinguished presence was having on the ground was clear to see: inside the fenced area and between the trees where the wind-flow was disturbed, the ground surface was firm, while outside, the sand was still ankle deep.

Near the village of Batadio, a dune that was moving and menacing an area of irrigated rice has been fixed and successfully planted with about 17 ha of trees. The experience with village woodlots, however, has been mixed. Three of the six villages included in the original programme have done a good job, but the others have been less successful. The conditions are far from favourable for young seedlings to establish, and even if they are well planted, they require regular attention for the first years of their life. In exposed places, they need protection from the searing *harmattan*, and this is usually provided by sticks driven into the ground with some old sacking tied to them. But above all they need water, about 10 litres per plant every week during the dry season and until such time as their roots have penetrated the ground deeply enough to be able to tap the moisture there. This may require three years or more.

In the main reforestation areas close to Gao, watering is done with a tractor and tanker trailer, and a gang of men with buckets. The tractor and tanker drive very slowly between the rows of saplings and the men walk to and fro, filling their 10-litre buckets and pouring the water into the depression dug around each tree. In the village reforestation schemes, it is not always so easy to organize the watering effectively, and this is one reason why they may have less success in establishing the trees. As a matter of fact, when you walk among the planted areas at the height of the dry season, you are forced to wonder how the trees manage at all in those harsh conditions, but manage they do if they are helped to a good start.

More impressive, at least to look at, are the areas of doum palms that have been closed off to allow them to regenerate. As mentioned earlier, the doum palm is a very valuable local tree species that provides good timber and also nuts. It had almost been wiped out until fences were put up to protect it from animals and signs were erected to remind people that "forest is a source of life and it must be saved". Now, the open wastes between the few remaining doum palms are spiky with thousands upon thousands of green fronds forcing their way through the sand, tomorrow's forest in the making.

All over the Sudano-Sahelian belt, reforestation and environmental improvement projects are getting under way. Most of them are helped along by food-for-work programmes.

A major project is one centred at El Obeid in the Sudan, about 350 kms south-west of Khartoum. El Obeid has been called "the gum arabic capital of the world". Gum arabic is the sap exuded by certain types of acacia tree, in particular *Acacia senegal*. When the trunk and branches are deliberately gashed with a sharp tool, the sap oozes out, hardens in the air, and can then be scraped off and collected as a crystalline-looking, yellowish substance. This water-soluble gum is a valuable product that is used in the pharmaceutical, confectionary, and other industries.

The gum-arabic acacias in the area of El Obeid have been degrading and becoming fewer in recent decades. The so-called Gum-Belt Project, with finance provided by the Netherlands through UNSO, and with WFP food-for-work, is rehabilitating and expanding the area of gum-bearing acacias, both as a means of environmental protection and as a source of income for rural people.

However, despite these hopeful signs that can be seen near Gao and El Obeid and in many other places in the Sudano-Sahelian zone, so far they only appear as a puny stance against the desolation, diffident dapplings of green that hardly seem to break the vastness and harshness of the sandy wastelands. A small step in the right direction has certainly been taken, but the work will need to stride out boldly in the coming years if it is going to reverse the degradation in those areas.

★   ★   ★

Reverting to Mali, some progress is also being made in food production near Gao and in other sites along the River Niger. Small irrigated areas, of about 20 ha each, have been created for rice production. Water for each area is lifted from the nearby river by a diesel-powered pump parked on the bank. The growing of vegetables under irrigation is also being promoted with some success.

During a meeting with the Governor of Gao, Lieutenant Colonel Koureissy Aguibou Tall, he said:

> We are trying to rebuild the economy of the area after the drought. Everyone is so poor, so lacking in purchasing power, that the food-for-work programmes play a very important role. We are receiving support from World Vision and from WFP for these programmes.
>
> All the people engaged in reforestation, soil conservation, and creating new irrigated areas receive rations of food in return for their labour. And the farmers who start cultivating in the irrigation areas get rations until they can harvest their first crops. Without this food aid, people would have to go elsewhere for work and we would have no chance of developing the region.

The governor touched on an important issue when he mentioned the lack of purchasing power in the Gao area. The pastoralists used to be wealthy, relatively speaking, but they have lost everything as a result of drought, and now there are few people who can afford to buy the produce from the irrigated areas. Rice is the most important commodity to be affected by this market situation. Yields are still rather low, and this contributes to high production costs. In fact, rice produced anywhere in Mali faces cost problems. It was estimated in 1987, that to grow a kilogram of rice cost about 50 CFA Francs per kilo, *excluding* any cost for the farmer's labour. At the same time, Thai rice could be brought into Bamako and sold for 88 CFA Francs per kilo. As a basis for comparison, traditional cereals such as millet were selling for about 22 CFA Francs per kilo in the same period.

However, in the Gao area, it is not competition from Thai rice that makes things difficult; it is simply the fact that if people are unable to afford to buy it, there is nowhere else it can be sent, for Gao is so isolated that the cost of transport to other markets would be prohibitive.

These facts are mentioned only to illustrate the practical obstacles to increasing food production in such disadvantaged areas. It was hardly surprising that the farmers we spoke to, as they weeded in their paddy fields under a broiling sun, were depressed about the prospects of being able to sell the fruit of so much labour at a price that would only cover their cash costs.

The largest food-for-work project in Africa is in Ethiopia. The erosion problems in the highlands of that country were described in Chapter 4. Suffice it to repeat here that the deforestation and the annual loss of soil are so great that the future ability of large areas to go on growing crops is in doubt. At the same time, about 38 million of Ethiopia's 42 million people live in those highlands, already impoverished almost beyond imagination. It is not rare to see a farmer cultivating a patch of land so steep that he must cling to a rope to avoid falling, so desperate is the search for cropland. Overgrazing is also a serious factor. It is estimated that Ethiopia has about 76 million head of livestock, almost twice the human population.

Charles Stewart, a British film-maker, went to live in rural Ethiopia in 1983 to make a film about soil conservation. He was caught up in the intensified drought of 1984 and 1985 and made the well-known TV film "Seeds of Despair". Stewart, who knows Ethiopia very well, reported that many of his highland farmer friends were only growing enough food each year to last them and their families 6–7 months, and that was in the years before the great and recent drought.

Given these circumstances, and whatever westerners like to say about the Marxist government of the country, it deserves credit for having decided to *do* something about erosion, water conservation, and reforestation. In fact, its development plan for the ten years ending 1993–94 hinges on the rehabilitation and conservation of resources. One practical step has been to decree that all rural people will donate a day each week to conservation work; hardly democratic some might say, but nor was China when it mobilized its millions to carry out the building of infrastructures which today provide the basic needs of all its people.

A large conservation programme with external assistance is in progress in 44 catchment areas with a total area of about 2 million ha. This programme, which grew out of some pilot work done after the 1974 drought, primarily in Eritrea and Tigray, got fully under way in 1980. The food-for-work component is supported by WFP with 80,000 tons a year, the EEC with 30,000 tons a year, and Australia with 10,000 tons a year, making a total of 120,000 tons. All the catchment areas in which conservation work is supported by food-for-work programmes are areas that have had food deficits for years.

The first phase of the project beginning in 1980 foresaw 23.3 million person/days of work per year. The second phase which began in 1987 has increased this to 26.7 million person/days per year. The total cost of the food-for-work component for the three years of the present phase comes to about $105 million, of which just over $22 million are going to subsidize half of the cost of the internal transport.

The standard food ration being provided is based on the assumption of a total of six family members requiring 500 grams of cereals per day each and 20 grams of edible oil each. Thus the total ration for a day's work consists of 3 kgs of cereals and 120 grams of edible oil.

However, there are many inputs other than food aid to this conservation project. For example, West Germany is providing expertise, training, equipment and vehicles worth about $1 million a year; Sweden is providing a total of $2.75 million for tools and equipment, silviculture research, seedling production and training; the UN University in Tokyo and the University of Berne in Switzerland are carrying out research into soil erosion and conservation under Ethiopian conditions; UNDP and FAO have a project assisting soil and water conservation; and Oxfam is providing construction inputs for small-scale irrigation through such measures as stream-diversion canals.

As you drive along the main road that leads north from Addis Ababa, you see hillside after hillside that have been traced with terraces and bunds along the contours. In fact, it is estimated that since 1979, 836,OOO kilometres of bunds and terraces and over 3OO,OOO kilometres of farm access roads have been built, and 5OO million trees planted. It is an impressive sight: whole landscapes where millions and millions of days of human toil have left their mark, where erosion is being checked and where, in many areas, trees are growing again.

Near Kombolcha, in Wollo, there is a mountain called Mount Yogoff which rises steeply to a summit that is at 3,OO2 metres elevation. The people in the area are particularly proud of it, and use it as a showcase, because its 3,OOO ha of flanks are now covered by fine stands of cypresses, eucalyptus, and other trees, all of which have been planted, or which have regenerated in the last few years as a result of closing the area to grazing and cutting. A track that can be negotiated by four-wheel-drive vehicles and leads to the summit has been excavated by hand in the steep slopes. It rises in a series of dizzy meanderings and hairpins.

Mount Yogoff is indeed an impressive sight, for every other mountain in the area has been denuded of its tree cover, apart from one or two large trees left on the summit ridge of each. No one seems to know why the local people have this habit of leaving one or two trees uncut near the summit: perhaps it is a sign of respect or of nostalgia, or it might have a religious origin. The only other place where large trees are left uncut is around the unique octagonal churches. (Those trees near the churches are a valuable source of seeds for the tree nurseries of which there are now over a hundred in Ethiopia producing about 13O million seedlings a year.) Whatever the origin of the habit, it gives an idea of what the hillsides must have been like not so long ago when they were all covered by such fine specimens.

Also near Kobolcha is an example of the water conservation work being undertaken. The Ambo dam is a small earth structure that was built in 1985–86. It traps the run-off from a catchment area of 3OO ha and creates a lake covering 3O ha. It is estimated that it will provide irrigation for about 4O–5O ha. It is interesting, in this connection, that the dam was planned on the basis of aerial photographs taken during the 195Os, and it had been estimated that much more than 5O ha would be irrigable. However, in the intervening years, so much land has been eroded away that the irrigable area has been significantly reduced. In 1987, work was still going on to level the land and build the irrigation canals. Farm access roads were also being built.

The dam itself took 17,659 days of work by men and women to complete which, using the standard food-for-work rations, meant an input of 53 tons of cereals and just over 2 tons of vegetable oil. There were also about $1,OOO-worth of non-food items, in particular the pipes and gate-valves which were donated by the Red Cross.

The households that will ultimately benefit from the scheme are 1,114 in number, amounting to over 6,3OO people. A small part of the area is already under irrigation and three crops a year of cabbages, tomatoes and peppers are being grown and sold, mainly in Assab.

On the day of our visit, there were about a hundred people working on an access road across a hillside. Its length was to be 56O metres and they were expecting to finish it in a total of 32 days of work, for which the input would be 9.6 tons of cereals and 384 kgs of oil. The people were very happy with the dam and were anxious to bring more land under irrigation as soon as possible

There are considerable achievements in the area of soil and water conservation and reforestation in Ethiopia. In addition, the point should be made that much conservation work is also in progress in other areas of the highlands *without* any support from foreign donors.

★　　　★　　　★

Despite these notable achievements, there are many problems associated with the Ethiopian conservation programme – and a few polemics surround it too. But first, let us look at some of the problems.

The soil conservation works began before there was a programme of research into erosion and soil conservation in Ethiopia. As Kabede Tatu, the impressive man in charge of the Community Forestry and Soil Conservation Development Department of the Ministry of Agriculture said to me:

Because of the urgency, we began the work without any prior research, and so research has been trying to catch up, and has been trying to improve on what we are already doing. A lot of research data has been collected and we now have to analyze it. Frankly, I am worried because we don't have enough trained manpower in research.

This lack of research shows up in the field and in the discussions that go on about the work. For example, it is argued that much of the terracing that is going on high on the hillsides, in areas that are to be planted with trees, is unnecessary and that merely closing off the area and planting trees, or even just letting the vegetation regenerate, might achieve the same results. It is an important issue, for if the work being done is using more labour than necessary, the same number of person/days could cover more area.

It is also said by some that disturbing the slopes by digging terraces or bunds in the areas to be reforested may add to erosion in the first year or so. There are discussions too about the tree species being used. In the main they are eucalyptus, which certainly do well in Ethiopia, but there is little data on other fast-growing species that might complement them. And it also has to be remembered that there are different ecological zones within the highlands, and what works well in one may not in another. Research in the different zones has not been systematically undertaken as yet.

Farmers are initially reluctant to undertake terracing work because it reduces the area available to cultivation by about 1O–12%. However, in areas where terraces have been built and the benefits in terms of crop yields are becoming evident, this resistance is disappearing. Many farmers told us that they had noticed that their crops were better on the terraces.

The resistance to terracing and bunding because of the loss of 1O–12% of the land surface would have been reduced had the technicians been able to propose suitable fodder grasses or legumes for planting on the scarp of the terraces or on the bunds to make use of that "lost" area. In addition, proper vegetative cover for the bunds and scarps would stabilize them and prevent them from breaching, as they often do now. Kabede Tatu was very open in talking about the matter.

We are late, very late, in this question of planting vegetation on the bunds, You see, we didn't have the know-how. It's an agronomic matter and in this Department we are engineers rather than agronomists. But we think we now have some solutions and we intend to carry out a very aggressive policy of seeding on the bunds.

It ties into the maintenance problem too. It is our policy not to provide any food-for-work for maintenance of the bunds and terraces. If farmers appreciate having terraces, they will maintain them. If they don't, then there is something wrong. But the need for maintenance is reduced if the bunds are planted rather than being left bare.

The quality of the work being done is is also called into question. The quality mainly depends on the supervision of the work by technicians, and the Ethiopians freely admit that there is a shortage of qualified field staff to provide the degree of supervision required. So the quality is patchy, but even the best-built terraces will breach and crumble without maintenance. On the other hand, even terraces and bunds that have not been well built will resist through time if they are reinforced and protected by vegetation planted on them.

The issue of closing off areas of hillside to protect new plantations or to allow vegetation to regenerate is a vexed one. For cropland and pasture are so much in demand that taking any land out of use creates local problems, and sometimes resistance too. The authorities tend to be autocratic and probably do not have the staff to carry out the intensive contacts required to persuade and convince the rural people of the value of conservation work, and to seek local solutions to local problems in its execution.

Despite the impressive conservation works that you see as you travel north from Addis Ababa, in fact only about 3% of the total area of the highlands that needs such works has actually been treated so far. There is a sort of ribbon-development along that main road, whereas in the interior far less has been done. An enormous scaling up of the operation is required and is in fact planned.

With regard to polemics about the activities, the question that attracts the most argument concerns the beneficiaries of the work. Before the revolution of 1974, a mere 2% of the Ethiopian population owned 90% of the land. After the Marxist government came to power, it simply nationalized all land and allocated its usufruct to newly-created Peasant Associations. When reforestation is taking place on this land, even though technically it does not belong to the people engaged in the work, they are clearly the most likely beneficiaries. A complication, however, arises with the reforestation that is taking place high in watersheds and on land which has *not* been allocated to Peasant Associations. These areas figure as state forest land, which has connotations of state forests for commercial exploitation, even if in fact they are "conservation" forests which form a vital part of the whole conservation system of the watersheds and will never be exploited commercially.

The overriding complication, however, is that at the time of writing, the government had not introduced legislation to determine the rights of rural people to use the forest resources they are creating once the trees have reached the stage of growth when some harvesting can begin.

Quite apart from affecting the enthusiasm with which rural people go about reforestation, these matters also pose some legislative problems in connection with food-for-work. The ILO regulations covering food-for-work stipulate that only when the people engaged in it are also the beneficiaries can they be paid in food alone. For public works, at least half of the daily pay must be in cash.

Opponents of the Marxist regime in Ethiopia are quick to take advantage of this situation. The US has even tried to scuttle the WFP food aid project to support soil conservation and reforestation works. This attempt took place in May 1986 when the current WFP project was on the list for approval by the Committee on Food Aid Policies and Programmes, known as the CFA. The CFA meets twice a year in Rome and must approve WFP projects before they can go into effect.

The US delegation lobbied to have the Ethiopian project dropped from the list before it came up for discussion. When it was not withdrawn, the head of the US delegation, Millicent Fenwick, an elderly and strong-willed, pipe-smoking Reagan appointee, asked publicly for the project to be withdrawn, saying that she had the support of the anti-slavery league in London. She found little support in the CFA, however.

In May 1987, I questioned Kabede Tatu about the legislation concerning who would be able to benefit from the newly-created forest resources being planted with food-for-work support. He had this to say:

There is a practical issue we have to look at before we talk about legislation. So far, we have not had the capacity to develop a plan to use those resources properly, and we cannot continue to use the forest as we have in the past. We have to use it rationally, and we must learn to use it according to a plan. From a technical point of view, we should be able to develop a planning procedure at the lowest level in the field to deal with, say, a woodlot on the land assigned to a Peasant Association. We are working on that now.

From the legislation point of view, I agree that the existing legislation does not clearly identify the responsibilities of the community and the benefits for it. But in the new legislation which has been drawn up and which is now before the Council of Ministers, these have been clearly defined. This new legislation is complex because it also covers a lot of other aspects, including the new structure of the Ministry of Agriculture which up to now has not had full authority to deal with forestry matters, which were the responsibility of a different unit dealing with forestry and wildlife. We are pressuring the government to finalize the new legislation that will bring it into line with the ten-year programme we have for conservation, and which depends entirely on community involvement and the rights of communities over the new resources being created. For sure, these rights will be formalized.

It is a pity that what goes on in Ethiopia cannot be looked upon without political colouring. Two other programmes of the government come in for even more heated criticism. One is the resettlement initiative under which the authorities are reducing the pressure on the highlands by moving people to more fertile and emptier areas in the lowlands to the south and west. From a purely common-sense point of view, this must be a correct policy. The government has been accused, probably rightly, of carrying out this programme with total disregard for people's wishes, loading them into Russian and East German cargo aircraft, flying them away without even ensuring that families stay united, and causing deaths by packing them into the unpressurized holds when the aircraft will be forced to fly at high altitudes and low temperatures.

The other programme that is much criticized is that of "villagization" under which people are being moved from their scattered hilltop dwellings and made to rebuild their houses in villages for which the layout has been established by the authorities. Such villages are immediately recognizable by the straight lines along which the round, thatched huts, *tokuls*, are built. It is said that "villagization" is merely a way to facilitate political indoctrination and control, and that it moves people away from the land they are cultivating, with the result that they have to lose time walking many kilometres to and from it each day.

All these criticisms may be valid, but those who make them may be losing sight of the fact that it is difficult to provide services such as health, education, agricultural extension, credit, farm inputs, and so on, when people are scattered in tiny groups of dwellings, over vast landscapes, often several days walk from the nearest road. Therefore, "villagization" may make sense. However, the authorities would do well to remember that it has hardly been a roaring success even in countries under more tolerant regimes, such as Tanzania.

If only the Ethiopian government could be less doctrinaire and could try these programmes with more sensitivity, in a less authoritarian way; and if only it had the resources to provide basic services in the new villages and settlements! In that case, perhaps the government would not lay itself open to such virulent criticism. It might even get the external support it so desperately needs. As Tom Grennell, an ex-Roman Catholic priest who looks after the WFP food-for-work project, as caring a person as one could ever hope to meet, said, "Drastic problems require drastic solutions." As things are, however, it is all too easy for opponents of the regime to promote the notion that the worst features of Stalinism are reborn in Ethiopia.

All over Africa there are multi-purpose WFP food-for-work projects aimed at supporting rural development. Under these projects, food can be provided to encourage rural people to engage in almost any type of activity that will benefit the rural economy and improve standards of living.

Of course, food-for-work must be provided in the context of well-planned development activities if it is to be useful, and unfortunately this is not always the case. For example, after a serious drought in Turkana, in northern Kenya, in 1979–8O, a large Turkana Rehabilitation Project was launched with support from the Netherlands and the EEC and with food aid from WFP. The people in the area are almost entirely pastoralist, but any attempt to help them resume an improved pastoralist life went by the board in favour of turning them into sedentary farmers in irrigated areas which they were creating through food-for-work programmes. The project has been less than successful and has been severely criticized, and food aid with it, though it was the development approach that was flawed rather than the food aid.

On the other hand, there is a project in Niger, near Keita, where a broad-based rural development initiative shows all the signs of becoming very successful. It is financed by the Italian government and FAO is implementing it. The Keita area is seriously degraded and the project is carrying out much soil conservation and reforestation work, in addition to many other activities. The local population has been mobilized to remove rocks, create bunds, plant trees, crops, and so on. Food-for-work is an important element in this mobilization, which is transforming the area. Many of the women work with a child slung on their back.

In much of Africa, women are now the primary work force in rural areas: many of the men, unable to make a decent living in agriculture, have gone to seek work in the urban centres, and it is estimated that 6O% of Africa's food is now produced by women. Taking this into account, many food-for-work programmes that WFP supports are specifically tailored to helping rural women.

Some innovative uses of food aid are being pioneered in a few countries. For example, Mali has been trying an interesting use of food as a catalyst in the development process. The experience is not well known because many donors to WFP have reservations about activities that involve the sale of food, as this one does, and so WFP is rather coy about it.

The approach consists of selling food aid to government field-staff working in rural development at a subsidized price. Stated so baldly, such aid could appear aberrational, but the system has some interesting features which, in effect, make it very rational. Firstly, we have to understand that a government development worker in the field, for example an agricultural extensionist, was earning about 16,OOO CFA Francs (US$52 approx.) per month in 1987. This salary would just – and only just – allow him and his family to live. WFP provides him with a monthly ration as if he were a peasant farmer engaged in a food-for-work programme.

In Mali, again at 1987 prices, this ration had a value of about 12,5OO CFA Francs, but the government development worker is charged 3,OOO CFA Francs for it. He is thus receiving a salary supplement of about 9,5OO CFA Francs each month. The 3,OOO CFA Francs which the development worker is charged for his monthly ration goes into an account in the National Agricultural Development Bank. The credits that build up are available for the purchase of agricultural inputs, and for services to farmers such as the provision of spare parts for irrigation pumps, small credit schemes, and the like.

In this way, the scheme generates cash for the provision of various inputs, but just as important is that it provides a real incentive for good technicians to work in rural areas. Government salaries for such development workers are abysmally low all over Africa, and as mentioned earlier, they are usually even lower for people working in the country-side because the cost of living is lower. Add to this the hardship of living in remote rural areas where amenities are poor and where there may be no adequate schooling for the technicians' children, and it is hardly surprising that staff prefer to stay in the city.

Turning food-aid into cash as described in Mali is called "monetization". WFP donors tend to resist it for a variety of reasons, among the most important being that it might dilute the efforts of WFP to reach its primary targets, who are the poor, the hungry and the vulnerable. However, with the economic problems that have been disturbing much of the industrialized world in recent years, funds for development have remained more or less static, while many Third World countries have fallen on desperate times as they struggle to service their debts. There is therefore increasing interest in monetization of food aid.

Numerous other approaches are being tried to harness food aid for rural development in Africa. Also in Mali, there is a project to re-structure the national cereal market. The donors are the US, Canada, the EEC, France, Germany, and WFP who jointly are providing 150,000 tons of cereals over three years, or the equivalent value in cash. The basic idea is to import cereals in years of shortage and sell them on the market, and provide cash or other inputs in years of surplus to allow for the purchase and stocking of the excess. In either case, the aim is to even out the supply and demand equation and stabilize prices for both producers and consumers. The project also foresees the possible donation of in-kind inputs such as fertilizer instead of grain if such inputs could help in the market restructuring process.

That, at least, is the theory behind this innovative and experimental project. In practice, it is not working too well at the moment, because with 80–90% of the population engaged in farming, the supply/demand equation is heavily weighted on the supply side. In such circumstances, it is not too difficult to stabilize consumer prices, but it is very difficult to stabilize prices paid to producers. However, the project is only a first shot in the long battle needed to improve the market situation of basic foods in Africa, for producers and consumers alike.

While on the subject of this project, it is worth mentioning one of the many cases of uninformed journalism that was perhaps based on the currently fashionable bias against food aid: in June 1987, no less a paper than *Le Monde Diplomatique* published an article by François de Ravignan about food self-sufficiency in Africa. In it, he mentioned the Mali project to stabilize the cereal market. He wrote that the national strategy for food self-sufficiency was based on the premise that the prices paid to producers were too low for them to be an incentive to produce more, and went on: "So thanks to European food-aid sold in the country, the claim is to be able to subsidize prices paid to producers .... It is simply being forgotten that this food aid, which is costing the country nothing, contributes strongly to lowering prices!"

He either did not know, had no interest in finding out, or chose to ignore, the fact that the project consists of food aid, *cash*, or *in-kind inputs*, according to what may be most appropriate to the situation at a given time.

Several countries in Africa have food-aid projects that are attempting to help local dairy industries get off the ground. Dried milk powder is given to dairies to be reconstituted and added to local milk. When this milk is sold, it generates cash that can go into services to local dairy farmers. A few years ago, this sort of input was important in launching a major and successful dairy industry in India under the name of "Operation Flood".

There are many imaginative uses to which food aid can be put, and indeed has been, but they are not always as well known as they deserve to be. An example is an approach that has been used, particularly in Kenya, at the beginning of droughts and when pastoralists realize that their animals are in danger. They are offered food in exchange for the animals, which are then slaughtered, and the meat is dried. That dried meat, which has good keeping qualities, can be used for a variety of purposes, including relief feeding if necessary. The pastoralist has received a fair price for his animals in the form of food which also keeps and can be consumed over the following months, and the pressure of livestock on the range has been reduced in a critical period when overgrazing would cause serious degradation. When this type of intervention has been carried out, the hides from the animals have paid for all the administrative costs. This is surely more ingenious than letting the livestock starve on the range, with the loss of both their meat and their hides, and leaving their owners destitute, as more usually happens in times of drought.

Experience of food aid in development work has ranged the whole gamut from excellent to abysmal. Those experiences show that it must be used with imagination and flexibility in development projects that are themselves well-conceived. There is no such thing as an off-the-shelf project design that will work in many different situations. Each situation has to be studied carefully and the food aid inputs tailored precisely to the needs. When they are, food aid can be a powerful prime mover for development, and when they are not, there are people always ready to castigate food aid *per se* rather than the *manner* in which its use was planned and implemented.

11
PROBLEMS WITH FOOD AID

Some of the criticisms that surround food aid – other than food provided during an emergency – have been mentioned. However, instead of condemning food aid out of hand, as many people do these days, we should at least know where the real problems lie, and be discerning and constructive in our criticism.

One of the charges levelled at food aid is that it leads to corruption, and tends to go astray. In response to this potential problem food aid donors, such as WFP, have monitoring operations which aim to ensure that the food reaches the intended beneficiaries. However, no one would ever deny that some food aid does go astray, or that it may sometimes be used for purposes other than those for which it was planned. The simplest of such alternative purposes is when a bag must be dropped off a truck to ensure its safe passage through areas infested by rebels, bandits, miscreants, or whatever they may be called. This has been a regular feature of trucking food through Uganda of late, and it also happens in other places.

A similar incentive was instituted by Jamie Wickens in Chad during the 1984 emergency. Rapid turnaround of trucks bringing food into N'Djamena, and taking it from there to regional bases and distribution points, was vital. Wickens therefore gave a bag of food to each gang of

---

Plate 12   Ethiopia – drought victims await the delivery of food rations.   (WFP/Dennis Craig)

workers for every truck they loaded or unloaded. Apart from being an incentive for fast work, the idea was also to reduce losses and costs. When people pilfer, they open or slit the bags, so it is not only the quantity they have stolen that is lost; additional work is required to repair the bags.

Wickens' initiative brought the desired effects, but even so, the measure has been criticized as being the thin end of the wedge in making pay-offs to ensure that people work well and behave honestly – things that, in a perfect world they should do anyway, without inducements beyond a normal day's wage.

Examining corruption that surrounds food aid compared to other forms of aid, we find that food aid may actually be less prone to malpractice. Food is bulky, perishable, highly visible, and hardly the easiest thing to stash in a Swiss bank account. Furthermore, food is also much easier to trace, should it go astray, than money.

There is also the question, which concerns all types of aid, of who is most likely to benefit from diverting aid from its intended beneficiaries. The smell of money is especially attractive to those who already have it, and to those who have the skills imparted by education, and the power and influence, to get their hands into the cash till. Local businessmen, politicians, and officials are ideally placed and equipped to exploit any development aid that can be parlayed into cash spin-offs. Although there certainly are cases when officials divert food aid for their own benefit, more usually it is the poor that cluster around when there is a possibility of some food being diverted their way.

Walking around the Chaguoua store complex in N'Djamena one day with Piet Winnubst, now the Chief of Operations for WFP in Chad, we saw about twenty ragged children hovering around, awaiting an opportunity to make a lightning grab at some momentarily unguarded food item.

"If kids steal food it is because they and their families need it," Winnubst commented. "The amounts lost in that way are very small. You see that wall?" He indicated the perimeter wall that runs at head-height around the store complex. "A man went over that one day carrying a fifty-kilo sack. The people who saw him said he seemed almost to jump it. Can you imagine? That's the sort of feat you can only pull off in desperation!"

Winnubst is tolerant of such petty pilfering, perhaps because he too knew hunger as a child. His home in Holland was occupied by German troops during World War II, and a soldier caught him trying to steal some of their bread. He was terrified and expected dire punishment, but instead the soldier gave him a piece, recognizing his need just as today Winnubst recognizes that of those impoverished children around the Chaguoua store.

On the other hand, though Winnubst may be tolerant of these misdemeanours, he is certainly not of the major corruption with food aid that has been rife in Chad of late. In fact, he and the highest level of government have fought a major battle against it.

After the emergency period in Chad, it proved difficult to return to routine operations of food-for-work, school feeding programmes, rural development activities such as the building of home and village grain stores, and the like. In fact, most of these development programmes were virtually abandoned during the crisis when relief food was distributed with a minimum of checking and cross-checking – time was simply too short. The result was that in the post-crisis period, there was a continued feeling that food aid was available as a hand-out. This phenomenon was not unique to Chad; it usually follows any emergency relief operation.

Even more serious in Chad was that local authorities often believed it was their prerogative to dispose of food aid as they saw fit. One local official even threatened to jail a young Chadian, employed by WFP to manage one of its stores, if he did not give him access to whatever food he wanted. Local authorities were often selling food, totally disregarding the provisions of the project document and the type of use foreseen for the food.

During the period of my stay in Chad, Winnubst called a three-day meeting of Chadian officials from all over the country who were concerned with WFP food aid. During the meeting, Winnubst was calm, kindly and humorous on the one hand, while on the other, he was steely in his insistence that the rules be observed. He talked openly of the abuse and misuse that were going on, of his role as a food-aid adviser and at the same time, as an inspector. He did so with such aplomb that much of the time the Chadians around the table were nodding their understanding and assent.

He was on thinner ice when dealing with higher level officials in N'Djamena who had been authorizing removal of commodities from the Chaguoua store without all the proper approvals, and for purposes not spelled out in the project document signed by the government and WFP. About 5OO tons of commodities were removed in this way during the first 3 months of 1987.

Eighty tons of sugar were among those commodities. When Winnubst was informed of the removal of this sugar, he telephoned the official in charge of the food-aid programmes in Chad. Winnubst asked him if he knew about the removal of 8O tons of sugar. The official assured him that he did. Winnubst replied in that case, there was no problem. However, there were proper procedures for the borrowing of commodities, and it would be easier for all concerned if they were observed in future. And when could he expect the sugar to be replaced?

Winnubst later determined through various channels that the President's office was not aware of the abuses that were going on, and slowly but surely, pressure was applied to bring things back into line. President Hissan Habré, who is widely regarded for his sobriety and integrity, fired one highly-placed person, and appointed a national director of WFP programmes in the country. Mohamet Hassan Moundou, a respected ex-minister from the early days of independence was called out of retirement for the task. His record and personal probity are beyond reproach.

Most of the monitoring work that uncovered the irregularities in Chad was done by a young Ghanaian called

Holdbrook Arthur. He often became upset over Chadian malpractice with food aid, and on one occasion, just after he had discovered a major discrepancy, he indignantly told the Chadians responsible for it that he was ashamed to work with them.

"You are *too* dishonest!" he exploded, in rounding off his diatribe.

It was a nice implication that a little fiddling in the African context could be ignored. At the same time, it was a scolding that only a fellow African could have given them.

Some countries have set up excellent control and monitoring systems of their own. Niger is an example. At each distribution of food aid, representatives of the local civic authorities, the military, and the farmers' associations are present. The quantities of each commodity are carefully checked by all concerned, and they then sign a declaration of the amounts distributed. Central government receives this declaration and passes a copy of it to the food donor.

When Winnubst was in Benin, prior to his assignment in Chad, he mobilized a Beninois computer specialist and an Italian volunteer, who also had experience in computers but who was cooling his heels in Cotonou, to set up a computerized distribution control system. Local staff were trained to run it, and it proved enormously helpful in keeping track of food aid and giving transparency to the operation. The distribution plan for the coming period was computerized. Copies of it were sent to every national and local authority involved, and to every community that was to receive food. Since everyone was informed of the plan ahead of time, the intended recipients would soon start asking questions if their allocation did not appear. A quite small investment in micro-computers and programmes for them ensured this total information coverage, and its resulting transparency in food distributions, in a way that would be almost impossible with more traditional methods.

Winnubst has an innovative viewpoint with regard to food-aid programmes: he believes that the national authorities, rather than the donor, should take the full responsibility for their effective implementation. This means, in effect, that national staff must be trained in the management of the programmes, imbued with an understanding of the philosophy behind them, and of the need for punctillious attention to the way in which the food aid is used. Not everyone in WFP agrees with Winnubst's stance; some prefer a more interventionist approach in which WFP's international staff play the key role in overseeing all aspects of the operation.

Winnubst's way of operating calls for subtlety and patience, but it is the best approach in the long term. A core group of local people who have taken the food aid programmes to heart and been trained in their administration will be best placed to monitor and manage them, with support of course from the WFP staff in the country. It is easier to pull the wool over the eyes of expatriates than it is over those who are part of their own society and culture.

Another reason for trying to build up the local capacity to administer food aid is that, within food-aid programmes, there is often room for manoeuvre by national staff in such issues as what quantities of food to send to different parts of the country. The project document may outline such matters, but no project document – for any type of development project whether it concerns food aid or not – can ever be totally specific in all details and followed to the letter. There are too many variables over time, and without some flexibility and intelligent interpretation of the effects of changing circumstances, development projects would turn into more fiascos than they actually do. Well-trained local people are better placed to fine-tune a project's activities than expatriates with less knowledge of the country.

There have been cases in many countries of dubious practices concerning food aid, and even if WFP has established criteria for the number of monitoring staff posted in a country according to the size and complexity of the programme there, monitoring may be far from easy. Somalia is an interesting example, and it is similar to many other countries in that it is in economic straits and poorly organized. Corruption will burgeon if given a chance.

The WFP Director of Operations in Somalia is John Murray, a young British economist with development experience in several countries, including four years in China where he began WFP's operations. He highlights the problems of effective monitoring in Somalia, pointing out that about 60% of the rural population is nomadic, and even those who are not nomadic are very scattered through-out a large country. Thus, many of the food-for-work programmes are small and involve only a handful of people. After the thousands involved in each programme in China, this came as something of a shock to Murray when he began his assignment in Somalia.

In order to monitor numerous small project components in a country like Somalia [he said,] the monitors must go into remote areas over very difficult terrain. It may take them a couple of days to reach the general area, and another day or so to reach the project site, where ten workers are supposed to be, say, planting a shelter belt. They may turn up on a day when the ten workers are doing something else, and all they may see is a few pits that have been dug for planting the trees. Chasing up lots of little project components like this is very frustrating. They are almost imposs-ible to monitor properly.

Any abuse of food aid in such small development activities, while difficult to ascertain, will also remain relatively contained. However, there was a recent large-scale food-aid abuse problem in Somalia that involved a refugee camp. It had an interesting outcome and is worth recounting.

Many of the refugees in Somalia have come in from Ethiopia in recent years. No one knows for certain how many there are, but an agreed planning figure for 1987 was 850,000 refugees spread over 41 camps. Most of these camps are in rangeland areas of harsh and dry climate, and there is no possibility of resettling the people and having them grow crops. Since Somalia has no spare arable land, there is no humane alternative but to provide food aid for people in the camps until such time that they can return to their homelands.

There was an outflux of refugees from Ethiopia, partly as a result of people voting with their feet against the government's "villagization" programme. They flocked into Somalia, and one camp for them was in a place called Tug Wajale, in the south and close to the Ethiopian border. The plight of these destitute people living on a barren plain, that was windswept during the dry season and a sea of mud during the rains, drew a lot of media attention, and many aid agencies became involved in helping in the camp. It became a showcase for the appalling living conditions of so many refugees in Africa and for the work of relief agencies trying to help them.

As the people came across the border towards Tug Wajale, both the UNHCR and the Somali authorities were, in theory, keeping track of the numbers swelling the camp population. Over a period of several months, the records showed that it had built up to a total of 90,000 people. However, if one moved around in the camp, it appeared to contain many less than this number.

In addition, the water consumption of the camp indicated that there were less people than the official figures indicated. All the water being used in Tug Wajale camp was being transported to the site, so daily water availability was easy to ascertain. Calculations based on this showed that there was not enough water being taken in for 90,000 people. Furthermore, the available water was not only sufficient for drinking, cooking, and minimal washing, but people were also washing their clothes regularly and showering under buckets.

Clearly, the figure for the number of people in the camp had been grossly inflated, but the government continued to maintain that 90,000 people were there, and so food aid for that number of people was being provided.

Gradually, the figure of 90,000 people became so obviously incorrect that pressure was put on the government to have a head count of the people in the camp. The UNHCR made two unsuccessful attempts to organize the count before finally succeeding on the third try. It revealed that there were only about 32,000 people in the camp!

It was evident that the figures had been inflated for a long time, even before the peak of "90,000" was reached. After the head count, the supply of food was immediately cut back to reflect the real needs, but the question hung in the air, begging an answer: what had happened to all the extra food that had been provided over the preceding months? It was easy to think the worst, that merchants or the authorities had enriched themselves. However, informal inquiries showed that the majority of that extra food had gone over the border into Ethiopia, carried there by the camels of the local nomads. Such irregularities cannot be condoned, but we can hardly say that the food was wasted, and given the famine situation in Ethiopia at the time, it may even have saved lives.

The monitoring of food aid programmes occasionally involves risk. The risk may be quite subtle, at worst endangering reputations or careers, but in the rare extreme, it may endanger life itself. In 1984, a WFP man in an African country had his career put at risk. There was some evidence that the government had for several years been understating its food reserves so that it could obtain more food aid, which it then sold to raise more cash. The WFP man was new to the country, and so were his monitoring staff, but in preparation for the annual exercise that is carried out each November in many African countries to calculate the cereal deficit for the coming year, they paid special attention to assessing the amount of food being held in stock. And sure enough, when the government presented its official figure of food in stock to enable the next years deficit to be calculated, it was lower by a large margin than the figure calculated by the WFP staff.

The WFP man therefore called the other food donors' representatives in the country and told them of his finding. Hitherto, the donors had been divided over the question of food stocks in the country, but faced with the evidence resulting from WFP's monitoring work, and the size of the discrepancy, they were all convinced that the government was deliberately misrepresenting the facts.

So the WFP man went to the government official responsible for food security and told him that WFP and the other major donors could not accept his figures. The official's response was to tell the WFP man that he was under the influence of subversive elements who were trying to discredit the government!

Fortunately, shortly after that, there was a WFP meeting of the countries in that region. James Ingram was briefed about the problem of official food stock figures in the country in question, since it was predictable that the delegation from that country would complain to him about the WFP man posted in their capital and try to have him removed. Sure enough, the delegation asked for a meeting with Ingram and made their complaint. Ingram, who tolerates no nonsense, gave them short shrift.

However, the government was not prepared to let the matter rest at that: the WFP man was queering their pitch and, once back in their own country after the meeting, they were determined to have him removed in one way or another, and as soon as possible. A diplomat heard of their plans and reported the matter to the UNDP Resident Representative, who went to see the government official in charge of food security. While he was actually talking to him about it, at midday on 12 December 1984, a coup took place. The Resident Representative watched as the food security official, who was the president's right-hand man, was arrested by the military. As the WFP man said later, he was saved by the coup!

It can be far more dangerous trying to ensure proper use of food aid in countries that are afflicted by civil strife and general chaos, as is much of Uganda. Mons Swartling is a Swedish WFP official who was stationed in Karamoja. His work there almost cost him his life.

Swartling, who is in his late fifties, has long experience in Africa, both as an agricultural and forestry specialist, and as a man with military training in logistics. The situation in Karamoja was extremely unstable and difficult when he was based there from 1981 to 1984 and charged with organizing the WFP programme of relief feeding and food-for-work. He had to safeguard the food both in the store in Moroto, and again during its transport. A store keeper could divert a whole truck of food and then say that it had been stolen, and there was no way of proving otherwise. There was a battalion of the Ugandan National Liberation Army stationed in Karamoja. They were indisciplined and corrupt, and since they seldom received food or wages, they often lived off the land, taking whatever they wanted from the villages, killing, looting, and burning if they met resistance.

They would turn up at the WFP store and demand that it be opened and food supplied for the troops. Swartling always refused, telling them that the food was for the needy, the old, the infirm, and for development, and that it could not be used by the army. His Ugandan store keeper and staff, standing by during these tense exchanges, often closed their eyes, expecting a bullet in the head at any moment.

The civilian sector of the government in Karamoja was also diverting all the food it could from the intended beneficiaries and selling it, and Swartling was trying desperately to put an end to that situation as well.

It was against this background of chaos and anarchy, with Swartling virtually the only person trying to prevent corruption with food aid in Karamoja, that he set out from Moroto on Christmas Eve 1984, alone in his old Landrover, to drive to Kotido, about 1OO kms to the north. He had gone about half way when he was ambushed.

There were two of them, [Swartling recounted.] They were so stupid that they ran out of the bush from opposite sides and couldn't shoot freely without hitting each other. The one coming from the left managed to put two of his shots through the door on his side. It was a right-hand-drive vehicle and one of the bullets grazed my left wrist, but both of them hit my right wrist and smashed it. It was very lucky that they didn't hit both of my wrists or I wouldn't have been able to get away. That shot was half a centimetre from causing total disaster.

It's funny but I had two thoughts almost at the same instant. Of course, one was to get away as fast as possible, which I did, and the other was that if I were their sergeant major, I'd have them punished for their incompetence!

He may joke about it now, but the agony of the next hours, indeed of the next days and weeks, still came through as Swartling talked. The blood was gushing from the arteries in his shattered wrist as he accelerated away from the ambush. He had a piece of rope in the back of the Landrover and after a few minutes, when he was sure he was not being followed, he stopped to fit it as a tourniquet.

His main concern was to reach Kotido where a doctor friend was working for the Lutheran mission. He realized that if he tried to go too fast, he might go off the road or cause mechanical damage to the Landrover which he would be unable to cope with in his incapacitated and fast-weakening state. He fainted three times, the world turning into dense pea soup and strange noises, but he fought back to consciousness and struggled on over the bad road towards Kotido. He managed to drive the Landrover right up to the door of the building where his doctor friend worked.

After some first aid there, the doctor drove him another 8O kms to a colleague who was better equipped for emergency surgery. They did their best in the primitive conditions to remove the pieces of deformed bullets and to save his hand despite the shattered bones, arteries and nerves. It took the government more than a day to make a helicopter available to fly him to hospital in Kampala, where he then spent 3 weeks in extreme pain. His weight dropped from 8O kg to 56kg, and gangrene set in. He was at death's door when he was finally evacuated to Europe for the amputation of his hand.

At the time of writing, Swartling works for WFP in Ethiopia and is based in Dessie, the capital of Wollo, to help with the soil conservation programme. His tall and rangy figure, with a baseball cap crammed over his long white hair, and a hook to replace his right hand, is a familiar sight in the Dessie area. He is respected and liked by all. He has some profound insights into development problems, and some interesting ideas concerning the soil conservation programme in Ethiopia. However, it seems unlikely that he will stay in Ethiopia long enough to have his ideas influence the approach of that programme, for he still suffers much pain from his amputation and is thinking of retiring early.

★   ★   ★

Let us revert to looking at some of the problems of food aid. It is often reported that donated food has been seen on sale in shops in developing countries and, therefore, it must have gone astray and is being mis-used. This issue is important and warrants a closer examination.

Before considering food aid that is sold, we must remind ourselves of the two basic types of food aid: "programme" food aid, and "project" food aid. As mentioned earlier, "programme" food aid is an indirect form of financial assistance to a country. Donors give food or sell it on concessional terms to governments to dispose of, usually through their own market outlets. If the commodities provided are ones that the country would normally have to import, such food aid results in the saving of foreign exchange. If the country could not afford to import the commodities, they may fill what would otherwise be a serious gap in the country's provisioning.

There are usually agreed conditions between the donor and the recipient concerning the use of the so-called counterpart funds that are generated when the government sells the food aid on the local market. The most common agreement is for the counterpart funds to be used for agricultural and rural development activities. However, it is possible that any recipient government, if it is determined and unscrupulous enough, could use these funds for almost any purpose, including the purchase of arms.

However, the important point is that "programme" food aid is normally sold on the local market; those people who report in critical tones that they have seen bags of food aid on sale often seem unaware that local marketing of "programme" food aid is a common practice.

Were they specific in their accusations concerning the depressing effect that the sale of programme food aid may have on the prices of locally-produced commodities, and on the eating habits of people, we should listen more carefully, for these can be two serious consequences of ill-considered "programme" food aid.

We should also remember, when we see a bag with a donor's name containing food for sale in a market or shop, that the commodity inside it may not be the one that it originally contained. Bags are in short supply in many countries and they may well be re-used many times.

In contrast with programme food-aid, there is "project" food aid. This is food that is donated mainly by WFP and by some private aid agencies. An example is CARE, a large US private organization that administers aid programmes with surplus American food. "Project" food aid is provided for specific development purposes, and it is targeted to defined beneficiaries. This food, and food donated for emergencies or humanitarian purposes, is not usually sold. Therefore, reports of the sale of food aid that was donated by, say, WFP give rise to more concern.

In fact, WFP and such organizations as CARE do have a very limited number of agreements that permit the sale of food aid to generate local funds in certain countries, as we have already seen. But what if the items on sale were distributed as part of a food-for-work programme? No one will deny that this happens and that food aid from this type of operation sometimes finds its way onto the open market. However, there may be little justification for the righteous attitude that critics often assume when condemning food aid because even some of the food-for-work is found to be on sale.

Pause for a moment and consider recipients of food-for-work. They are usually the rural poor, people living on the verge of destitution, and people who have very little cash. Yet, their needs go beyond the cereals, tinned fish, and edible oil they are usually paid in return for work. For example, they will need sugar, tea, salt and cooking utensils. So if they trade some of their food aid – in effect their pay – for these other essential items, should that be thought of as abnormal, as a breach of the principles of "project" food aid?

Another criticism of food aid is that it is wasteful. In April 1985, it rained in Assab, wetting 12–14,000 tons of emergency food aid that was stacked on the quay in the open because all the covered space was full. There were media reports of large quantities of food rotting in the harbour at Assab while people were starving in the interior of the country, a waste of precious resources.

It was not mentioned that it virtually never rains in Assab, for the annual precipitation is only about 25 mm, and that the freak storm that hit the port was a stroke of extreme bad luck. Nor was it ever made known to the general public that a grain storage technologist sent by WFP examined the damaged food about three months later, and a month or so after most of it had been dumped outside the port area and condemned as unfit for human consumption. He stated in his report that "much of it was apparently wrongly condemned and was indeed fit for human consumption at the time of dumping".

Clearly, the grain storage consultant should have been sent there earlier, for he would certainly have been able to

227

save most of the food, but even so we need to keep a sense of proportion: the amount of food dumped because it had been damaged by rain was only about O.7 per cent of the 1.96 million tons of emergency food that Ethiopia received in the years 1984–86 inclusive.

When considering waste, we should remember how it also figures in non-food development assistance. Sometimes this waste is visible, as in the case of a hospital given to Chad under a bilateral aid programme. The hospital was equipped with a beautiful institutional kitchen, all stainless steel and oil-fired cooking ranges. It has never been used because the local custom is for members of a patient's family to cook meals for their sick relative on fires they light in the area around the hospital; and quite apart from that tradition, fuel oil is scarce and very expensive in Chad. Another bilateral donor is mounting an anti-tuberculosis project in a remote area of Mali. It has provided two mobile X-ray units at a cost of more than US$2OO,OOO each, but the vehicles have insufficient ground clearance to function in the sand.

Stories of visible waste are legion: cargoes of donated cement left in the open and when it rained they hardened into a permanent monument to inefficiency; totally inappropriate equipment of all kinds being provided; new irrigation schemes that are never fully utilized, or out of use within a few years for lack of maintenance; equipment out of use for lack of a spare part, or of people properly trained to use it, and so on.

Anyone concerned with development could provide lengthy lists of such cases of visible waste, so there is no point in expanding on it. However, mention should be made of some of the invisible waste that often takes place. For example, what about the expensive overseas training or study programmes that are often provided for people from developing countries? Of course, some are very useful, but the participants are not always selected according to their ability to take best advantage of the training. It is wasteful if a trainee is chosen only because he or she, or the family, have influence and the person does not have the required aptitude. It is also wasteful if a newly-trained person is not placed in his national administration where his knowledge and skills can be best used.

It is also wasteful, but not very visible, when a highly-paid foreign "expert" is assigned to a project and does not perform as required; it may also be wasteful when a government asks for aid, and receives it, for a development project in a particular politician's electoral area, irrespective of whether that area is economically and technically suited to the project. Yet, this sort of thing frequently happens.

★   ★   ★

The disincentives to local food production that food aid can cause provide the basis for the most serious of all criticisms. Tony Jackson in his book *Against the Grain* was among the first to draw a bead on this aspect of food aid. For instance, he quoted the case of Guatemala after the earthquake of 1976 had killed about 23,000 people and left over a million and a quarter people homeless. The country was having a bumper harvest at the time, and of course, the crops were not damaged by the earthquake. There were only a few food items that were in short supply immediately after the disaster, such as salt, but basically, there was no need for massive imports of food. Rather, building materials were required once the reconstruction period began.

Despite this, the US sent more than 24,000 tons of grains and blended foods into Guatemala during the months following the earthquake, helping to knock the bottom out of the local market, and thereby causing serious problems for local farmers. (WFP's intervention there was to buy locally any food that was required to relieve hardship.)

There have also been numerous cases of food aid going on too long after an emergency, and here we should remember the comment made by Alan Jones, mentioned earlier in this book, when he said, "Relief operations always begin too late, grow too big, and go on too long."

Indeed, once relief operations have overcome their start-up inertia, they tend to become institutionalized and gather the unstoppable momentum of a juggernaut. Many people are working in the operation, shippers and truckers are making money from it, surplus food is being disposed of for a just and humane cause – or for what was such a cause at the start – so who is interested in turning off the tap? Who is going to take into account the livelihood of the local farmers? Yet it is just as important to halt relief operations at the right moment as it is to start them at the right moment.

Food aid may have a negative effect if it arrives too late after an emergency. A press report recently stated that emergency food supplies donated by the EEC in response to a hurricane disaster in Mauritius arrived no less than 15 months later! By that time, anyone who had really needed the food would have either made other arrangements, or died, and the arrival of food aid into a situation that will probably have returned to normal in the intervening months may cause market distortions.

There is little evidence that project food aid causes any major impact on local markets. This is largely because most donors of project food aid have become rather sensitive to its potential disincentives. There is a growing tendency to provide project food aid in areas that have chronic food deficits year after year, and attempts are also made to time the food inputs so that they arrive in the months of scarcity before the harvest. Furthermore, the total quantities are relatively small when set against the total national consumption. And as already mentioned, the studies carried out by Simon Maxwell indicate that, although the problem may arise, careful monitoring can correct it.

WFP has been a leader in trying to promote purchases of food aid in developing countries that have surpluses, and in programmes of import substitution. To quote one example, in recent years there has been a clever arrangement with Kenya. Kenya needs large quantities of wheat each year, which normally it would have to import commercially. On the other hand, it usually has surpluses of maize, beans and other local commodities. WFP provides certain quantities of wheat to Kenya in exchange for a credit of maize and beans.

Then, when there is a food-aid need for which those local commodities would be appropriate, usually in project activities in the country, WFP calls them forward for delivery.

As can be imagined, calculating the "exchange rate" between the wheat and the local commodities is fairly complex, but overall, the arrangement works admirably. It is interesting that during the severe drought of 1984 in Kenya, when the country had a cereal deficit of more than a million tons, a shortfall of roughly half over normal years, WFP was able to advance food from the stocks of local commodities it was holding in stores in many rural areas of Kenya. It was precisely in those rural areas that the food was urgently needed. Having food on-site proved an important factor in helping Kenya overcome its large cereal deficit and in coming through the drought without any crisis ever developing.

So-called "triangular transactions" and "local purchases" have also become a feature of WFP operations in the last 7–8 years. Triangular transactions are when WFP uses cash donations to purchase commodities in one developing country, for delivery in another. "Local purchases" differ only in that the food may be delivered in the same country.

These operations are growing, and have been developing particularly rapidly since 1984. In 1986, a total of about 900,000 tons of food were bought in developing countries. However, this still represented only about 9% of all cereal aid.

The countries in Africa that provide most food for triangular transactions are Zimbabwe, Kenya, and Malawi. Local purchasing has taken place in a number of countries, including Mali, Burkina Faso, Niger, the Sudan, Ethiopia, Cameroon and Zambia.

Beginning in 1981, Zimbabwe has provided enormous quantities of maize for triangular transactions. The first of these resulted in the first large-scale overland logistics operation organized by WFP. In April 1981, Zimbabwe had a million tons of maize stockpiled. If some of it was to be purchased and used in other parts of Africa, it had to be brought out through Mozambique. Tun Myat was one of the instigators of the famous Maize Train Operations that went on for over two years and brought out about 5OO,OOO tons of maize that were used in Tanzania, Mali, Chad, and Niger. Africa was feeding Africa, but organizing the transportation was no mean feat. There were the usual problems of shortage of rolling stock and locomotives and weak management in Mozambique. In fact, when WFP undertook to organize the operation, the authorities in Zimbabwe did not think it could be done.

Irrespective of transportation problems, local purchases are not always as simple as one might expect, even when the funds are available. In fact, they may be fraught with problems. Some developing countries, even when they have surpluses, do not have the organizational capacity to be able to market them easily or efficiently.

Mali is an interesting case in point. The WFP multi-purpose development project there has an annual allocation of 12,OOO tons of food, but in the last two years, about 6,OOO tons of that food have been bought locally in Mali.

Francis Valere Gille, the man in charge of WFP operations in Mali, negotiated the first purchase with OPAM, the Office des Produits Alimentaires du Mali, in effect the parastatal organization responsible for most of the food in the country. The market control system operated by OPAM, or more exactly by its National Cereals Office, results in official cereal prices in Mali being higher than they are on the world market. In fact, for that first purchase, the Cereals Office quoted prices that were above those of the world market for the same commodities. However, since the operation was seen as a pioneering move in local purchasing, WFP agreed to pay the higher price.

But in addition to the higher price, there were other irritating problems. For example, the sacks in which the grain was delivered were old, of poor quality, and not all of the same size. Nor were they properly marked. In effect, the

Cereals Office did not live up to its contractual obligations in several respects, even though the grain itself was good.

WFP could have been indemnified for the contractual deficiencies by the Cereals Office, had they wished to press the matter home. However, WFP did not wish to do this, for it was the first purchase in Mali and they wanted to encourage the Cereals Office. Instead, they decided that the following year, Valere Gille would put WFP's purchase out to tender, including potential private sector suppliers such as cooperatives, in addition to the Cereals Office.

The private sector was very business-like, responding within a matter of 3–4 days to the tender, with realistic prices, and agreeing to all the conditions stipulated by WFP. The response from the Cereals Office was equally rapid, but less business-like. It consisted, firstly, of a telephone call to Valere Gille, followed by a letter, from a very angry official to say that WFP had no right to request tenders from the private sector, that WFP's role was to support the Cereals Office, and that what had been done was intolerable. To this Valere Gille replied that the WFP invitation to tender was a normal practice for consulting a market, a market which in this case included OPAM as well as other operators.

After a couple of weeks, the Cereals Office sent its proper response to the invitation to tender, in which it said that WFP knew that it could only sell cereals at the official price, which was about 96 CFA Francs per kilo – against a current market price of only 6O CFA Francs.

A little later, Valere Gille had a meeting with the newly-appointed Minister for State Enterprises. He suggested to him that the various parastatal offices should be much more market oriented in all aspects of negotiations and sales. They should offer realistic prices, be able to make offers and reach agreements quickly, use good sacks, and generally provide all the other services that a buyer has the right to claim of a vendor, rather than expect the buyer to accede to their conditions. He informed the Minister that the Cereals Office was refusing to mark the sacks, a WFP condition, or to deliver the commodities to the buyer's stores, a quite normal request from a buyer and one to which all the other tenderers had agreed. He politely pointed out to the Minister that his various offices could only be successful if they marketed properly. For how could they ever sell abroad if they could not even do so within their own country?

The Minister was impressed by the arguments. He took the matter up with the Cereals Office, and ultimately, they made an excellent offer, dropping their price to the market level, and even improving on the conditions that WFP had requested, for example providing new sacks rather than the first quality stipulated in the invitation to tender.

Thus local purchases although often difficult, may lead to improvements in the the marketing and services of cereals offices in developing countries which, in time of surplus, will help them to sell on the world market.

We have looked at a few of the problems and criticisms surrounding food aid. There are more: for instance that school feeding programmes do not always reach the poorest of the poor and that they may ultimately favour the children from more prosperous households. (It is probable however that the more prosperous send the children to private schools that are not eligible for food aid.) Or that the work carried out under food-for-work programmes is of low quality, or that it benefits the local landowners or authorities more than the rural people.

If we really want to be objective about these problems and criticisms, I believe it will emerge that it is not food aid *per se*, as an idea, that is at fault; rather, it is the way the food aid has been planned and administered in some cases. Many of the criticisms attached to it apply equally to other forms of aid when they are ill-planned and administered. However, there can be no doubt that "programme" food aid has more potential for causing all the problems that we have mentioned than does "project" food aid. Given the generalized nature of the former, it is far more difficult to monitor; and without the benefit of the torchlight of constant monitoring, many shady nooks will remain in which all manner of undesirable things may be going on. Food aid targeted to specific sectors of the population, for specific purposes, as it is under "project" food aid, is far less likely to have undesirable side effects and is easier to control.

If we take a step back and look at the world food situation on a macro level, we find that there are increasing surpluses in many regions, while at the same time there are also many areas of grave food shortages, under-development, and poverty, especially in Africa and parts of Latin America. The surpluses in the traditional high production areas such as North America, Australia and Western Europe are causing increasing concern. In one way or another, most of these surpluses are paid for by governments through subsidies and price-support mechanisms. It seems that total world cereal surpluses are now reaching some 400 million tons annually. A recent forecast for the EEC alone is that, by 1990–91, it will have production in excess of requirements of 40.3 million tons, and 89 million tons in stock, whereas in 1986–87, excess production was only 29.5 million tons, and stocks were only 36.5 million tons. The fact that countries such as India and China, which were large importers of foreign cereals in the past, have now become surplus producers, or are at least self-sufficient, must also be taken into account.

Certainly, efforts will be made in the near future to curb agricultural production in the main surplus countries, for surpluses are costly not only in terms of the subsidies paid for their production, but also in terms of storage costs. At 30 August 1986, the food being held by the EEC was costing 1,428 million ECU (about $1,500 million) annually to store.

However, even if there is a drive to reduce this excess production, the world cannot be safe without a regular reserve of surplus food. What if there were to be a series of natural or man-made catastrophes, for example droughts and Chernobyls that compounded each other? In the absence of such disasters, however, it behoves mankind to use those surpluses in a creative way to alleviate the poverty and under-development in other parts of the globe, not as a hand-out, but rather as a force for sustainable improvement of the conditions in those areas.

In many cases, food aid began with the aim of dumping surpluses, thereby protecting domestic markets, while at the same time creating future export markets. This may still be the tacit aim of some food donors, but the majority are becoming more altruistic in their food aid programmes. The criticisms of food aid have helped force this change for the better. The existence since 1962 of WFP has also helped, for WFP has no commercial interests or markets and no political positions to defend. It can therefore more easily apply the resources it receives with the sole benefit of the recipients in mind.

This does not mean that WFP has not made mistakes too. In fact, further refinement in food aid programmes by WFP is still required. Every input of food aid must be carefully planned according to the specific development circumstances that surround it. This implies that the planning of food aid programmes requires people with an understanding of development issues and problems. I believe that a criticism which can be fairly levelled at WFP is that not all of its field staff have enough experience and understanding of development. Some do, and these are the ones who are the most thoughtful and creative about the use of food aid in their countries of assignment; but some do not have this capacity and are only at home while handling the organizational and administrative aspects of the programme.

Some of those with development experience before joining WFP show considerable inventiveness when discussing food aid possibilities. For example, in certain countries, and in areas where basic cereals are not in short supply, why provide cereals at all in food-for-work programmes? Highly-valued commodities such as tea and sugar alone might be better. And with regard to monetization, one WFP man suggested to me that there are many surplus commodities that could make a contribution to development through careful import substitution.

"Even that infamous wine-lake in Europe!" he said. "Many countries in Africa import considerable quantities of wine. If the EEC gave us some of that lake, we could import it, in quantities small enough not to upset the commercial market, sell it, and use the cash for rural development."

Aid of any sort, food or other, cannot hope to make a useful contribution unless it is based on the needs of the recipient, rather than on the needs of the donor. In the past, many development projects have been set up in such a way that they bring guaranteed business back to the donor country in the form of experts, construction contracts, supply of equipment, and the like. Some countries continue this approach in their bilateral aid projects, usually with poor results in development terms. The same self-serving approach can easily be applied to food aid, if the donor is cynical enough not to care about the effect in the recipient country as long as a problem at home has been resolved. Fortunately, there are signs that most donors, of food and of other types of development support, are generally becoming more attuned to the needs and possibilities of the recipients: a couple of decades of relative failure in development in Africa, brought into horrendous focus by the famines of 1984–85, have been forcing a soul-searching of late! And in respect of food aid, surplus food is an important resource that has shown its value in development when correctly applied. Globally, it constitutes about 10% of the value of all official development aid at present, but in Africa, it represents about 20%. The argument as to whether it might not be better to donate cash instead of food is irrelevant, for the cash does not exist, while the surplus food does.

12

AND THE NEXT FAMINE?

No one doubts that there will be more droughts and potential famines in Africa. In fact, in September 1987, the situation turned ominous in Ethiopia yet again. The government appealed for 950,000 tons of grain to see the country through to the 1988 harvests. The rains which had arrived early (in fact during my stay in Ethiopia in late May), and which had given cause for some optimism, lapsed into sporadic showers in many areas of the country. In Eritrea, Tigray, Wollo, and Hararghe, these showers were insufficient to keep the already-planted crops growing, and in some areas there was not enough rain even to allow planting.

The widespread rains that finally arrived in August enabled the drought-stressed crops in some areas to make a partial recovery, and allowed for some planting of short-cycle crops such as chickpeas. In Eritrea, however, the rains were too little and too late, and a total crop failure was expected. Overall throughout the country, the situation was estimated as being similar to that in 1984; and we hardly need to remind ourselves of events following that failed harvest.

So the question we need to ask now is what have we learned from the two major crises of the last 25 years? Did the drought of the early 1970s in the Sahel, and the even

Plate 13   Mozambique – the face of hunger. (WFP/Riccardo Cueva Rap)

greater catastrophe of the 1984–85 period in many parts of Africa, give us the knowledge, skills, and organizational capacity to avert so much suffering and death in the future?

When describing the Sahelian drought of the 197Os, Per Ivarsen said, "It was only when the bodies began to pile up that the cry for help went out."

It is reasonable to hope that such a situation will not arise again, for there have been improvements in the technical aspects of detecting potential famines on the horizon, even if they still need refinement. There is nothing new about the idea of trying to forecast famines and take remedial action in time. As mentioned earlier in this book, the British colonial administration in India was much exercised by the issue and developed a series of parameters and administrative measures to ward off crises before they turned into famines. More recently, the mistakes, problems, and delays in mounting relief operations have focussed more attention on the fact that early warning and quick action are the essential keys to preventing a potential famine from becoming a real one.

We must remember that it will always be at least 3 months, and more often 4 or 5 months, from the moment of a cry for help to the time when food can actually be distributed – at least as long as the traditional shipping and transportation methods are used, and as long as food has to be called forward from donors and moved over great distances. If a crisis can be detected in the offing, pre-positioning of food in the region can lead to vital time saving if, and when, the crisis begins to materialize

One example of good pre-positioning took place in West Africa in the 1978/79 cropping year. The Sahelian drought of the early '7Os returned, though in a milder form. There were indications that there would be serious food shortages again, so WFP quietly brought forward shipments of 5O,OOO tons of wheat from its less urgent requirements elsewhere. Sure enough, food shortages did begin to materialize, but when they did, 5O,OOO tons of wheat were already in West African ports and could be quickly moved into the interior. The crisis was nipped in the bud. It is a reflection on the type of information provided by the media that, since there was no crisis, the general public did not even know one was in the making in the Sahel that year.

If all goes well in the prediction of a crisis while it is still in the making, in the pre-positioning of commodities, and in rapid action to distribute them as the situation deteriorates, it may be possible to help people before they are compelled to leave their homes in search of food or work. If the crisis can be forestalled in this way, numerous problems will be averted. There is a very real human problem once people leave their homes: to their physical distress is added the emotional distress of the breakdown of their social structure, of having to leave their familiar environment and head off into the unknown in search of salvation.

Let us try to transpose ourselves into the hearts and minds of a family in an area of Africa stricken by drought: it has rained, the first brief and scattered showers of what should become the rainy season, so they have toiled to prepare their fields for planting, optimistic in the hope of normal rains. But those first showers are not followed by others, so they never sow; or maybe there are some further showers, so they do sow, only to watch the seedlings wither.

Faced with the prospect of having no crop, they husband their resources with even more care than usual in already frugal peasant societies. There is no real hope of a solution, for there can be no crop until the end of the next rainy season. They discuss what they can sell to be able to buy food; they seek work or any activity that can raise a little cash to be able to support themselves and their children with the bare essentials of life. They begin to sell off their meagre assets. The prices they obtain are at rock bottom because everyone around them is also selling for the same reason – "hunger prices", as Italians still routinely say today when referring to low prices, a sure indication of much less prosperity in quite recent times in Italy.

African parents see their own thin bodies become even thinner. Particularly distressing, they must watch their children suffer and become more gaunt. They have sold all of their most precious possessions. Their food reserves dwindle fast, despite their frugality.

One day, the awful finiteness of those food reserves becomes inescapable; there is no option but to leave home or to die. Other nearby families may already have left, but of course there is no news of the fate that they encountered.

So they set off into the unknown, into the vastness of a drought-stricken African landscape, with a minimum of pitiful belongings, with only their diminished strength to carry them to salvation, and yet with no assurance of finding it. Many of us, well-fed and travelling in the comfort of a jetliner, our children snug at home, are apprehensive about the unknown ahead of us. Imagine the mental anguish of those people as they set out, leaving everything they know behind, and suffering physically too.

Even when people, who have been forced to leave their homes, do find salvation in some feeding camp, their presence there poses grave practical problems. Firstly, there is the issue, mentioned earlier, of health when many are crowded into confined areas with little or no sanitation. Relief agencies have to deal with this, in addition to finding and distributing the food that is required. In the longer term, there is the problem of rehabilitating people for a normal life, of getting them back onto the land with seeds and tools in time to resume cultivating when the next rainy season arrives.

The conclusion can only be that if we are to forestall suffering and starvation, and the need for hordes of distressed people to set out looking for help, a timely alert to the impending crisis is of the essence. Only then will it be possible to mount effective relief operations. Physical and mental suffering, and life and death, hinge on this.

★   ★   ★

The experience during the Sahelian famine of the 1970s led to the creation of a Global Information and Early Warning System by FAO. This System, with which WFP

242

works closely, uses satellite imagery to try to detect droughts and famines in the making.

The era of satellite imagery, or remote sensing, for this type of work was born with the launching of Landsat in 1972. The first attempt to use it was in connection with a screwworm study in the southern United States and Mexico. Screwworm is the larva of a blowfly which sometimes lays its eggs in sores or wounds, or in the nostrils of mammals, including man. The larva is armed with rings of small spines which allow it to bore into flesh, with serious, and even fatal, results.

The reproduction of this parasite depends on temperature conditions on or near the ground. Landsat was used to measure these temperatures and correlate them with screwworm activities, but the exercise was found too costly to be economic.

FAO first became involved with remote sensing for the prediction of plagues of desert locusts. These plagues originate when there has been abundant vegetation growth following rains in the semi-arid areas in which locusts live, and in which in their normal state, locusts are non-migratory and solitary "grasshoppers". The favorable conditions allow their numbers to multiply so much that overcrowding may occur when the conditions turn unfavourable again. When this happens, the locusts enter a gregarious and migratory phase in which their appearance changes, their metabolic rate rises, and they become more active and nervous. They take to the sky in huge migrating swarms, devastating crops where they land. They also lay egg fields that will hatch into future swarms when the rainfall conditions are right. In 1869, locust swarms even reached England, probably from West Africa.

Since locust plagues are so closely related to vegetation changes in their desert breeding areas, Landsat imagery was applied to following these changes and to forecasting possible outbreaks. Some success was achieved, and from there it was a small step to applying Landsat to monitor vegetation as an indication of drought. Later, after Meteosat was launched, it also became possible to monitor cloud movement and cover. Adding this imagery to that of Landsat provides indications of likely conditions on the ground in the drought-prone areas of Africa.

The information emerging from satellite monitoring, coupled with information gathered from governments in the countries concerned, is the basis for the FAO Global Information and Early Warning System on Food and Agriculture. The System puts out regular telexes and bulletins on the food situation and prospects in countries at risk. FAO and WFP also put out joint alerts on certain situations. More routinely, WFP sends out a weekly telex to donors on the subject of changing food aid requirements, shipping arrangements, and desirable schedules.

Remote sensing technology via satellites is improving continuously. However, the ability of scientists to interpret the images has not kept pace, even in industrialized countries, let alone in the developing world. There was a fiasco in Ethiopia during 1985 when UNDRO announced that it had rained in parts of the Highlands and that prospects were looking better. At the same time, however, all the other relief agencies, on the basis of their experience on the ground, were announcing disaster conditions in the same areas. It is alleged that UNDRO's statement, which lost them much credibility, had been based on faulty interpretation of satellite images.

There is, therefore, much current interest in an experiment involving more than a hundred scientists which is taking place on the plains of Kansas. The scientists are observing a tract of land and the overlying atmosphere at ground level and from aircraft and helicopters while remote sensing satellites pass over. The scientists will compare the data collected from the ground with the satellite images in order to determine how the interpretation of those images can be improved.

However, effective early warning requires national systems to supplement the satellite data with information gathered on the ground, for famine does not depend only upon crop production. It is often thought that people starve merely because food production has been inadequate, but this is not so. One of the last great famines in Europe occurred when blight hit the potato crop in Ireland between the years 1846 and 1850. Potatoes were the staple diet of the poor in Ireland, and it is estimated that almost 2 million people died, and almost as many emigrated, in those years. During the same period, however, it is also estimated that there was enough food in Ireland to feed twice the population of 8 million people, and the huge and regular exports to England of cereals, meat, butter, and eggs continued at their usual rythm as if nothing were amiss among the starving Irish peasantry. So famines can take place without there being any major failure in food availability, and they often do take place in such circumstances.

In fact, poverty is at the root of most famines, rather than a simple lack of food production in an area. People starve when their economic, political and social status is too weak to allow them to command the food they need, and so it is the already impoverished and emarginated who go to the wall when the going becomes rough. People with money and social power do not starve, except perhaps in a blockade or siege situation resulting from strife. It can therefore be said that famines are economic disasters, and not just food crises.

This thinking was first propagated widely in 1981 by Amartya Sen in his fascinating book *Poverty and Famine: an Essay on Entitlement and Deprivation.* It provides the basic strategy behind the Early Warning Systems (EWS) that have been set up in a few African countries in recent years. They are still in the experimental stage.

The Early Warning Systems apply a three-stage process in attempting to detect famines in the making, and as a basis for deciding what action should be taken to pre-empt disaster. The first of these three stages is the relatively obvious and traditional one of monitoring the progress of crops and forecasting likely harvests. Crop assessment is a somewhat arcane field. To the outsider it appears rather hit-or-miss, but experts in it achieve surprising accuracy,

245

especially if they know the country well. To a large extent it is based on talking to farmers and field technicians to find out how they rate the forthcoming harvest compared to previous ones. They also discuss the incidence of pests and diseases. Comparing this information with known past performance is already a good indication of what to expect.

The area under crops for the current year also has to be assessed. This is usually done by actual measurements in sample villages or communities, followed by upward extrapolation for the whole region being assessed. In addition, the assessors themselves look at the crops and apply their knowledge and experience in the mental gymnastics that go into determining the likely food production figure for the area being examined. This figure will be modified as necessary as the season progresses and in the light of events such as good or poor rainfall and attacks by pests. This assessment of probable harvests leads to the identification of areas at risk, the first stage in an EWS.

Once an area has been identified as having a potential food production shortfall, phase two begins. This phase takes into account numerous factors in an attempt to monitor the trends and to ascertain whether a famine is likely. Households are sampled to see what food reserves are being held in the area and to ascertain how long families think they could hold out after a poor harvest. Surveys also attempt to find out what other resources the people have that could help to see them through a crisis. For example, do they have assets they could dispose of to be able to buy food? Do they have a chance of earning money through work or handicrafts, and so on?

At the same time as this sort of enquiry is being made, those working with the EWS are on the alert for the first evidence that a crisis is actually developing. The prices of food in the local markets is a sensitive barometer, as are also the consumption patterns in the area. That is to say, are people eating the same staples that they would normally be eating at that time of year? If they are eating other commodities, it may be an indication of an actual or expected shortage of staples.

A little later, the first so-called stress indicators may begin to show. For example, increased attendance in schools where there are feeding programmes, or more people turning up for food-for-work programmes, may be a first sign. More livestock being sold than usual, the arrival of nomads in an unusual place or at an unusual time, doctors seeing cases of incipient malnutrition in their clinics, veterinarians and animal health staff finding livestock in poorer condition than normal for the time of year, unusual movements of people, the increased sale of household and personal possessions, for example jewellery – these are the sort of warning signs that begin to ring the alarm bells.

If those alarm bells begin to tinkle faintly in the distance, the third phase begins. This consists of nutritional surveys among the children under five in the area. Attention is focussed on the young children, for they are the most vulnerable sector of the community and quickly show the effects of food shortage.

During the 1984–85 emergency, nutritional surveys were a cause of contention. Different methods were being used by different international and private relief agencies, and not surprisingly, with different results in a given region. With each agency claiming that their findings were correct, and making proposals for action based on them, dissent and discussion sometimes obstructed the task in hand.

This raises a point about the private agencies. Most of them do outstanding work, with dedicated and selfless people operating in conditions of extreme hardship. They often provide eyes and ears in remote areas for the bigger national and international relief agencies, and thus, much of the flow of information for early warnings and situation reports comes from private agency staff. However, it is a fact, that during major emergencies, some of the volunteers who go to the field for short periods of work with private agencies lack experience. They are often horrified by the suffering they encounter. A member of an international agency, when describing the relief work in Darfur in 1985 said:

> Some volunteer would come rushing up eyes popping out of his head, and say that he had just seen people dying like flies, that it was horrible, and that something had to be done at once. So you would ask exactly where he had seen them, how many people there were, and what the access to the area was like. But it was difficult to get a coherent answer out of those volunteers until they became battle-hardened.

This understandably emotional reaction of volunteers may have contributed to the chaos in trying to reach correct assessments of the levels of malnutrition in drought-stricken areas. Now, however, there is general agreement among all concerned regarding the procedures for carrying out nutritional surveys. Measurement of upper-arm circumference as an indicator of nutritional level has been dropped; all now use the weight-for-height method and the same basic criteria for interpreting the data that is gathered. However, the statistical sampling methodology still varies somewhat from one relief agency to another.

The method and the criteria generally applied are as follows: children in the height range 65–115 cms are surveyed, and the results compared with standard weight-for-height (or length) figures for boys and girls established by the World Health Organization. These standards, which were published in 1983, are based on surveys of very large numbers of healthy, well-fed, male and female children.

In practice, children in the 65–85cm height range are usually measured in a horizontal position, and the taller ones are measured while upright. They are measured to the nearest half centimetre, and then weighed to the nearest tenth of a kilogram. The child's weight is then expressed as a percentage of the standard weight for his or her length.

A perfect nutritional status would theoretically produce survey results with 100% of children having 100% of their standard weight-for-height, but this never happens of course. In reality, even in a population of well-fed children, natural variations occur. However, for the vast majority of children, when they are 80% or below of the standard weight for their height, the risk of mortality increases sharply. Up to 2–3% of children with only 80% of their standard weight for height is usually accepted as a natural variation. As the proportion of children in the under-80% category rises above this 2–3%, it is assumed that there is a proportionately serious problem.

As long as there are only a few children as low as 85% of standard weight-for-height, the situation is still considered normal. A first sign of impending trouble and risk is usually recognized when a significant proportion of children reach the range 80–84% of standard weight-for-height. Real concern begins when a survey reveals that 20% or more of children are below 80% of standard weight. Assuming that there has been no other cause, such as an epidemic of measles, these levels of malnutrition among the children are considered serious.

When children go below 70% of standard weight, it is usually a foregone conclusion that there will soon be deaths related to malnutrition in the community, if they have not already occurred.

The Early Warning Systems try to combine all the issues described above into their operations. The way they actually go about it varies. The gathering of the basic information in the field that will enable areas at risk to be identified, the first phase, is carried out by more or less formalized arrangements in the different countries that have an EWS.

In Ethiopia, the EWS of the RRC, which was first set up in 1976, long before any other in Africa, relies in the main on the field staff of the Central Statistical Office. They are spread all over the country, and they provide 10 days of work each month to the EWS, with RRC paying the expenses. The smallest administrative unit in Ethiopia is the *woreda*, and there are 550 of these in the crop growing parts of the country which support 80% of the population. At the time of my interview with Birhane Gizaw, the impressive chief of the EWS, they were obtaining monthly crop assessments and other information from 44O of these *woreda*.

The EWS has set up a committee in each *woreda* as the contact point for the monthly review of the crop, weather, and pest situation. As the harvest approaches, they try to assess the prospects in terms of likely surpluses, self-sufficiency, or deficits for the main crops. These *woreda* committees are also the grassroot-level units that advise the EWS, if prospects look poor, of the number of people likely to be at risk, what stocks and other resources could be mobilized, and for how long they could probably hang on without help. The EWS is not so well organized in the nomadic areas of Ethiopia as yet, but even so, they correctly raised the alert for the damage that was to be caused by the drought in the Ogaden in the early months of 1987, and identified the requirements if starvation was to be avoided.

The Ethiopian EWS has only recently started on nutritional surveillance. They are being helped by the Save the Children Fund (UK) in Wollo, and at central level by Sweden which is paying for a nutritionist.

In some countries, government staff such as extension workers and other field technicians are the backbone of the EWS. They do the work in their spare time for a small payment from the EWS. This is the case in Chad, where an EWS was started recently with financial support from the EEC and with the involvement of Medecins sans Frontières (MSF). About 6O part-time people gather the information. They check market prices of food every week, and during the growing season, they check the status of the crops every 1O days. At all times, they are on the alert for stress symptoms or unusual happenings that could indicate impending or actual shortages.

In Mali, where again the EEC and MSF are involved, there is a mobile team of the EWS in each of the four administrative Regions. They travel 25 days a month gathering intelligence, and they are in regular radio contact with their headquarters in Bamako.

All of the Early Warning Systems have core staff in their headquarters. The data which comes in from the field is processed by computer and published in synoptic form in a monthly bulletin. This bulletin is circulated widely among government and donor staff. When an area which is at risk has been discovered, it is usual for the in-depth investigations of phases two and three to be carried out by staff from headquarters.

The Early Warning Systems have no authority in respect of relief operations once they have identified a need; in other words, they can only provide the alert and a recommendation as to what should be done, and it is then up to government and relief agencies to take the appropriate action.

The recommendations made by an EWS can cover a range of possibilities. If the EWS has done its job properly, its recommendation may be that food be moved into the area as a precautionary reserve (because shortages arc foreseen before the next harvest), or that food-for-work programmes be started, or that food be brought in for normal or for subsidized sale, or that income-generating activities be launched for the longer term, and so on. Emergency calls for immediate and free distribution of food indicate that the EWS has not functioned properly or that the government or relief agencies did not respond properly at an earlier stage in the alert.

In the short time that Early Warning Systems have existed in Chad and Mali – they were both started in 1986 – they have begun to make interesting progress. They have trained their staff, perfected their questionnaires, and become operational in the field. Furthermore, they have been able correctly to raise alerts on several occasions. However, there have been some response problems following the alert. In Mali, two recommendations for immediate and free food distribution were made. One was for Almoustarat, north of Gao, where serious malnutrition levels had been revealed by the ESW. It was almost two months before food was distributed by the national office for aid to drought victims, despite the fact that there was plenty of food in the country, Almoustarat is less than 150 kms from Gao, and trucks can easily reach Gao by tarmac road from Bamako in two days.

In Chad, in the first year of operation, eleven cantons needed phase two studies in the field, after having been identified as being at risk; and in three cases the EWS recommended inputs of relief food to forestall suffering. In two cases, where family incomes were reasonable, millet was brought in and sold at subsidized prices. In the other case, where families had almost no resources and insufficient stocks of food to see them through to the next harvest, food was distributed free. CARE, the American private agency, distributed 120 tons of sorghum, 15 tons of edible oil, and 20 tons of dried milk.

As in Mali, however, the response was less than perfect. For in the area where food was distributed free by CARE, the EWS had advised that the livestock were in good condition and that milk was available. For this reason, the EWS recommended that no dried milk should be sent. However, the committee made up of government and donor representatives decided differently, and the 20 tons of CARE milk powder went there anyway.

Early Warning Systems, whether on the global scale operated by FAO, or at the national level, can have a crucial role in averting famines. They must progress further, however, particularly in respect of information gathering at the field level. This is difficult and expensive in Africa. However, the best EWS will resolve little if there are no emergency preparedness structures in famine-prone countries. Part of such structures is the creation of emergency food reserves.

This may sound an obvious step to take, but like so many things concerned with food aid and famine, it is not as straightforward as it might appear. In early 1987, Ethiopia agreed with donors to set up an emergency food reserve of 180,000 tons. The problems of holding food reserves are connected with the fact that the stocks have to be rotated regularly to prevent deterioration. And in addition, the annual storage cost in Ethiopia is estimated at $35 per ton.

Unfortunately, the availability of food nearby may not help if bureaucratic delays intervene. We have already seen how it took two months for the Mali authorities to distribute food in Almoustarat after the alarm had been sounded. A similar incident happened in Ethiopia in April/May 1987 in connection with refugees from the Sudan.

In mid-April, some 20,000 people flocked into Ethiopia from the Sudan. Their villages in the Blue Nile region had been burned by the Sudanese army. They fled towards Ethiopia, walking anything from 3 to 14 days to seek refuge near Asosa, where they congregated.

When news of this new influx of destitute people reached the outside world, the UN High Commission for Refugees (UNHCR) sent a mission to assess the needs. It went to Asosa on 1 May, a remarkably rapid response for an international body.

There was no immediate follow up to the UNHCR mission with regard to an official request for food. Small amounts were provided to the refugees but nothing like enough. For six weeks, the refugees waited, suffering terrible hardship. Eva Wallstam, the Swedish nutritionist working with the RRC's Early Warning System, visited the refugees when they had been at Asosa for five weeks.

"I went to that camp at Asosa last week," she told me on 28 May. "It was awful, absolutely awful. Many of the kids were under 60% of standard weight for height. There was a four-year-old girl who weighed only 6.2 kilos. They're probably beyond saving at that point. People were dying. In fact, they told me that forty people had died since they arrived."

The very next day, 29 May, I was talking with Brother Augustin (usually known as Gus) O'Keefe, the canny Irishman from the Holy Ghost Congregation who is the head of the Christian Relief and Development Association in Ethiopia. With poise and calm, he effectively coordinates most of the activities of forty-seven different private relief and development agencies working in Ethiopia. He has a staff of about fifty people and runs a fleet of 65 trucks. After almost 15 years of relief and development work in Ethiopia, he is a doyen among the expatriates concerned with this field, and he certainly knows more about it than almost anyone else.

During our conversation, he casually let drop that he had *just* been asked what could be done about the Sudanese refugees at Asosa. He told me that some of the private agencies had immediately agreed to help, and that the first trucks were being loaded as we were talking. He adroitly, and with poker face, refused to be drawn into a discussion about why 2O,OOO Sudanese refugees had been forced to wait six weeks for food, when there was plenty of it available in Ethiopia at the time, as well as trucks that could move it. It was 28 days since the UNHCR mission had visited Asosa and before those trucks were loaded.

Obviously, the sending of assessment missions by donors is a normal step before relief operations. Governments have often made exaggerated requests in the past, and therefore donors are wary. Once a country has an Early Warning System that is known to be reliable there will be credibility added to a call for help. Potential donors' first reaction can then be one of willingness to believe that there is a real need. They can start mobilizing, even if an assessment mission will still be required to determine the exact dimensions of the need. In the past, and in the absence of such credibility, the first reaction is often one of scepticism, which leads to an assessment mission and delays before anything is done at all.

In respect of logistics, the rapid supply of additional trucks when required remains an unsolved problem. Even with advance warning, it is difficult to find donors prepared to give trucks, to deliver them to the country, and to set up the trucking operation within the time-frame required to ensure that food distributions keep pace with the needs as they develop during an emergency.

A partial solution could be for an agency such as WFP to have a fleet of trucks mothballed in a strategic spot in Africa, ready to be moved into an emergency and hold the fort until other trucks could be donated. The hundred four-wheel drive BM 9O military trucks provided by Italy for the Sudan emergency, and later passed to the government, would have been perfect as the nucleus of such a fleet. Their sheer ability to go anywhere would have enabled their rapid movement to the scene of any emergency in the continent.

It is a sad truth that when truck fleets are donated to government services in Africa, they often have high rates of unserviceability and short working lives. This means that in countries with recurring crises, such as Ethiopia in recent years, trucking capacity needs to be repeatedly strengthened. In a joint FAO/WFP Special Alert issued on 24 September, 1987, regarding the deteriorating situation in Ethiopia, the following is stated: "A recent survey by a transport capacity study team indicates that the present distribution capacity for emergency relief is well below that of 1985/86; in order to merely raise the internal distribution capacity to the previous level, additional support is needed urgently for the purchase of vehicles, spare parts, and fuel...."

Of course, no truck can last for ever, especially in African conditions, but private truck owners perform miracles in keeping their vehicles operating. They show extraordinary feats of improvization in repair work; they cobble, modify, and adapt to great effect, and probably smuggle in spare parts too! Their livelihood depends on the trucks, so there is every incentive to keep them running. And run they do, although anyone who knows Africa will confirm that they often look and sound as if they should have been allowed to expire and rest quietly under a baobab years before.

Perhaps international donors should be exploring ways of supplying trucks to private operators in countries where private trucking exists, as it does in most of Africa. The operators could receive them on easy credit terms, and their repayments could go into a fund for purchasing spares, and ultimately, replacements. Since much trucking is done for relief and development agencies who can pay in foreign currency, at least part of the repayments by truckers could be credited in foreign currency. In this way, imports of spare parts, tyres, batteries and the like, which are impeded in so many countries by a lack of foreign exchange, could be made easier.

★　　　★　　　★

All those who have worked in a managerial capacity in one of the recent relief operations agree that the greatest problem in getting an operation under way is the lack of experienced people. The excruciating inertia that Alan Jones described in the early days of the relief action in the Sudan resulted from this shortage of experience and skills among most of the agencies, and from a lack of coordination of effort.

In one relief operation after another, the tendency is for the same mistakes to be made as were made in the previous one; the wheel is continuously re-invented, even to the point where, in the past, each new relief operation wasted time designing new forms and administrative procedures for running and controlling the operation.

The first 4–8 weeks are crucial, for if the operation gets off on the wrong foot, it will be difficult to put it right later. This proved to be the case in Karamoja in 1981. The Swiss have a Disaster Relief Unit that is specialized in the immediate actions required to get the ball rolling, and the increasing belief is that WFP needs to be the instigator and central point for a similar UN "start-up team" of professional, highly experienced people. It would consist of a coordinator, and specialists in the fields of: transport, logistics and storage, maintenance, nutrition, and telecommunications, and they would be backed up by an adminstrative clerk-cum-accountant.

The leader of that team would need considerable freedom of action, and also authority, and herein lies the rub. For if that team were to lay down guidelines – for example that a maximum of two makes of truck should be donated and come with 10–15% of their value in spare parts, or that drivers must be trained before they are turned loose on new trucks – would the relief agencies in general accept those guidelines? Unfortunately, past experience shows that donors and relief organizations are often pre-occupied with questions of their own identity and prestige, and do not want to be coordinated by anyone.

After the tragedies of recent years, particularly in Africa, experienced people certainly exist, and they could be called in to form "start-up teams". There can be no justification in future for sending in people who do not have the experience and skills required to run key aspects of relief operations. This often happened in the 1984–85 emergency, sometimes for lack of anyone who could do the job, but also through faulty decision-making. WFP was guilty of it too. A good example is that of Helen McNaught, a young New Zealander who had worked in her country's overseas aid programme. In Ethiopia, there was an urgent need to keep track of food shipments, of arrivals in port, and of forecasts of future arrivals. As in many African countries, WFP played the central role in this coordinating work, and Helen McNaught was despatched to Addis Ababa to look after it. Although she was a development specialist, she had never worked a computer in her life. Her predecessor overlapped with her for three days to introduce her to the system, but he himself had received limited training from someone sent for a short stay by WFP in Rome. She did a truly excellent job in the end, but not before she had gone through weeks of anguish and frustration to master the system and run it properly.

An important lesson was learned in Ethiopia during the last crisis concerning the relationship between relief food and food-for-work during a famine situation. The decision taken in Ethiopia in 1985 was to give priority to distributing relief food to the camps and feeding centres, and so people engaged in food-for-work programmes, many of them in drought areas too, found their rations cut off or much curtailed. The consequence was that many of those people were forced to leave their homes and become part of the hordes making their way to camps, adding to the overall problem of relief work.

There was also a longer-term negative effect: people involved in food-for-work felt that they had been let down, that the RRC had not lived up to its obligations towards them. After all, they had done the work, so where was the food? This would be bound to affect the future relationship between the people and the RRC. In fact, there was so much bad feeling that as late as mid-1987, WTOE, the WFP trucking operation, was having to deliver the food-for-work in certain areas to avoid scenes of protest and clashes were RRC trucks to appear. In future, relief food and food-for-work are to receive equal priority. Even if the work the people are doing is unlikely to produce much benefit, for example planting trees in drought conditions, at least the rations will enable them to stay where they are, suffering less than if they have to undertake a stress migration, and ready to resume normal agriculture when the drought finishes.

Technical progress is being achieved, and experience has been acquired, in famine prevention and relief. Human disasters and suffering on the scale of 1984–85 do not need to happen again in Africa. If politics, pride, and prejudice can take second place to the interests of the poor and the hungry, if donors are as generous as in the past, Africa can be helped over the probable droughts and crises of the next years. But however good famine prevention and relief work become, it must not become an end in itself. When famine conditions repeatedly arise, it is proof that development has failed. In the longer term, rehabilitation and development are the only solution for Africa. With the economies of African countries as embattled as they are, there is little prospect that they can finance their own rehabilitation and development. Africa desperately needs assistance. The world surpluses of food, if carefully and creatively used, can make an important contribution to helping its people into a more prosperous future.

Epilogue

As this book goes to press, the situation in Africa remains grim and threatening. Drought, although not as widespread as in the years leading up to the 1984 catastrophe, is still severe in many parts of the continent. In some areas of the Kordofan and Darfur regions of Sudan there was an almost total crop failure in 1987. For Sudan as a whole, sorghum production in 1987 was below half its 1986 level. In fact, at 1.4 million tons, it was close to the 1.25 million figure of the worst drought years of 1983 and 1984. The Beja nomads in the Red Sea Hills have never properly recovered from their loss of livestock in 1984–5 and over 400,000 of them are receiving emergency food aid.

In June 1987, Ethiopia has seemed to be heading for a reasonably good year – relatively speaking. An FAO/WFP Crop Assessment Mission estimated that there would be an overall deficit of 609,000 tons and that the country would need emergency donations of 400,000 tons. Then in late July David Morton, WFP's Director of Operations in the country, travelled to Eritrea and Tigray and was appalled by the conditions he saw there. All the signs of impending disaster were clearly visible. Those northern parts of Ethiopia were again gripped by drought. Morton sent a telex to WFP in Rome to raise the alarm. Conditions seemed to be as bad as they had been in 1984, or perhaps even worse.

This warning from Morton was taken seriously at once by all concerned, including the government, major donors and private relief agencies. Within two weeks the US had a mission in the area and they confirmed Morton's findings. At the time of writing, it is estimated that 1.05 million tons are required for emergency relief to people in Eritrea, Tigray, northern Wollo and Hararghe. This, plus non-emergeny food aid, brings the total requirement to 1.3 million tons.

In contrast to 1983–4, donors have been quick and generous in their response, and only 95,000 tons of this amount still remains to be promised. However, the situation is less satisfactory in respect of supplementary (non-grain) food. Of an estimated need of 45,000 tons, only 4,000 tons have been pledged to date.

For the first time the Soviet Union has pledged food. It is to provide 250,000 tons of wheat and has bought the first tranche of 50,000 tons from the EEC. So far, however, the Soviet Union has not provided detailed information regarding its schedule for delivery. This is of concern to WFP because of its widely accepted role in coordinating shipments to avoid congestion and ensure efficient distribution.

Donors have also been quick to respond to other needs such as air-transport, warehouses, storage tents, pallets and tarpaulins. In commenting on the prompt response from donors compared to 1983–4, the head of WFP's Disaster Relief Service, Bronek Szynalski said:

I only hope that the good response from donors has been because they think that the figures have been calculated by people who know what they are doing, and are therefore correct, and not just because they are afraid of running into the same situation as they did in 1984.

As I see it, there are much better efforts now to coordinate relief work than we have ever had before. There has been no need to call donor conferences. We feel that if we provide correct information that appears credible, we will get the response. So we make a great effort to ensure that the emergency information sheets we telex to donors are correct, and that they do not raise issues that could cause controversy – in other words that their content has been informally approved by the government of the country concerned.

When a situation is growing critical, we try to provide a lucid telexed piece each Friday that covers food requirements, how they have been met so far, non-food requirements related to food movements, and logistics for port arrivals and within-country movements. Recently we had received promises for trucks but there was little action to deliver them. We told donors in our telexes that promises were fine but would they procure them *immediately* and get them to us. All this has worked marvellously, much better than in the past.

Drought has not affected the Sahelian countries to any noteworthy extent, but some of those few countries in Africa that traditionally produce surpluses have been seriously hit. Zimbabwe and Kenya are usually net sellers of cereals, but Zimbabwe has banned the export of maize, and Kenya is selling only small quantities. Malawi has often sold surpluses too, but this year, for the first time in history, Malawi itself needs food aid (drought and mealy bug infestation in the cassava crop are the causes). The drying up of these usual sources of local cereals makes it more difficult to find suitable food aid for neighbouring countries and adds to the cost and complexity of transportation.

Malawi's problems of feeding its own people have been exacerbated by an influx of regugees from Mozambique. There are now 420,000 of them in camps, and the number is expected to swell to 600,000 by the end of the year. In Mozambique itself, over 3 million people are displaced and need help. Although drought has also affected Mozambique, the major cause of the problem there remains the civil war. Very little food is being grown and almost the entire population is dependent on imports or food aid.

Political and tribal strife appears to be leading to even greater insecurity in some countries. In addition to the dramatic and expanding problem of refugees and displaced persons it is creating, strife is gravely affecting relief operations. Access to South Sudan is as difficult as ever. Many of the towns are in desperate straits, with more and more displaced people from the countryside arriving daily. For example, the town of Aweil is harbouring more than

50,000 displaced persons whose numbers are swelling by 50 to 100 per day. It was recently reported that over a thousand people there had died of causes related to hunger and malnutrition. Barges with commercial goods and relief supplies sent up the Nile to Malakal were attacked twice on the way. And if the conditions are bad in the towns, no one knows how desperate things may be in the countryside, since no one can travel in safety to have a look.

In Ethiopia, strife is making it very difficult to move food to where it is needed. Supplies are beginning to pile up in the ports. Air lifting is in progress from Assab to Asmara, and to other points in the north when possible. According to one report even Asmara airport was attacked recently. Some of the flight crews refuse to overnight there.

The vital north-south roads cannot be kept open, or even opened for short periods with any regularity. WTOE trucks have sometimes arrived at a point, been unable to proceed and after waiting some days, have had to return to their departure point and unload.

Since the Eritreans rocketed 16 WTOE trucks in October 1987, Probably to make a political point, they have destroyed a further 90 trucks. Most of them were government trucks from the RRC. None belonged to the UN, but 7 belonged to CARITAS. Now Band Aid, USAID, Germany and Italy have come forward to provide WTOE with 85 new long-haul trucks, a vital input because more food will have to be moved in Ethiopia this year than has ever been moved before.

The logistics for Malawi are also problematic. Its main and traditional access to the sea has always been via Mozambique, and food can still be moved via Tete into Malawi through the so-called "Tete Corridor". This corridor might be cut off by anti-government forces at any time. Food is being transported via Tanzania using the Chinese-built Tanzam Railway, but the capacity of this route is limited. Shipments are also being made via Durban. When human lives are on the brink, WFP is politically pragmatic.

Bronek Szynalski is deeply concerned by the situation in Malawi and by the growing refugee problem. He spent much of his childhood as a refugee himself. Deported from Poland to Siberia in 1940, he and his family trekked to Iran. There, in 1942, they were picked up by a relief organisation that shipped them via India to what is now Zambia. His father joined a Polish unit in the British Army, fought and was seriously wounded in Italy, while Szynalski lived with almost five thousand other Polish children and their mothers in a camp in the bush near Ndolo. In 1948 the family was reunited in Britain but continued to live in a refugee camp until 1951. For him, dried skim milk is not just one of the commodities he helps to provide to those in need. He has eaten it himself. He knows about camp life, about eking out rations, and making up meals from odd ingredients.

"The refugee and displaced people situation in Africa is much worse than it was in 1984–5," he said, "and it is continuing to worsen. We feel that we have it under control, but our control is on a very thin edge. In Malawi we are more or less hand-feeding the people. If we have stocks, they are only enough for two weeks. That is just not enough in a landlocked country. It's extremely dangerous and we're very worried."

This book has been about the African situation. However, we cannot ignore what is happening in other parts of the world and the effect it could have on the availability of resources for African relief and rehabilitation. Szynalski wound up our conversation by telling me of his concern for Asia. Last year, the monsoons failed in much of the Indian subcontinent. Before that failure, India had accumulated surplus stocks of 23 million tons of cereals. It has now used most of them for famine relief and is beginning to import cereals. Previously, India was a food donor. Pakistan too is importing cereals for the first time in some years. Even if there were to be a *partial* failure of the next monsoon, the traditional food aid donors could be pulled to full stretch. And what if the Soviet Union withdraws its troops from

Afghanistan and there is a flood of millions of returnees to the country? They will need food aid in large quantities to re-establish themselves. To add another ingredient, due to the wet summer last year the EEC had a very poor cereal crop. It was low both in quantity and quality.

Truly, we live in a global village.

Rome, March 1988

Index